PUIG ANTICH
ASSASSINAT

Salvador Puig Antich
Collected Writings on Repression and Resistance in Franco's Spain

Edited by Ricard de Vargas Golarons

Translated by Peter Gelderloos

Salvador Puig Antich: Collected Writings on Repression and Resistance in Franco's Spain

Originally published by Editorial Descontrol as *Salvador Puig Antich: 45 anys després* (2019)

This edition published under a Creative Commons 3.0 License

ISBN 978-1-84935-401-1
E-ISBN 978-1-84935-402-8
Library of Congress Control Number: 2020933426

AK Press   AK Press
370 Ryan Avenue #100   33 Tower Street
Chico, CA 95973   Edinburgh, EH6, 7BN
USA   Scotland
www.akpress.org   www.akuk.com
akpress@akpress.org   akuk@akpress.org

The addresses above would be delighted to provide you with the latest AK Press catalog, featuring several thousand books, pamphlets, audio and video products, and stylish apparel published and distributed by AK Press. Alternatively, visit our websites for the complete catalog, latest news and updates, events and secure ordering.

Cover design by Margaret Killjoy, birdsbeforethestorm.net
Printed in the United States of America on acid-free paper

CONTENTS

1. Prologue—Ricard de Vargas Golarons 1

2. The Context and Significance of Salvador Puig Antich, the 1,000, and the OLLA—Peter Gelderloos 7

3. Multi-Hued Sensations from Barcelona—Jean-Marc Rouillan 33

4. Nothing That Seemed Like a Goodbye—Bru Rovira 43

5. What We Chose to Live—Felip Solé 49

6. Salvador's Memory—Imma, Montse, Carme, and Merçona Puig Antich 63

7. Chronology of Salvador Puig Antich's Life (1948–1974) 75

8. Chronology of the Autonomous Workers' Movement in Catalunya 85

9. The MIL and the OLLA—Ricard de Vargas Golarons 97

10. Salvador Puig Antich in the MIL-GAC: A Brief Political Biography—Sergi Rosés Cordovilla 163

11. Remembering Salvador Puig Antich Over the Years—Ricard de Vargas Golarons 191

12. The Letters of Salvador Puig Antich 203

13. The Texts of Salvador Puig Antich 213

14. Glossary 249

15. Photos and Documents 271

Index 293

Prologue to the 2019 Catalan Edition

Ricard de Vargas Golarons

In 2014, on the fortieth anniversary of Salvador Puig Antich's execution, the Madrid publishing house Klinamen published a speech I gave about the MIL and the OLLA in April 2010, as part of a conference on Workers' Autonomy held at the Universitat Complutense of Madrid.

Despite the original intention and the commitment of the publishers to also publish the Catalan version of the book, in the end it was not to be. For this reason, on the forty-fifth anniversary of Salvador's death, we thought it appropriate to republish the text in Catalan in order to contribute to recovering Salvador's memory and that of so many others who confronted the dictatorial, capitalist regime in the final years of Francoism.

Despite a continuous effort over the past years to recover the historical memory of struggle and resistance, the pacts of the Transition have prevailed. Now, more than ever, we find ourselves in a situation of powerlessness, despondency, and confusion, fostered by a constant erosion of rights and liberties, sustained by an authoritarian Spanish nationalism that is exclusive and repressive, and by a global context in which capitalism is universal and ever more brutal.

In this general context, the aforementioned compromises of the Transition—which enabled the survival of the regime's economic, political, and judicial structures—have seen parties and unions adapt to a political system subordinated to the interests of the dominant oligarchy.

Given the current crisis suffered by the popular classes, in order to get out of this dead-end, we need to find new strategies, autonomous and self-organized, with firmness and determination, that allow us to face the system that oppresses us.

There is no other way.

It is in this light that the struggles of Salvador and his comrades in the MIL-GAC and the more radical part of the working class take on their full meaning. That is why I think it is essential to reclaim their contributions to anticapitalist struggle and social transformation, which were negated as much by the Francoists as by those who made deals with them.

Given his personal integrity, his political honesty, his revolutionary conviction, and his determination as a fighter, Salvador's life and struggle can help us reflect and propose new paths for overcoming the difficulties we now face.

Aside from the aforementioned speech and several articles published in different media, this book contains new material about Salvador: historical and political texts, biographical and personal accounts, as well as two chronologies, texts by Salvador himself, and a collection of photos, posters, flyers, and documents that demonstrate the reaction, both national and international, to his arrest, trial, and execution.

Many thanks to Manel Aisa, Jordi Banyeres, Olga Díaz, Josep Font, Rafa Iniesta, Eduard Márquez, Genoveva Munell, Josep Lluís Pons Llobet, the Puig Antich family, Carles Sanz, Felip Solé Sabaté, Jordi Solé Sugranyes, Gemma Soriano, and Joan Vinyoles, for all the labor of editing, translating, and transcribing that made this book possible.

Barcelona, January 2018.

Salvador Puig Antich, Forty-Five Years Later

Who would have thought that forty-five years could already have passed, today, the 2nd of March, since the execution of Salvador Puig Antich in the Modelo prison of Barcelona. A great many years have passed, and on the other hand, it seems like time has stopped, like it just happened. Over the last years, some of his comrades and friends have begun to disappear. Truthfully, there are few of us left who are living witnesses to the era of struggles and hope and the end of Francoism. How would Salvador react, what would he do, "the Doctor" as we knew him in clandestinity, if he could see the current political and social panorama of repression and control, ever more authoritarian and devoid of freedom?

Salvador Puig Antich, member of the MIL (Movimiento Ibérico de Liberación, or Iberian Liberation Movement), was an anarchist, anticapitalist fighter beloved by his companions and by all the people who had the opportunity to know him, for his human and solidaristic qualities. He did not limit himself to participating in expropriations and in the revolutionary writings that were a consequence of the social war, the intensification of the class struggle and the autonomous struggles of workers and neighbors; he also had a direct relationship with a variety of workers' collectives and neighborhood associations, like the Comissions Obreres or Workers' Commissions of the neighborhood, where he maintained contact with feminist collectives and committed to putting out a recording in which the women demanded free abortions and spoke out against patriarchal society.

It was an era of radicalization for the workers', neighborhood, and popular struggles, in which a new generation that had not suffered under the war confronted a capitalism that, in the Spanish state, was sustained by Francoism. They created ruptures for an anti-authoritarian, libertarian, and emancipatory practice—above all in the workers' struggles—aiming for an individual and collective liberation that would surpass the bourgeois democracies of the time and avoid a future Spanish democracy that would serve as the heir to Francoism, which is exactly what a large part of the anti-Francoist opposition was preparing.

It was a time when many autonomous struggles emerged, wildcat strikes throughout Europe, various armed organizations around the world, and a new generation that, on a cultural level, broke with the conservatism of their parents' generation. Many things happened that made us think it was possible to put an end to the capitalist system and begin a new society, liberated and egalitarian, without exploitation or oppression. At the time, almost all the struggles and resistance arose from the working class and the class struggle.

The MIL arose from the experience of May '68 in France, from Situationism, the wildcat strikes in Europe, more than twenty years of guerrilla struggle in Catalunya, from the revolutionary conquests of the collectivizations during the Civil War, from the workers' councils in Central Europe during the 1920s, and, above all, from the experience of autonomous workers' struggles in Catalunya, with a libertarian, anti-authoritarian, and revolutionary practice, that appeared at the end of the '60s and beginning of the '70s. The MIL's well-known expropriations served to provision Ediciones Mayo del 37, our publishing project that enabled the self-education of workers, and to bankroll solidarity funds for fired workers.

It was, as we have said, a time when it seemed that anything was possible; times of solidarity and hopes of liberation that were completely dashed by the bargains of the Transition. At that time, there were many like Puig Antich who were strong and enthusiastic, ready for anything. Marcel López, who was born in Barcelona in 1939, a worker at the Bultaco factory, connected to the MIL, left us last year. He was a fine example of a combative and solidaristic youth. He, like others, traveled clandestinely from the Pyrenees to Barcelona, hauling illegal pamphlets and books that were distributed in factories all over the country. He also wrote a study that was widely distributed against the stopwatches of the company efficiency experts (*How to Fight the Stopwatch*).

Over these past forty years, many things have happened that have corralled us into the current situation of powerlessness and selfish and unsolidaristic individualism. It is ever more widespread amongst the popular classes, under the heel of a corrupt financial capitalism that provokes the current economic crisis in order to enrich itself further and to sow misery and discord while increasing its control over the working class with the worldwide growth of a reactionary and philofascist authoritarianism supported by the State. This situation owes a great deal to the submission and the managerial role of the institutional left on behalf of a predatory capitalism, and its lack of responsiveness to the basic needs of so-called social welfare.

It is also necessary to emphasize the role of new technologies or the technological revolution, which favor social control and individualism. Over the last few years, the Spanish state has also suffered a regression in rights and liberties of all kinds (human, social, and political), with the growth of authoritarianism and Spanish nationalism, the exclusive heir of Francoism.

I remember they labeled us idealists. Even the soldiers, as they interrogated me after my arrest, commented, "This one is an idealist." And it is true, we were idealists, with transformative social ideas that we tried to put into practice with our actions and in our daily life. A little later, once Franco died, during the Transition, we fought for a democratic rupture against the Franco regime but it was not possible, because a wall was raised before us, and guarding it were not only the Francoists but also a good part of the leftists and democrats, who conspired in the white-washing of the totalitarian regime, giving the new regime a democratic façade though it was, for the most part, the heir of Francoism. Evidently, these examples of collaboration and submission do not provide us with a good reference for political struggle, which might help us advance and get out of the trap we currently find ourselves in.

We have fallen many years behind, and we need new references of struggle that will put us on a path to new spaces of freedom, that break with old and new forms of submission. Perhaps we need to look a little further back, to the guerrilla and workers' struggles of the 1970s that were self-organized and autonomous.

The political, liberatory project of Salvador Puig Antich, and of so many other youth of forty-five years ago, still remains to be completed. The youth of today, oppressed more and more by the most brutal capitalism, must organize themselves and struggle even harder against submission, control, and growing misery. We must learn from our struggles and our defeats to continue the fight for a truly free and solidaristic society. That is when Salvador Puig Antich will remain alive, amongst us all.

Barcelona, March 2, 2019.

2

The Context and Significance of Salvador Puig Antich, the 1,000, and the OLLA

Peter Gelderloos

The name Salvador Puig Antich and the events of the so-called Transition are famous within the Spanish state, but virtually unknown elsewhere. This introduction to the English translation provides the historical background necessary for understanding the events and names mentioned throughout the book.

When Ricard de Vargas Golarons asked me to help him get his recent book translated and published in English, I cleared my agenda and agreed to help. The book was about Salvador Puig Antich, an old friend and comrade to Ricard and to so many others in the anticapitalist movement that rocked the Spanish state at the end of the Franco dictatorship. The book was originally published in Catalan in March of 2019, the forty-fifth anniversary of Salvador's execution at the hands of the fascist state.

Ricard and I worked together five years earlier to organize a weekend of events to mark the fortieth anniversary of Salvador's execution. We were part of a small assembly of anarchists, both young and old, fighting for the preservation of *historical memory*. That term, a recent introduction to English from a handful of Mediterranean languages, implies a belief that has not been so common in English-speaking revolutionary movements: that history is not a matter of record, but a matter of memory—corporeal, living, and passed on from generation to generation rather than entrusted to professional historians and archivists.

Memory, in this sense, transcends a single lifetime, and history is a living thing that must be fed and exercised continuously and, preferably, in the streets.

There is an incredibly strong history of radical struggle in North America and in the United Kingdom, but it is precisely where these struggles are not *remembered* that our movements are the weakest, and they are forgotten precisely where State policies have been effective at stomping us down or buying us off.

Spain is a State on the cusp between remembering and forgetting. A brutal war, a long dictatorship, and an insidious transition to democracy, which boosted the leaders of popular movements into the halls of power, almost erased the memory of the revolution that has been bubbling beneath the surface for centuries. That revolution erupted most famously in 1936, but also in the '70s, in 1934, 1932, 1909, 1873, 1821, 1640...

The memory has been preserved, at least in part, because each generation has struggled, fought tooth and nail, to pass it on. Though a book is a poor substitute for presence, I will try to relate this history as it has been told to me.

In May 1936, the nearly one million members of the Confederación Nacional de Trabajo (CNT)—the radical confederation of labor unions—approved a declaration in favor of anarchist communism: they weren't just fighting for scraps, they were fighting for a revolution. One and a half months later, there was a military coup inspired and supported by fascist governments throughout the rest of Europe. The coup only succeeded in half the country, and in many areas like Madrid, Barcelona, and València—the three biggest cities—it was largely anarchist workers who rose up and defeated the military.

Whereas the government and police forces had largely rolled over or openly supported the coup, self-organized workers were able to defeat the military in the streets, thanks to months of specific preparation, as well as the preceding years of insurrectionary and clandestine struggle against unfavorable odds, which left them armed and experienced. The end result of July's days of street fighting was that the lower classes were armed, exuberant, and aware of their own power. In the countryside and in the city, they began collectivizing land, factories, hotels, hospitals, and other workplaces. In some areas, the anarchist CNT organized this revolutionary activity, whereas in other places it happened spontaneously. A revolution was underway.

The dominant liberal narrative portrays the military coup as an unprovoked aggression. This view is as victimistic as it is inaccurate. It is a fallacy based on the liberal idea that the democratic Republic could satisfy everyone's needs if they only learned to cooperate. But the truth is, the interests of a despotic Catholic Church, a bloated colonial military, a land-monopolizing aristocracy, and profit-driven factory owners were simply antithetical to the vital needs of millions of peasants and urban workers. The military leaders were justifiably worried that an anarchist revolution would break out and put an end to the oppressive society they defended. This is why the Spanish bourgeoisie and landowners supported either the fascists or the authoritarian elements on the Left capable of reining in the anarchists. This is key to understanding the defeat of the revolution and the victory of the fascists: both the fascist side and much of the antifascist, or Republican, side were united in prioritizing the defeat of the revolution, whereas the antifascist side was a mix of revolutionary and counterrevolutionary elements.

The most powerful force of the Republican faction was the CNT and its allied political organization the FAI (Federación Anarquista Ibérica, or Iberian Anarchist Federation); followed by the Socialist Party and the union they controlled, the UGT; and then by a smattering of small Marxist groups like the POUM and pro-autonomy parties from Catalunya and Euskadi. At the beginning of the conflict, the Communist Party was all but absent in Spain. Communists quickly grew in influence, though, as the Soviet Union was the sole country besides Mexico to give military support to the Republic; however, they did so only in exchange for Spain's vast gold reserves. As Stalinists flooded Spain in the form of military advisers and *cheka* (secret police), they gained considerable influence in the Socialist Party and proved themselves to be the defenders of the Spanish bourgeoisie *par excellence*, consistently protecting the wealthy from anarchist expropriations, discouraging talk of revolution, and even recruiting fascists who had found themselves behind Republican lines when the war broke out.

Of all of the antifascist elements, the only to support a revolution besides the CNT and the FAI were a part of the rank and file of the UGT, and the dissident Marxist POUM, which, however, was not above participating in various conspiracies with the bourgeois political parties to limit the power of the CNT. Regardless, in less than a year they would be liquidated by their Stalinist rivals.

With half the country in the hands of the fascists, and much of the working class armed, the anarchists held an urgent strategic debate. They had lost their strongholds in Cádiz and Sevilla, where the fascist onslaught was fiercest as Franco's colonial "African Army" arrived from Morocco. In Zaragoza, where the CNT had focused on union organizing more so than insurrectionary strategies over the previous years, the working class was poorly armed and inexperienced, and their most radical members were quickly put up against the wall. In Madrid, the anarchists were fighting alongside socialists and loyal government troops to keep the fascists from taking the capital, and in the countryside of Aragón, peasants were not waiting for anyone's permission to burn property titles and declare anarchist communism. In Catalunya, the anarchists had comfortably defeated the fascists and could easily take over, but also shared the stage with multiple powerful left-wing organizations. It was here where the strategic debate had its most influential iteration.

Unlike Aragón, where the revolution was happening spontaneously, in Catalunya the anarchist movement was effectively organized within the CNT, and it was at an emergency meeting of the Catalan Regional Committee of the CNT where the key strategic decision was made: to form a joint antifascist committee not only with other workers' organizations like the UGT, but also with the political parties (the Comitè Central de Milícies Antifeixistes de Catalunya). Despite some internal dissent, the CNT adopted the slogan "First we win the war, then the revolution." However, this was not to be. A conflict between capitalism and revolution had morphed into a conflict between fascism and antifascism, and the antifascist side itself would destroy the revolution long before the fascists won the war.

The favorable aspect of this anarchist strategy was to demonstrate that revolutions do not inevitably produce monsters. Unlike the Jacobins and Bolsheviks before them, the anarchist revolutionaries of the Iberian Peninsula intentionally avoided taking power. In Catalunya and much of the rest of the Spanish state, they could have easily banned all the other organizations and parties, censored their presses, jailed their leaders, and imposed their will. Not only did they do none of that, they crafted a power-sharing committee in Catalunya in which they did not have majority votes, and institutionalized their commitment to working together with the other parties. And they did this despite having more popular support and nearly all of the guns. The reason for this strategy was the popular anarchist reading in Spain of the failure of the Russian Revolution: they believed the revolution had been destroyed by authoritarianism because the Bolsheviks had acted unilaterally.

This is of course a misreading: the Russian Revolution was destroyed by the Bolshevik counterrevolution because the Bolshevik strategy centered on controlling State power. States are incapable of making social revolutions, as a State is a permanent war measure against society, and intrinsically requires the exploitative economic organization of society. Since the Bolsheviks had tied their destiny to the Russian state, they continuously had to make the State stronger, and the revolution weaker.

The antifascist militia committee could have included only workers' organizations and militia representatives, to the exclusion of political parties—an inherently bourgeois institution. The committee could have—and should have—abolished the government rather than existing in parallel to it. The CNT, after destroying the government, would have had to abolish itself if it were to follow its decision from May 1936 in favor of anarchist communism, as the need for labor unions disappears when private property and the owning class disappear. This was the key mistake: the CNT did not have to *take over all of society*, it simply had to destroy the government and step aside, getting out of the way of the collectivizations and the new forms of organization that were already being created spontaneously by the lower classes. Instead, tragically, this organization that had made the revolution possible also strangled it, supporting the government and eventually joining it, formalizing collectivizations and later discouraging them, and thus completing the historical function of labor unions: to formalize, manage, and ultimately pacify workers' struggles.[1]

It was also ironic that the Comitè Central dovetailed perfectly with the Stalinist "Popular Front" strategy. This seemingly benign concept that all groups concerned should work together against the fascists was developed by the German Communist Party a few years earlier, after their practice of working together with the Nazis to destroy the Social Democrats backfired. In Germany as in Spain, the Popular Front would be far more effective at policing the Left than at defeating the fascists. Plenty of exiled German anarchists supported the revolution in Catalunya and brought their experiences with them, but in July of 1936, there were few Stalinists to speak of in Catalunya, and the minuscule Communist Party had no representation on the Committee (part of the reason why the Stalinists would take over the Socialist Party rather than acting through a party of their own). However, the danger of counterrevolution was not of Stalinist provenance alone. It was present in any participation with government and in the very functioning of a Popular Front.

Part of the anarchists' error was naïveté and part was an honest, and perhaps accurate, fear that they were not strong enough to go it alone. Yet another part was the bureaucratization that had beset the CNT, or the formalism of the FAI. Stuart Christie has authored a lucid study of the latter organization, created by

---

1. Agustín Guillamón points out throughout his work on the Spanish revolution that collectivization was simply a cooperative management structure whereby workers ran the factory, often out of necessity, as many factory owners fled the zones where anarchists were strong. Socialization was the true revolutionary practice, whereby workplaces were made communal property and their product shared out according to the maxim, *to each according to their need*. To keep the tenuous antifascist coalition together, the CNT agreed to discourage socializations, whereas much of what happened in the countryside exhibited a fully communal logic and could be described not just as collectivizations, but socializations.

the grassroots to prevent reformists from taking over the CNT, but preserving itself after that task had been accomplished and eventually becoming a reformist organization in its own right: the second generation of the FAI were responsible for launching the careers of the so-called anarchists who would become government ministers, authoritarian intellectuals like Frederica Montseny and Diego Abad de Santillán.[2]

As we shall see, this process of bureaucratization played a major role in preventing the CNT from exercising any radical influence in the autonomous movement of the '60s and '70s. Nonetheless, it can be heartwarming to underscore that they did not try to take power or liquidate their opponents. Another revolutionary accomplishment they can take credit for—until now unpublished and unknown in English-language historiography—was to make contact with members of an anticolonial independence organization in Northern Africa (the CAM, Comité de Acción Marroquí) and propose the liberation of Spain's colonies and a joint struggle against Franco. The plan, however, was shot down by the pro-colonial Socialist Party. The CNT agreed to shelve their plan so as not to upset the united antifascist front. By favoring colonial democracy over anticolonial struggle, the socialists changed the face of World War II and potentially set back anticolonial struggles around the world by two decades. Once again, we can see in hindsight that there were more similarities between the fascists and the antifascists than between the anarchists and the left-wing parties in the Popular Front.

The Republic was doomed. The stingy support of the Soviet Union could not outweigh the military generosity of fascist Italy and Germany. German aviation and Italian tanks and volunteers crushed the poorly equipped Republican army, divided as it was against itself. And with its increasingly dictatorial tendencies, the Republic could scarcely motivate its defenders. Using the *cheka* and the International Brigades, the Communists killed off thousands of anarchists and dissident Marxists. The *falange* and

---

2.   Stuart Christie, *We the Anarchists! A Study of the Iberian Anarchist Federation (FAI), 1927–1937* (Oakland: AK Press, 2008).

Franco's troops, for their part, killed 175,000 Republican soldiers and militia volunteers in combat and 130,000 civilians behind the lines, mostly for political reasons. After their victory in March 1939, the fascists executed around 200,000 more people, again mostly for political reasons. It is also important to note that no exact figures are known, since the Franco regime effectively hid the extent of the killings, and there was no interest in the West to document them either, given the complicity of Western democratic governments with the fascist regime.

This bloody repression murdered the aspirations of a generation and silenced a large part of the people who had directly experienced years or even decades of some of the most effective revolutionary struggles in Europe and Latin America (taking into account the longstanding affinity and exchange between anarchist movements in Spain, Italy, Argentina, and Uruguay, in particular). Perhaps the scope of the killing only becomes clear if we consider that the Franco regime murdered a much larger portion of the Spanish population than the Nazis killed in Germany. Though Spain had only one-third the population of Germany, Franco's Nationalists killed 475,000–575,000 people, whereas, of the twelve million victims of the Holocaust, 400,000–500,000 were from Germany, and all the rest were from territories conquered by Hitler.

As though this level of violence were not enough to produce a generational rupture and erase a collective experience of struggle and revolution, the people of the Spanish state were to carry on their fight for many more years, and they were also in for a great deal more suffering.

With the ineluctable victory of the fascists in the Spanish Civil War and the Nazi-Soviet Non-Aggression Pact, World War II was inevitable. Still, governments on both sides of the coming conflict shared counterrevolutionary priorities.

The French government locked up 550,000 Spaniards, Catalans, and Basques fleeing the advancing fascist army, constructing a series of concentration camps to house them. When World War II broke out, some of the interned escaped, others were handed over to the Franco regime and re-imprisoned, and others were sent to Nazi death camps: some 5,000 died at Mauthausen.

As with the war, the effects of this repression should not be understated, nor should it be understood strictly as a death toll. Those who survived also bore its marks. For example, the French placed Ricard de Vargas's father in a forced labor camp, irrevocably damaging his health. He died before Ricard was old enough to speak. Salvador Puig Antich's father presents a similar case: handed over by the French authorities to their Spanish counterparts, he was sent before the firing squad for his activism in a Catalan independence group. Yet just before they were to pull the trigger, his life was spared. The episode had a tremendous physical and psychological effect on him. His heart never recovered, and when he found out the regime had given his son a death sentence, it was too much for him, and he withdrew, unable to be present for Salvador's final months.

Amidst a general climate of loss and trauma, many parents decided not to tell their children at all about the struggles of the previous generation, afraid they might be inspired to join the cause and suffer the consequences. In fact, it was the Juventudes Libertarias (FIJL), the anarchist youth, who reanimated many of the neighborhood struggles starting already in 1939, when Franco came to power in the entirety of the Spanish state. Starting as teenagers, a generation of youth who had not served in the militias and had not emigrated to France launched a campaign of bold actions, including rescuing hundreds of radical prisoners awaiting execution in Franco's concentration camps. Throughout the '40s and '50s, the FIJL would be at the forefront of the resistance, just as they had during the Civil War after the CNT's conservative turn in '36.

In the meantime, though, most of the anarchist movement was in exile in France, where World War II had broken out in earnest. Catalan, Spanish, and Basque anarchists were instrumental to the French resistance, helping organize the partisans and liberating cities like Tolosa (Toulouse). In 1945, unaware that the future NATO countries wished an alliance with Franco, they expected the Allies to continue and sweep the fascists out of power in Spain as well. When the democratic West let them down, the *maquis*, or guerrilla combatants, kept on fighting. The CNT organized itself in exile in Tolosa and hundreds of militants adapted their smuggling routes over the Pyrenees to support a guerrilla struggle in Catalunya. There were also important guerrilla movements in much of the rest of the Spanish state, though they did not attain the intensity and penetration of the movement in Catalunya.

The guerrillas supported strike actions by workers, spread anti-Franco propaganda, sabotaged capitalist infrastructure, and organized assassination attempts against police figures or Franco himself. A key precedent to the MIL and the OLLA, they continued the practice of "armed agitation," developed by the anarchist affinity groups in the 1920s. "Armed agitation" is wholly different from the strategy of "armed struggle," in which a specialized armed group acts as the vanguard of the movement by constituting the nucleus of a future army (e.g. Castro and the 26 July Movement), serving as the military wing of a clandestine political party (e.g. ETA [Euskadi Ta Askatasuna]), or by carrying out the most spectacular actions and using its position to attempt to influence and direct a mass movement (e.g. the Red Army Faction or the Weather Underground). On the contrary, the groups that carry out armed agitation understand themselves to be simply a part of a broader movement, increasing that movement's capacity for communication, self-defense, and self-financing by organizing and funding clandestine printing, attacking the forces of repression, and expropriating money from capitalists to support the families of strikers, prisoners, and the victims of the police. They also seek to generalize their practice rather than centralize it, distributing weapons among the lower classes and encouraging the horizontal proliferation of armed groups.

A key example from this period helps illustrate the difference. On more than one occasion, a group of anarchist *maquis* would break into a factory to assault an infamously brutal manager. Whereas a vanguardist armed struggle group would assassinate the manager in such a circumstance, the *maquis* would strip the manager down in front of all the workers, perhaps beat and humiliate him a little, and loudly warn him, for all to hear, that if word got to them that he continued to be abusive, they would come back and kill him.

The former action creates a spectacle, turning the workers into passive spectators and instilling in them the clear message that the armed group were the protagonists, the saviors, the ones who would deliver the solution. And for any workers who disagreed, perhaps the only saviors were the police, since there is little use debating with one who is better armed than you and executes their opponents.

The latter action, however, maintains the workers as the protagonist of the struggle, putting them on a stronger standing but making it clear that it is up to them to get rid of the bosses. In this view, the most important struggle is that of the workers themselves. It places a lower premium on illegal action and a more accessible ladder towards the more powerful tactics: not all workers are armed at a given moment, but with a little creativity they could all find a way to beat up their bosses. In this way, armed agitation creates a stronger complicity between everyone in the struggle, whether they are regular people trying to make a living and sometimes raising their voice in protest, or those who dedicate their entire lives to the most dangerous aspects of a struggle. Armed agitation makes it clear that everyone's contributions are needed: the workers could be inspired to form their own such groups, or they could continue fighting in the workplace and the realm of daily life, fighting harder, more bravely, knowing they are not alone.

The difference in the lethality of the two actions is also significant. Though the practitioners of armed agitation—the affinity groups in the '20s and '30s, the *maquis* in the '40s and '50s, and the autonomous combat groups like the MIL and the OLLA—sometimes did take lives, they never did so lightly or gratuitously. This reticence towards executing those who could easily be identified as enemies is no small matter: anarchism has always distinguished itself as an ethical revolutionary current that does not make excuses for separating ends and means, and it is no coincidence that it has not resulted in the totalitarian States or systems of gulags and mass executions created by other revolutionary currents.

The anarchist guerrilla movement had far-reaching consequences that have been left out of a hostile historiography. In fact, anarchists who participated in the revolutionary experience in Spain, and then the resistance in France, and then the *maquis*, wrote one of the first chapters in the book on guerrilla struggles in the twentieth century.[3] Exiles who fled to Cuba, Mexico, and Uruguay shared their experiences with the movements that would blossom there over the next two decades; one exiled anarchist, Abraham Guillén, wrote one of the two principal manuals on urban guerrilla warfare. ETA got their first weapons from old anarchist resistance fighters who had fought Franco in Spain and Hitler in France. The Tupamaros and the Red Brigades got their forged documents from CNT counterfeiters. Many of those first armed groups on two continents after World War II followed an. anarchist model, but some of them made key changes to prop up their vanguardist politics. Subsequently, these were the only groups to be remembered in the histories written both by establishment academics and by professed anticapitalists.

Armed agitation helped foment a powerful movement for a few years in Catalunya, but in 1949, with the tacit approval of the NATO bloc, Franco took the repression to a new level, authorizing the extrajudicial murder of suspected anarchist sympathizers and brutally dismantling the support network the *maquis* depended on. Ricard de Vargas estimates at least five hundred *maquis* were killed, with many more imprisoned, and the guerrilla movement lost much of its reach. Nonetheless, the groups of Marcel·lí Massana, Josep Facerias, and Quico Sabaté continued until 1951, 1957, and 1960, respectively, and Ramon Vila Capdevila, working alone, continued until he was finally shot

---

3.   Arguably, this experience constituted one of the two main roots. The other, arising in parallel and having more of an impact in the rural sphere, were the anticolonial struggles waged by Indigenous peoples as well as peasant/bandit resistance throughout the world, which merged with anarchist movements in places like Mexico, India, Ukraine, and Korea.

down in 1963, after some thirty years of near continuous armed struggle.

The *maquis* were an explicit influence and inspiration for groups like the MIL and the OLLA. But they were not an isolated phenomenon: Sabaté's group in particular helped set up resistance groups all throughout Catalunya during the '50s. Nonetheless, some five years elapsed between the time when the old guerrillas gave up the ghost and when the new generation of the autonomous movement would begin their revolutionary struggle. Other lines of possible continuity from the powerful revolutionary struggles of earlier generations were even more broken down.

The CNT in exile outlived the Franco dictatorship, though not as a revolutionary organization. Centered in Tolosa and Paris, it commanded substantial strength, and throughout the '40s supported both labor organizing and the guerrilla struggle within Spain. However, as repression continually frustrated these activities, the organization abandoned confrontational strategies and became increasingly conservative. It did not help that the Confederation retained much of the bureaucracy from its days as a million-member organization, and that the worst opportunists to join the Republican government in its name—particularly Frederica Montseny—had turned the organization in exile into their personal fief. Eventually, the *maquis* broke their ties with the CNT in order to continue the guerrilla struggle, even though they never forswore their beloved Confederation.

To make matters worse, the organization did not develop an internationalist practice or even take a stand in the labor struggles occurring in their adopted home in France, quite the contrary to the anarchist exiles of 1939 who formed an integral part of the French resistance against the Nazis. They maintained the old view of the interior (Spain) and the exterior (France), with the latter supposed to be a base of support for struggles in the interior, even as they lost contact with those struggles. Notably, the MIL adopted this same language of interior and exterior, and even experienced some of the same problems, albeit on a smaller scale and a more accelerated timeline.

The once glorious CNT was in no position to hand off the torch of so many decades of revolutionary experience. The rupture in the continuity of struggle was almost complete. However, in a last breath of rebelliousness, anarchist delegates from Europe, North Africa, and the Americas agreed to the creation of Defensa Interior in 1962. The delegates included old anarchist exiles like Cipriano Mera and Joan Garcia Oliver, representing a more action-inclined sector of the CNT and the FAI, together with younger anarchists from the ever ready FIJL, the Libertarian Youth, like Octavio Alberola. Inside Spain and across Europe, Defensa Interior carried out actions against the Franco regime such as symbolic bombings, kidnappings of regime figures, and assassination attempts against Franco. Two members of the group were executed, and many more were arrested. Democratic and Francoist police forces collaborated to repress the group, but its membership and scope were international. After just a few years, in 1965, it was dissolved by the CNT due to pressure from the action-averse leadership. Nonetheless, the experience of armed resistance continued, now free from the control of the Confederation.

Together with others, veterans of Defensa Interior formed the 1st of May Group in 1966 to continue attacking the interests of the Franco regime. Active until the mid-70s, the group occupied the Vatican Embassy, machine-gunned the Spanish Embassy in London, and bombed the Spanish Cultural Institute in Dublin. If Defensa Interior was the first urban guerrilla group as we understand that term today, the 1st of May Group was the bridge that adapted and spread the model to so many others— though only a few of their heirs, like the Angry Brigade, were faithful to their non-vanguardist practice.

Though organizations came and went—with the exception of the most stagnant—there were survivors to all these struggles, many of them living in France or farther afield. Ironically, though the epicenter of this revolutionary cycle, with its many aftershocks, was in Catalunya, an anarchist continuity within the Spanish state was completely destroyed by four decades of bloody repression. As such, radical youth coming of age in the 1960s did so in a social movement dominated by Marxism. Tellingly, the Franco regime had retroactively changed their bogeyman from the anarchists to the Bolsheviks, "Reds," so as to better comply first with Hitler and Chamberlain's and then with NATO's adversarial politics. But there had been no danger of a communist revolution sparking the fascist coup in 1936. The revolution had been an anarchist one. Completing this delicate dance, the Franco regime legalized the study of Marxist texts in the universities and entertained dialogue with communist and socialist organizations, whereas they banned anarchist texts and used the most brutal means to make sure the CNT could not reestablish itself on Spanish soil. Though they never hesitated before waving the flag of a Red Menace, when mentioning the *maquis*, Franco's newspapers never spoke of anarchists, only "bandits," perhaps taking a cue from *Izvestia*. The invisibility of anarchists in those decades, the fact that they were *unmentionable* for the regime, whereas the communists were the promoted adversary, speaks volumes to where the true danger lay.

But, anarchism springs eternal. A part of the rebellious youth in the Spanish state, raised on Marxism, turned back to an anti-authoritarian politics. Ironically, French youth growing up in Tolosa, who would also play a role in this story, were closer to the anarchist tradition, as many of their neighbors were old exiles from the CNT. But their comrades across the border learned to express their anti-authoritarianism in a Marxist vocabulary.

Throughout the 1960s, workplace and neighborhood struggles grew in Spain as elsewhere. But whereas the democracies of Western Europe had myriad ways of training people to be obedient in the way they rebelled, Franco's fascist regime had crushed workers' organizations and outlawed expressions of dissent. When factory and construction workers started to resist the growing exploitation, the State-instituted vertical unions permitted under the regime were not up to the task of channeling and institutionalizing rebellion. To organize their protests and strikes, the workers created a system of solidaristic assemblies and committees that would become Comissions Obreres. In its beginnings, Comissions or CCOO had more in common with the autonomous unions of the early CNT, and even more with the factory councils of the revolutions in Russia in 1917 and Catalunya in 1936 than with a bureaucratic labor union.

Though there had been earlier attempts, particularly in the Basque Country in 1956, Comissions Obreres in their permanent form were born in 1964 when workers in Madrid, Asturias, Barcelona, and the Basque provinces of Guipuzkoa and Bizkaia created committees coordinating multiple workplace assemblies.[4]

The Comissions were a tool to neutralize the Francoist labor bureaucracy and fight for workers' demands, but they were nothing without the practices of organization, solidarity, and wildcat strikes already being put into practice.

In 1962, thirty-five thousand workers joined in a miners' strike in Asturias. Other sectors like agriculture and construction joined the strike in solidarity, and though labor statistics at this point in the Franco regime are hard to come by, the repression was well documented: fifteen thousand workers in provinces outside of Asturias were punished for supporting or participating in the strike. And in Bizkaia, another 35,000 workers carried out a general strike. In response, Franco declared a state of exception.

In 1963, there were strikes in Barcelona and Oviedo (Asturias), subsiding the next year in Barcelona but remaining strong in Asturias. From 1966 to 1967, strike activity increased across the entire Spanish state. There were also major protests, like the eighty thousand workers who marched in Madrid on January 27, 1967, organized by CCOO. A major wildcat strike by eight hundred workers in Bizkaia lasted six months, from 1966–67 and sparked multiple solidarity strikes, like a general strike in Bilbao by at least forty thousand workers. There were fewer strikes in 1968, but they were harder and lasted longer, then another rise in 1969 despite the declaration of a state of exception in the entire country in January.

It is important to keep in mind that at the time, protesting and striking were illegal activities and CCOO was a prohibited

---

4. Some future members of the MIL and OLLA were present at the meeting where Comissions Obreres were created in Barcelona, illustrating how they very much came out of the workers' movement.

organization. The CNT, UGT, and other unions also existed in clandestinity at this time, though they were tiny and isolated, weakened by the decades of repression. Among the CNT sections operating in secrecy, some were autonomous from the organization in the exterior, given the difficulties of communication and the conservatism of the latter, while others continued to pay their dues. For whatever reason, the CNT maintained its strength in Barcelona among workers in the cinemas and on the fishing boats.

Sometimes it was these various organizations that launched strikes, and sometimes strikes broke out spontaneously in response to firings or bad conditions, or in solidarity with other strikes. Either way, due to the illegalization of all workers' organizations, most of these strikes can be described as wildcat strikes that required a high degree of horizontal, localized, and partially spontaneous organization, as well as a strong practice of solidarity. Though hierarchical organizations were not absent from the stage, repression and worker self-organization meant they had little control, and the strike movement was largely autonomous. Even as authoritarian parties struggled to take it over, CCOO's enabling of horizontal methods allowed it to grow exponentially.

Multiple tendencies existed within CCOO and competed for influence. It was not until 1968 that the CCOO in Catalunya were effectively brought under the control of the Partit Socialista Unificat de Catalunya (the Unified Socialist Party of Catalonia [PSUC]), itself effectively controlled by the Communist Party. But even then, many workers tried to push the movement in different directions, including the autonomous, anti-authoritarian current represented by Plataformas. While the authoritarians pushed a strategy of "entryism," using CCOO to run for election within the fascist labor bureaucracy, the CNS (Central Nacional Sindicalista)—that age-old mirage of *changing the system from within*—the more radical autonomists, including several of those who would form the MIL and the OLLA, succeeded in getting numerous factories to boycott the CNS elections.

This was the stew in which the MIL, the OLLA, and the Autonomous Groups were born: a growing workers' movement trying to find its feet and create adequate tools of resistance after decades of repression; an authoritarian Left trying to institution-alize the new movement and ride it to the negotiating table; a cen-tralizing Spanish state still trying to complete its nation-building project and stamp out all the other cultural-linguistic groups that inconsiderately existed within its claimed borders, giving birth to a slew of national liberation organizations; and a fascist regime modernizing its economy and seeking increased integration with Europe.

The revolutionaries who would go on to form the MIL and similar groups did not grow up in the anarchist tradition—in fact the French members of the group, in Tolosa, had far more contact with the CNT than the ones from Barcelona—but they could see how the Leninist organizations were destroying the movement, twisting it to their own ends in order to win a recon-ciliation with capitalism and a place at the negotiating table in the eventual Transition to democracy. They had an urgent need for theory and historical examples of practice to help them artic-ulate an anti-authoritarian critique of political parties and labor unions, to underscore and strengthen the autonomy of the work-ers' movement, and to point out a clear horizon: the destruction of capitalism and the State.

Being non-dogmatic and non-sectarian, they drew their the-ory from council communists, Situationists, communization theorists, autonomists, and anarchists like Camillo Berneri who were critical of CNT collaborationism during the Civil War.

Some sources have incorrectly identified the MIL as anar-chist, given that its most famous member, Salvador Puig Antich, identified as such. Going to the opposite extreme, certain left communist historians have denied any anarchist character in the MIL. The fact of the matter is that, while their rhetoric was largely Marxist, their "actual practice was entirely anarchist," that being a wholesale adoption of armed agitation.[5]

At the end of the 1960s, faced with the growing strength

---

5.   In the words of Ricard de Vargas Golarons, personal conversation on February 14, 2020, and many other occasions.

and radicality of the wildcat strike movement, the increasing effectiveness of authoritarian political parties in taking over that movement, and the increasing brutality of fascist repression, revolutionaries across the Spanish state, but especially in Catalunya and Euskadi, confronted the need for more tools of theorization, communication, collective self-defense, and counterattack.

They began forming autonomous groups to publish and distribute illegal texts, carry out sabotage actions in support of wildcat strikes, knock off banks to raise money for printing, strike funds, and the purchase of weapons, preparing for an impending revolutionary confrontation.

Some of these groups, to avoid protagonism and a specific identity, never gave themselves names. When the police discovered the existence of such clandestine cells, they often assigned them invented names. This was the case with the OLLA, an acronym for Organització de Lluita Armada, which simply means "Armed Struggle Organization" in Catalan. Others, like the MIL (1,000), which then became the MIL, Movimiento Ibérico de Liberación, Iberian Liberation Movement, did choose their own names, though the changes and arguments around those names reveal the latent tension between the project of creating a specific organization dedicated to the most dangerous tasks of the struggle, and the project of fighting vanguardism and isolation in a broad movement.[6] In fact, there were even arguments over who was a member of the MIL: was it only those who participated in the armed actions, or anyone who participated in any of their activities?

Authoritarian socialization and leftist politics would teach us to focus on a formal organization over an opaque, informal mass of resistance, and amidst a plethora of formal organizations, to home in on the most effective one. Lacking a clear criterion for what constitutes effectiveness in a revolution we still have not won, the focus in leftist historiography inevitably drifts to the

---

6. The original name of the MIL simply refers to the number 1,000 in Catalan or Spanish. In a controversial move, a part of the group later invented the name "Movimiento Ibérico de Liberación," turning MIL into an acronym, without consulting the others.

most famous formal organizations, and this is a question usually settled by the capitalist media themselves.

The revolutionary movement in the Spanish state in the '60s and '70s is not a story of CCOO, GRAPO, ETA, and the MIL. It is the story of millions of workers illegally going on strike, taking over the streets, facing police truncheons and bullets, making use of whatever organizations they had on hand; and it is the story of thousands of these workers trying to go further, clearly seeing how the dominant organizations were diverting and institutionalizing the movement for their own ends. These workers tried to develop the theories and practices that would allow them to simultaneously resist the repression of the police and the integration of the politicians, both left and right. If they could do this, the movement could grow, discover its own strength, and demand not just crumbs but the whole fucking bakery. And at that pass, they would identify the next hurdle to clear, onward towards the revolution.

Salvador Puig Antich was one of those revolutionaries. Ricard de Vargas Golarons was another. They were two among thousands. Both of them happened to participate in the MIL and the OLLA, though Salvador's life was cut short just as he was embarking on a new strategy that would sharpen the groups' revolutionary practice.

One of the strengths of this book is its focus on the context. Some of the writers describe the intense reality of life in an armed group, others on the political debates occurring in that group and the broader movement. Comrades speak of the contemporary strike movement, family members speak of accompanying Salvador as he awaited the *garrot vil*. Each writer speaks from their own perspective, following their own priorities. Sometimes these perspectives clash, which is also a testament to the conflicts, debates, and contradictions that form an integral part of this history of struggle.

The event we organized five years ago, on the fortieth anniversary of Salvador's execution, was also based on a multiplicity of voices. A comrade from the MIL, fresh out of decades in prison, dissident poets, Salvador's sisters, autonomous activists from

CCOO—all of them shared their story. And, like the movement itself, it was an interplay of organization and spontaneity. At one point late in the evening, an old man got up on the stage. He told how he worked at a Barcelona factory that went on strike in those combative days. A workers' assembly decided they needed to distribute and debate certain radical texts to improve their theoretical understanding of the situation and identify the best strategy to take. But under the dictatorship, they did not have the means to print illegal literature. They got in touch with a contact person in one of the armed groups and ordered a large print run of subversive literature. The armed group took care of the printing and smuggling the whole bundle across the border. Tears coming to his eyes, the old worker told us how a handsome young man showed up at the rendezvous, handing over the bundles of literature, and slipping in a huge wad of stolen cash for their strike fund. This was food, rent, and lawyers for the striking workers. It was resistance: it was life. And the young revolutionary was Salvador Puig Antich. A short while later he was arrested, the old man related, and executed a few months after that. Remember, he urged us.

That was the kind of action that gave the MIL and other combat groups their meaning. In the '70s, the strikes only grew, soon to become one of the largest wildcat strike movements in world history. And now, as the regime became more attentive, they produced more precise statistics. In 1971, 266,453 workers went on strike in 601 different labor conflicts. In 1974, the year Puig Antich was executed and the OLLA dismantled, the number climbed to 625,971 in 1,193 different conflicts.[7]

The MIL and other autonomous groups continued to support these conflicts, but repression took a toll, and every group faced a tension between a higher level of specialization and security and a higher level of connection with the broad movement. This debate eventually led to the dissolution of the MIL. Other problems abounded.

---

7.   Statistics from: http://historiadelpresente.es/sites/default/files/revista/articulos/9/9.2pereysaslaimposiblepazsocial.elmovimientoobreroyladictadura.pdf.

In the '30s, the anarchist women's organization Mujeres Libres fought simultaneously against patriarchy and the State, and throughout the Civil War they were consistently more radical than the higher committees of the CNT. But Franco's regime represented a patriarchal onslaught, reinforcing traditional gender roles with a vengeance. It did not help that the CNT in exile, under the watch of the homophobic, anti-feminist Frederica Montseny, did not allow the veterans of Mujeres Libres to find an integral place in the exile community.

As such, the struggle against sexism within the autonomous movement was starting almost from scratch, and this weakness is also evident in some of the writings of members of the MIL, who systematically referred to women comrades as "the companion of," a practice also adopted by many of the group's biographers like Sergi Rosés. Other autonomous groups, such as the OLLA, attached more importance to the struggle against patriarchy and had more central women members. Movement historian Irene Cardona Curco interviewed many of the women veterans of the autonomous groups that fought in the final years of the Franco regime and during the Transition, documenting their experiences and the changes in the movement they helped to bring about.[8] Needless to say, the MIL and OLLA had already been dismantled by the time most of those changes came about, and it is still, of course, an ongoing struggle.

In the end, the revolutionaries had too much ground to cover, whereas the reformists had all the advantages, not least of which partial support from the fascist regime itself. Franco's Spain and Salazar's Portugal hold the dubious honors of being the two longest lived fascist governments in the world. But in Spain, especially, a growing portion of the fascist leadership was coming to believe that their interests would be better served under a democracy.

Franco had always been an ardent defender of capitalism, which meant integration into the global economy, together with

---

8. Irene Cardona Curco, *Aproximació al paper de les dones als Grups Autònoms de la Transició* (Barcelona: Editorial Descontrol, 2016).

France, Britain, the Soviet Union, and all the rest. Politically, he was most closely aligned with the NATO bloc, and hoped for greater inclusion in Western Europe's political and economic structures. But he also hoped to give his regime continuity. To that end, he groomed Admiral Carrero Blanco as his successor, and also found a king somewhere amongst the parasitic class of aristocratic layabouts that lounge in idle wealth across Europe, centuries after the abolition of feudalism. Fitting propaganda for the tale that capitalism is a meritocracy.

But in 1973, Carrero Blanco was blown to smithereens by ETA, and Franco was getting older. And the wildcat strike movement was only getting stronger. Fascism had forestalled a revolution, but it had failed to permanently pacify the Spanish working class.

The history is contradictory on this point, as it often is. On the one hand, the fascists definitely chose to transition to a democracy. Already in the '50s, they engaged in intermittent negotiation with the Communists. There is also strong evidence that with the help of the United States military and intelligence services, they infiltrated and took over the Socialist Party to turn it into a neoliberal organization more in line with the European Economic Community, the EU forerunner that Spain hoped to join. After all, with a democracy, it was inevitable that the opposition would rule for a while, yet at that point, the Communist Party was the main institutional force in the opposition. The Socialist Party scarcely existed. And it hardly befit Cold War politics that Spain should be ruled by a "Communist Party." Socialists had proven reliable Cold War allies across Europe, and they would in Spain, too, once they swept the 1982 elections in what was described as a major "surprise."

Whatever the case, towards the end of his reign, Franco commented on the stability of the State with a famous phrase: "*atado y bien atado.*" *Everything was in place and tied down tight.* The fascists definitely supported the Transition to democracy, though the wildcat strike movement may have accelerated the timeline or weakened the position of fascists who wanted to continue the regime after Franco's death. Forward thinking members of the regime opened up more channels of dialogue with the Communists and Socialists. Franco died in November 1975. Over the next two years the PCE and PSOE were legalized.

The strike movement continued. In 1976, 2,555,900 workers went on strike, but now that the Communists and Socialists had control, the same actions took on a different meaning.[9] Especially from 1974, the strike actions, rather than opening the horizon to a possible revolution, pointed towards democratic reforms. In this context, it is especially significant that the Left increasingly began encouraging pacifist strikes, effectively leaving the workers defenseless, at the mercy of the police, and therefore dependent on a negotiated, political solution crafted by the fascists and the workers' new masters.

Unless they could specifically defenestrate the Socialists and Communists from their role as movement representatives, any mass action the workers took would be willfully interpreted as a protest in favor of the Transition to capitalist democracy. And legitimized by the regime and backed by a Europe-wide political apparatus, the representatives had a lot of support.

Together with centrist Catholic parties and nationalist parties willing to exchange independence for partial autonomy, they all sat down at the table with the fascists and agreed to form a democracy. They decided to keep the king as a symbol of stability: plenty of democracies had kings, showing how innocuous that system of government was to previously existing inequalities.

They legalized labor unions willing to receive government funding and to be managed by full-time bureaucrats. CCOO and the UGT quickly dominated the field. Hundreds of thousands of people flocked to the CNT, which still enjoyed a strong reputation, so many decades later, but the government targeted the anarcho-syndicalist union with heavy repression. The police force, after all, remained the same during the Transition. It may not have mattered: the CNT returned from exile with politics that had become obsolete forty years earlier. The groups from

---

9.   Statistics from http://diposit.ub.edu/dspace/bitstream/2445/12622/17/Annex3.pdf.

the exterior crowded out the interior CNT locals who actually understood the situation in Spain; they shunned the autonomous movement, failing to distinguish Marxist vocabulary from Marxist practice; and, failing once again to recognize a revolutionary situation, they adopted a defensive posture, pushing for legalization and union organizing rather than the insurrectionary general strike that was still just within reach.

In June 1977, Spain celebrated its first elections since 1936, and in October, there was a general amnesty affecting all political prisoners, essentially defined as those who had been arrested for crimes that would not be crimes under a democracy. Those who had expropriated banks, defended themselves from police repression, or gone on the counterattack, remained locked up. Much of the heaviest resistance in the Spanish state in the '80s was initiated by these prisoners.

Many of the most principled, committed revolutionaries, before, during, and after the Transition were killed or imprisoned. Some were relegated to silence and oblivion. Others were recuperated, and recast as heroes of democracy. Salvador was one of these.

The Socialists and Communists did nothing to save him while he was awaiting execution. Their protests began only after the fascists had already snapped his neck with the *garrot vil*. Alive, he was a threat to them. But dead, they could claim him as a martyr. The Left, the media, the official history books, claim Salvador Puig Antich as an anti-Francoist fighter, and by insinuation, a democrat. This could not be further from the truth. Like the anarchists who came before him and those who have come since, Salvador fought against capitalism in all its forms, whether the dictatorial capitalism of Franco, the liberal capitalism of the bourgeois democracies, or the red-painted capitalism of the socialist States. As Ricard de Vargas declared at a recent anarchist bookfair in València, "We were not antifascists, we were anticapitalists."

The Catalan nationalist movement has also tried to claim Puig Antich as their martyr. And though he was sympathetic to the cause of independence and opposed to Spanish nationalism, his priority was an internationalist anticapitalist struggle, and he would have fought against the creation of any kind of Catalan state. Likewise, the fact that he often wrote in Catalan, that this book you now hold in your hands was originally written in Catalan, are both political acts in the face of the suppression attempted by the Franco regime and by considerable forces under the democratic government—and as an anarchist translator I take specific pleasure in working with a language that has not been thoroughly disciplined as the official tongue of a modern State, and, as such, has been less homogenized. Nonetheless, Salvador's intention, the intention of the original book, and of this translation, are to communicate across borders, to destroy those borders with the sharing of experiences, ideas, and weapons in a growing revolutionary movement that recognizes no constraints to freedom and collective wellbeing.

This, reader, is the context this story arises from, and this is the intention with which it is shared with you. Take it, make it your own, place it in dialogue with other stories you know, but do not forget: this is a memory of our struggles, our aspirations, our lives. Memory of that kind cannot survive in a book. Its home, and ours as well, is in the streets.

I highly recommend a close reading of the Glossary on page 249, full comprehension of this book without it is improbable.

Multi-Hued Sensations from Barcelona

Jean-Marc Rouillan

For Salvador

1.

The bullets whistled. The echoing detonations resonated at the bottom of Passeig de Fabra i Puig. I ran. A winter sun splashed the road of compacted earth with a pale light. With each shot, I cringed smaller and smaller. My brain boiled with the obsession of just getting to the corner. The plainclothes cops were chasing me, not so far away. The sirens of the 091 ululated amidst the traffic.[1] The right-hand sidewalk was curved, following the slope. How to explain that a simple angle could make me feel so calm? I was no longer in their sights. And I saw him. He was coming towards me, also running. He had taken the other Sten out of the bag, the one we had left in the white SEAT.[2] And he had locked in a magazine...

At the wheel, attentive, he had to make good our escape. He drove fast and precise, even though we had shaken off the heat a while ago. The huge wagon of *greys* had crashed into the parked cars.[3] We... we were shouting a lot. When I started blazing away, my ears had whistled and they were still buzzing. And of course, he hadn't seen the blood on the mustard-colored carpet nor our copper footprints in the corridor...

---

1. Trans: The police.
2. Trans: A British submachine gun, also used by various insurgent groups.
3. Trans: Common name for the police during the Franco years, for their grey uniforms.

When he left me, with the bags, on the street above the asylum, he told me, in French: "*Je vais planquer la bagnole... Je serai là dans une heure.*" *I'm going to hide the car. I'll be back in under an hour.* As I walked down the sidewalk by the psychiatric hospital, the sea illuminated the horizon. The light had changed. The sun seemed to burn with all its flames. I was happy. We had confronted it and we had managed to escape the trap.

2.

Two years earlier, when I met him, it had just grown dark. He arrived on an old German motorbike with the airs of a false Belmondo.[4] We were waiting for him in front of Hospital de Sant Pau. Of that meeting, I remember the electric blue lighting of the marquee of a tool shop on carrer Sant Quintí. It flooded the wet sidewalks with a blurred irreality.

> *O, bleu...*
> *O, suprême Clairon plein des strideurs étranges,*
> *Silences traversés des Mondes et des Anges*
> *– O l'Oméga, rayon violet de ses yeux!*"[5]

From that moment, he would be one of us in joy and in suffering.

Handsome and talkative, he told me he was still doing his military service in a barracks in Mallorca, where he served as a nurse. I asked if he knew how to remove a bullet. "Sure, if I have the right material and it's not in a bad place." His nickname occurred to us in a flash: for us, he would be "the Doctor." No one ever chooses their *nom de guerre*. In a book published not so long ago, I read an entire lucubration, based on cheap psychology, analyzing why he would have called himself that. We hear so much nonsense, these days...

---

4.   Trans: Jean-Paul Belmondo, a French moviestar of the '60s and '70s.
5.   Rimbaud Voyelles.

3.

We were traveling at 100 kilometers an hour on a highway flanked by olive trees. He drove an orange and white Vespa. I sat behind him. The wind whipped at our long chestnut locks. Beside us, the earth was a monotonous ochre all the way to the horizon, just like the furrows that disappeared in the distance. And the breeze shook the silver and green foliage, the same tone as the Francoist uniforms. And, as always, the same sun, livid and cold.

We left behind the long walls of factories built of dirty bricks. Miserable colonies where proletarians scraped by. Behind walls leprous and mute.

At the gas station, an employee in a greasy smock filled our tank. Afterwards, they both went into the store. When he came back out, I saw that he had unbuttoned his brown velvet jacket. Neither words nor gestures were needed. They were right behind him. Two *Guardia Civil!* Their varnished tricolor hats scintillated like their dark glares. The sergeant scrutinized us through the dark eye of his Z45.[6]

> But the *Guardia Civil*
> advance sowing bonfires,
> where young and naked
> imagination is burned.[7]

We were only twenty years old, and life threatened to cut out at any moment.

4.

In the period when his mother lay at death's door, we lived in an apartment in Vallcarca, next to Baixada de la Glòria. In spite of our security procedures, towards evening we would head out so he could call. We walked to Gràcia. One night, I accompanied him to a place near his parents' house. We parked the car in a

---

6. Trans: A Spanish submachine gun similar to the MP 40, standard issue for the *Guardia Civil*.

7. Federico García Lorca: "Romance of the Spanish Guardia Civil."

discreet spot. And I followed him. Covertly, he handed me his gun. A little farther down, his little sister waited on the sidewalk. She wore a black and white skirt and a pale yellow jacket. I roamed the empty streets for two hours. I remember that I was hungry.

One night, he came back and he told me: "She died." Then he cried. He cried sitting in the entryway. Since I didn't know what to do, I passed him the bottle of Caballo Blanco and a glass. I had seen it done in a Hollywood movie once.

5.

One summer evening, in the kitchen of the apartment on carrer de Sales i Ferrer, he was decked out in a simple apron, cooking. The aroma of hot olive oil perfumed the apartment. He expertly seasoned two pieces of chicken and put them in the pan. Sometimes, I asked myself if we weren't eating the same thigh every day. On the way home, crossing Travessera de Dalt, we would buy them at a little shop with white tiles. The shop was next to a laundry where we got our clothes washed. The employee was an Andalusian girl as dark as an olive. It was impossible not to flirt.

On the table in the living room, the little red plastic television emitted black and white images, mute. I don't know why, but I get this image of a windmill. I set the table, plates, and cutlery. On the record player, a black vinyl with a blue sticker was turning round and round. Pink Floyd's *Atom Heart Mother*, maybe.

He came in with the pan smoking.

—C'mon, lunch time!

When one looks straight into
the vertiginous pale eyes of death,
one speaks truths:
the barbarous, terrible, loving cruelties.[8]

---

8. Gabriel Celaya: "La poesía es un arma cargada de futuro." *Poetry is a gun loaded with future.*

It was the moment when, without being brutish, we reflected on struggle and on death. We often came back to this question. We didn't put on blindfolds. Our decision was crystalline: we would stay the course until the end. As though the air of the vanquished streets commanded us to live free or perish.

Pensive, he muttered: "Now we just have to make ourselves really small." And I added, with irony, "if we don't want them to lop off our tops."

And we laughed...

6.

I don't think we spent any Christmas together. Nor any other holiday. Unless you count the meals in Tolosa as collective celebrations of guerrillas with suspended sentences. He liked eating at the restaurant L'Entrecôte, located on one of the avenues of the Rose City.[9] The cobbler, an ex-FAI and ex-*maquis*, had shown him a photo of some kids the same age as ourselves, taken just outside the place before a fatal journey to Barcelona.[10] And he simply told us: "They also went to L'Entrecôte...!"

Sometimes, in Barcelona, we would have supper at the restaurant Putxet, just to get out in the evenings and lighten up our day-to-day existence. I remember a long yellow wall and the steps we had to climb to get to "our" table, in the back, from where we could keep an eye on the door. Not long ago, a writer from that neighborhood told me a portrait of Carmen Amaya dominated one of the walls.[11] It's as though every memory lacked one or two patches... a blindspot... a moment... and we forget. But I remember well that he ordered an asparagus omelet and drank Sangre de Toro.

---

9.   Trans: A sobriquet for Tolosa de Llenguadoc.

10.   Trans: Tolosa was a principal staging ground for *maquis* active in Catalunya after 1945. They would prepare their missions on the French side of the Pyrenees before crossing into Francoist Spain. Many were ambushed and killed during the crossing, or shot down in action in Barcelona or another city.

11.   Trans: A famous *gitana* flamenco dancer and singer from Barcelona who died in 1963.

7.

One night, already late, he showed up with a girl with dark blond hair, quite drunk. He knew he was breaking our security norms. To calm me down, he said, "She's a friend." She wore her hair short and had on a green shirt. They spoke about school. And they kept drinking while they listened to a T. Rex album.

I stretched out on the bed and opened a book. The memoirs of Nestor Makhno. I heard them laughing. Suddenly, the girl burst into my room and, in one hop, feet together, jumped onto the mattress. The pillow fell away leaving the CETME uncovered. The girl looked at the assault rifle, her gaze adorned in glittery blue eyeliner. He gathered that I was not at all happy, so he lifted her onto his back and carried her back to his room. Later they made love and I went to sleep.

8.

One winter morning, we went to pick up a vehicle robbed by the Basque's group. They had parked it in a big vacant lot. On foot, we walked along carrer de Provença almost until the Modelo prison. The light was pale and serene. He wore his brown velvet jacket and I, a knee-length grey tweed. Our breath condensed in the cold air. An ETA activist had given me the jacket, used in the failed assault on the Iruña prison.

We took a detour to avoid passing in front of a bank guarded by two *greys*. The blood red gleam of their insignias matched the trim on their hats. I pulled a cigarette out of the violet pack of Celtiques.

> *Quand je fumerai autre chose que des Celtiques*
> *Moi, je suis con, ma foi, mes fleurs noires à la face*
> *Fini le temps des bombes, ajourd'hui on transige*
> *On groupuscule, on parlemente et l'on eixige...*
> *Alors, nous tirerons nos dernières cartouches*
> *Je veux mourir tout seul, là-bas, au bout du quai*
> *Tiré à quatre chiens dans la nuit, camarade...*[12]

---

12.   Léo Ferré: "Quand je fumerai autre chose que des Celtiques."

The comrades awaited us on the sidewalk. They showed us the car, a golden-brown 1500 Break, and they gave us the keys.[13]

9.

He arrived at Plaça Lesseps driving a blue Citroën 2CV... Or maybe it was grey... It was dusk and "at night all cats are grey," as they say. Jordi and I waited for him on the side of the road, next to a bus stop. Someone had passed us information on how to get a Cyclostyle from a school near Tibidabo.[14]

We entered and crossed the first classroom. The walls were decorated with children's drawings, like the walls of any school in the world. But their colors had disappeared, muted by the coating of sickly yellow light from the street lamp that illuminated the doorway. Even the ivy on the walls of the patio was dyed with that electric lemon tone.

The scene had the color of an old *noire* serialized novel. Black and yellow. Jordi and I lifted the machine. He opened the back door of the 2CV. The bodywork had that same yellowish hue.

A few months earlier, I had gone down this same street to visit some friends behind the amusement park. It had the effect of making the place seem familiar.

Then, up the highway, we looped around the large, sinister building. Driving, he commented in a monotone: "That place is a prison for children."

10.

I crossed carrer de Sardenya at the intersection. With a quick glance I confirmed the presence of the parked vans. He followed me some twenty meters back. It was the usual procedure when we met with a legal comrade. Well, I say that now, but in those times, no one on our side was completely legal. I carried a Sten under my grey three-quarter length tweed. An icy air flowed through the January twilight. A few days earlier, we had crossed

---

13. Trans: The Simca 1500 Break was a French station wagon manufactured between 1963 and 1966.

14. Trans: A rotary stencil copy machine useful for making fliers. Completely mechanical, the design dates to the late-nineteenth century.

the border at Collada de Toses, all covered in snow. The avenue was deserted.

I headed for the market. I saw our man in front of the gate at the entrance. He wore a red jacket and a large green scarf. He was the only person standing there. As I approached, he scrutinized me out of the corner of his eye. I had the look of an undercover. After passing by him, I turned. "The Doctor" was walking towards me. When we got close to the corner, I whispered, "There's the parrot..."[15] He smiled.

I went to a parked van and kept watch. After speaking one or two minutes by some green and grey metal poles, my comrade took a kraft paper envelope from his black wallet. The other guy took it and got out of there like he was carrying a hot potato.

As we drove home in the blue R8 with a Logroño license plate, I think he said something about a worker from the Corberó.[16]

11.

In the evening, when the weather was nice, we would go out on the terrace. We made sure no neighbor was hanging their laundry behind the red brick wall, and we got comfortable. We brought our bottles of choice. He always had the Caballo Blanco and I, the black bourbon. It was like being suspended over a Barcelona roasted by the evening. And on the horizon at that hour, the Mediterranean recovered, piece by piece, its customary aspect of marine blue.

When we were alone, he would only wear boxers with shrill print designs. We spoke of our operations. We deciphered rough maps drawn by a comrade. And we verified them against a city map spread out on the hot tiles. We spoke at a whisper.

The smells from the kitchens and the clatter of plates and tableware rose from below. The neighbors feasted like Muslims on a Ramadan evening. The great pine trees on the slopes of Guinardó were coated in dark green.

---

15.   Trans: A reference to one who copies or mimics faithfully.
16.   Trans: A stove factory in a village outside Barcelona.

One evening, he and I had a picnic with four other activists from Tolosa. Crowding together in the apartment, we shared a roast chicken. We always laughed raucously in our reunions. Dandy wore a blue and green Hawaiian shirt, Hélène, a cherry red gown.

12.

I always ask myself what he would have held onto in his memory if he had survived and I had gotten out of the Simca 1100 first, that 25th of September at 18:45, near the bar El Funicular.

He carried two guns, as we all did after the first arrests, two weeks earlier. A 6.35 in the inside pocket of his jacket and an old 9mm long under the belt.[17]

What impressions would he have threshed out for a text like this one?

Would he have affirmed (without cracking a smile) my innocence? Innocent for combating the dictatorship and its thugs?[18]

(Just as I received, this New Year, a portrait of his young face, would he have received a photo or drawing of my own face?)

Would he have saved these colors, imprinted, indelible?

After twenty-eight years in prison and thirty-seven years without going back to Barcelona, my memory is still full of our past. Today, I live the present from the outside, I'm afraid of forgetting, of being surprised by the amnesia of the march of time. As I'm still surprised by the absence of my old comrades... Memory is an unknown territory that one must discover traversing it like an explorer.

Last September, Jordi came to sleep at my house (he says he doesn't remember anything) and I showed him the galley proof of our magazine *CIA*, which was never printed. He remembered... forty-five years afterwards, he described an illustration we found. Olive, Popeye's companion, is walking with huge strides and over her sweater we had put the letters GAC: *Grups Autònoms de Combat*...

---

17. Trans: Both numbers are cartridge dimensions referring to pistols.
18. Trans: Here, "innocent" has the double meaning of "naïve."

Because we live amidst blows, because they barely let us
say we are who we are,
our songs cannot be, sinless, an adornment.
We're hitting bottom.

Damn the poetry conceived as a cultural
luxury by the neutral ones
who, washing their hands of it, avoid and evade.
Damn the poetry that doesn't take sides until it too is
stained.[19]

---

19.   Gabriel Celaya: "La poesía es un arma cargada de futuro." *Poetry is a gun loaded with future.*

4.

Nothing That Seemed Like A Goodbye...

Bru Rovira

Joaquim, Immaculada, M. Carme, Montse, and Merçona are the five siblings of Salvador Puig Antich.[1] That 2nd of March, Joaquim couldn't arrive in time, because he lived in New York. Mercè was thirteen and they decided to leave her at home. The father had heart problems and didn't find out until later; the mother died a year earlier.[2]

Immaculada, Montserrat, and Maria Carme were at their brother's side when he was called to chapel. "Going to chapel" meant that within twelve hours they were going to execute you. His sisters accompanied him during those hours. They awaited dawn and with it, his death, or maybe, a pardon. Only General Franco could give the pardon. They say a Barcelona doctor— Dr. Puigvert, it seems—called him at 8:30. "His Excellency," replied doña Carmen, "is resting, and he cannot be disturbed at this time."[3] The previous evening, the general had signed off on the order. Now, he slept.

Immaculada and Maria Carme told us about his final night. This is their account...

Oriol, the lawyer, never encouraged me to think that things would turn out well, quite the opposite. That Friday, however, he tried to

---

1. Text originally published in the magazine *Arreu: General Information Weekly of Catalunya*, no.19 (February 28–March 6, 1977): 43–45).
2. Trans: This is an understatement. Salvador's father had faced the firing squad during the dictatorship and had his death sentence commuted at the last moment. He never fully recovered, and could not deal with his son's impending execution.
3. Trans: Franco's wife, Carmen Polo y Martínez-Valdés.

cheer me up by telling me there was a decent chance of a pardon. I was completely calm, and so happy I went to have supper at the house of some friends. Oriol arrived with Maria Carme, and the first thing he said was, "No crying and no tears." The news left us all undone. You know when you feel like falling to the ground and curling up in a ball, but you have to get up and just force it all down?

We didn't tell our father because Salvador wasn't so close to him personally, and we also knew he would cause some drama, and Salvador didn't want any dramas. Aside from all that, he had a weak heart. We decided Merçona, the youngest, should stay at home. Merçona was the apple of Salvador's eye. Sometimes, when he came down from Tolosa de Llenguadoc, he picked her up at school and took her out for a snack. "What are your sisters up to?" he would ask, and after a short while he would have to head out. In the chapel, Salvador asked us how she was and said it was best that she hadn't come. It would have marked her for life, and with Merçona at his side, he would have completely fallen apart.

* * *

We got to the prison at eleven. It was full of police, *Guardia Civil*, you can imagine. Before we got to see him, they closed us in a room where they searched us from head to toe, they even kept our nail files. In the chapel, Salvador was alone with nine guards, the director, and one of Oriol's office colleagues. He seemed calm, and in the hour since Oriol had told him he was going to chapel, he had written three letters, none of which we received, by the way. It's said they were all burnt.

We put on a happy face to encourage him, and to avoid causing any dramas. I remember the first thing we said to him was, "Damn, brother, they're really making us sweat for this pardon!" He agreed, but you could see how he actually felt, whereas we were keeping it hidden. From the beginning, the situation was so brutish that we all started chattering. It seems that talk makes the time go by. I brought along many family photos I had enlarged and retouched that very day. It was really good, because for more than an hour we were talking about them, about this day, about that, there at the baptism...

Since he was so nervous, and in some people that provokes diarrhea, he kept going to the toilet. "I've never shit so much in my life!" he said. Every time he went it was a show, because all the guards mobilized, and, of course, they made him shit with the door open.

Among the guards, there were some who were kind, and others who were sadistic. When he was in the bathroom, one official said to Maria Carme, along with Montse and myself, "Do you know what the *garrote* is? It's a ring they put around the neck and then they tighten it, clack, clack, clack..." Salvador came back at that moment, and I didn't know what face to put on. The same guard complained constantly. "Let's see if we can finally get this over with. I've had it up to here with this..." His wife, who lived in the rooms set up for guards in the prison, would sometimes shout out to her husband, "Hey, is it over yet?"

There was another guard who was the one in charge of Salvador during his time at the prison. His name was Jesús, and Salvador thought highly of him. I remember he let us stay longer for visits, he read him newspaper articles, played chess or cards with him... When he had to go, the guard cried and told him, "They'll kill you, but you're going to be immortal." Salvador froze up when he heard this.

* * *

Towards morning, though we couldn't tell exactly what hour it was, since the one thing we never did was look at the clock, we were exhausted. Montse was dizzy and we sat her down in Salvador's seat. We also got some chairs and, for more than an hour, we didn't say anything. For me, it was the most beautiful part of the night. You know what it's like when there are five people who aren't saying anything, yet they're completely in touch?

His eyes were closed, and Maria Carme and I looked at each other and thought, "Four hours from now, he'll be dead." It was beautiful, because with just the slightest physical contact—Maria Carme stroked his hair—we were filled with a kind of electricity. It was that hour before dawn when you're sleepy, but full of thoughts.

* * *

Then Manero arrived and the situation changed. Manero was a chaplain and friend of Salvador, a great person, and the principal at the school he used to go to.[4] They had also visited a couple times after school.

Manero had come for a very specific reason. In the hour when Salvador was alone—before we had arrived—the prison chaplain, Pablo, wanted to come in and preach him some sermons. Salvador had already butt heads with him because he was underhanded, not just as a priest but as a person. He would pull him aside and get sanctimonious, those kinds of things. Salvador chewed him out and said, "I don't want to see your face, do me a favor and leave." The chaplain kept preaching, and then Salvador shouted out: "I'm going to start a riot God Himself couldn't withstand!"

This got Pablo as mad as a hornet and left. I don't know how on Earth he knew Manero, I suppose he had been keeping an eye on Salvador and had called the prison. In any case, the chaplain called him and said, "Come help me out, because this Salvador is going to Hell!" Manero came, all polite, and said he didn't want to visit as a chaplain, just as a person. The authorities asked me about the visit, and I checked with Salvador, without telling him about the chaplain's phone call—that was the only lie that night—and Salvador gave him permission to come in.

Manero was really nervous, but he cheered up when he saw us and we began to speak about memories from school, old classmates and so on.

That whole night we were waiting for the pardon. Salvador

---

4.   Trans: Under the Franco dictatorship, as well as before the Second Republic, the Catholic Church exercised a virtual monopoly on education in the Spanish state.

didn't seem to believe it would come, but he had that little pinch of hope so necessary to endure. The door to the room kept opening. Aside from Oriol, who never stopped coming and going, the guards came in often to give instructions, though we could never hear more than whispers.

Each time the door opened, Salvador's heart would race, as though someone were about to walk in and announce the pardon. He looked at the door obsessively, and after a moment, he'd turn his head as though to hide his anxiety.

Sometimes, the authorities would ask us to step out so they could ask us questions like where we were going to bury him, and so on. Those interruptions were awful, because when I came back in, Salvador would ask me, "What did they say?" And you'd have to cover it up...

* * *

At five in the morning, they wanted to kick us out, but Oriol managed to get us an extension. There were moments when our conversation reached utopian dimensions, like when he said if they didn't kill him, we should bring him his guitar, that he would finish philosophy and start studying medicine... You know when you talk just for the sake of talking?

At eight o'clock they got aggressive with us. They would come to kick us out and we kept saying, "Just a second, just a second." We didn't want to say goodbye to him, because we couldn't, it was impossible, it would be to accept that we would never see him again. He said, "Go on, go on..." and we replied, "No, we're not leaving, we'll wait for you right out here, we'll come right back."

Finally I told him, "Be brave and hold out to the very end." He replied, "Of course, beautiful, don't worry." No strong kiss, no forced embrace, nothing that seemed like a goodbye.

"We're right out here waiting for you," we told him.

* * *

Outside the prison we got seats in a bar. We each ordered a cup of coffee we couldn't even touch. Even though there were plenty of friends there, it was the greatest sense of powerlessness I've felt in my entire life: sitting in a bar waiting for them to come tell you, "Okay, we've finished."

* * *

His coffin was transported in a van. The three of us followed to the cemetery in a car. The cemetery was completely flooded with police. "All this for one body?" Montserrat got really anxious and we let her go in, but not to accompany us all the way to the grave. There it was just Maria Carme, Paco—a work colleague of Oriol—Marc Palmès, the father of Pons Llobet, we still don't know how he managed to get in there, and myself.[5] They opened the coffin for one or two minutes, which I remember as an eternity, a moment that left a huge impression. I wanted to tell him everything I felt, I couldn't have in the chapel because we would have just ended up in a sea of tears.

Since they had just killed him, he didn't look dead, it looked like he was sleeping. That put me completely at ease: seeing Salvador with such a tranquil face, eyes closed like he was sleeping... I just opened my mouth and started talking. I told him he was an amazing person, that I loved him so much, that he was worth more than all the gold in the world, so much more than those people... But he was dead, and they had killed him.

---

5.   Trans: Josep Lluís Pons Llobet, another member of the MIL, already in prison at the time of Salvador's arrest and execution.

5.

What We Chose to Live

Felip Solé

For Salvador

1. It must have been around 1968. Before, during, or after the May Days in France? I don't remember why nor how. Who had arranged it? Why was I the one to go?

Whatever the case, I drove out of Barcelona in my flaming black Stromberg, the 11 horsepower Citroën we called *the duck*. As I drove to Vic, I contemplated the landscape bathed in sunlight, the green hills around me and the different tones of blue in the sky above. Past Vic and Ripoll, my eyes strained as I kept a lookout for the unmistakable silhouettes of shiny black three-corner hats atop bodies deformed by that hated coat of disgusting green: the *Guardia Civil* at their checkpoints, both permanent and random.[1]

That day I didn't see any, not even going over the peak at Collada de Toses. Going down the descent to Cerdanya and all the way to Puigcerdà, I filled my gaze again, this time with a view of the valley. Just at the village entrance, on the right hand side, there was a dirt road to Osseja. Three hundred meters from the village, I stopped. I remember a long stone wall, a meter high, warming in the sun. That's where I had to await my contact.

Did I smoke a cigarette? I don't remember, but I definitely lit one. My body was warmed by the sun, and the air was fresh. After twenty minutes, a figure appeared coming towards me. It was Oriol Solé, my cousin. He had crossed the border using the shepherd's path from Aja to Osseja. He carried a big, heavy bag

---

1. Trans: Vic and Ripoll are two towns in northern Catalunya. The narrator is driving towards the French border.

full of material from the printer's. We shook hands and dropped the bag in *the duck's* trunk. With a decisive gesture he unzipped his jacket and pulled out a publication. As I leafed through it, he took three more copies out of the bag and handed them to me. I don't remember which book or pamphlet it was. Once we got back in the car, we conversed endlessly as *the duck* ate up all the kilometers back to Barcelona. At one point, we sang an old anarchist song from the Civil War: "On the mountain of Alcubierre, a lamp is lit / with a sign that says your permit's not worth shit." We inserted long pauses between stanzas to feast our eyes on the landscapes the sinuous highway offered up to our gaze.

After speaking of Tolosa, where he lived now, of revolutionary struggle, of Marxism and anarchism, of girls... we sang some more. In those days, it took three hours to drive from Cerdanya to Barcelona.

Once in Barcelona, I accompanied him to Badalona. Driving through the town, he directed me to a street where he had me stop in front of a brown apartment bloc illuminated by the light of the afternoon sun. "Remember this house," he told me.

Oriol got out of the Stromberg and he took his leave with "salut," as we shook hands.[2] I watched him until he went in through a door carrying the bag, and then I headed back to Barcelona.

That same journey would be repeated time and again, always following the same routine: Ignasi Solé would contact me, he would ask me to pick up Oriol at the border, and I would agree. Then I would bring him down to Barcelona, and I wouldn't see him again for a while.

I would not go inside that apartment bloc—more specifically, into the apartment of "Little Guy," Santi Soler Amigó—for another two years. And that would be the day I met Salvador Puig Antich, first getting to know him by his *nom de guerre*, "the Doctor."

...you will not use up all of Death's names.

---

2.   Trans: In Catalan as in English, the word for "goodbye" has religious roots, so revolutionaries would historically take their leave with "*salut*," or "health."

Only remember
it is called "old traveler" and "veil,"
and it wears my name, as I speak to you, and yours, as you
listen.[3]

I don't want to reflect on his death, but neither do I ever want to stop feeling it, at once serene and enraged.

2. Not long afterwards, I had to do my military service in Zaragoza. I left *the duck* with my cousin Ignasi Solé, my contribution to his clandestine political activities. I spent eleven months far from Barcelona, but I didn't miss it. In fact, I wanted to travel, to get away from my roots, discover other worlds. That's where I met many of the people with whom, three years later, we would create that autonomous group that had no pretensions of a name or initials, no ambitions of growing or recruiting members. A specific group that supported struggles of all types. Always against capitalist misery, and against the gloom of Franco's fascism. Once I was freed from the military—those officers who made themselves despicable with the way they forced us to live—destiny led me to Arrate, a *"baserri"* or farmhouse outside Beasain, thirty kilometers from Tolosa, a small city in Guipukzoa.[4] I became proficient in speaking Euskera, and then Oriol asked me to serve as a messenger with the dissident members of ETA. Once, I brought a letter to Baiona. I had to get creative in order to get across the border with it at Irun, and without a passport at that. Once in the city, I found the address where the members of ETA-VI Assembly lived.

Afterwards, I spent a few more months in the Basque Country with my obsession for learning Euskera. And I got it down pretty well; really it wasn't as difficult as everybody said. And though I didn't know it yet, my comrades of the future 1,000 would give me the *nom de guerre* "the Basque."

---

3.   Trans: Quote from the poem, "Noves paraules d'agur" or "New words of parting" by Salvador Espriu, a contemporary Catalan poet.

4.   Trans: Not to be confused with Tolosa de Llenguadoc in France, where the MIL was largely based.

I returned to a Barcelona darkened by the cloud of Francoism during Easter Week, 1971. I'm sure it was raining. In any case, the streets were completely empty of cars and people. It was a ghost city, with everybody vacationing in the Pyrenees. This had a positive effect on me. The city was mine, easier to recover despite all the closed windows and shuttered shops of Eixample.

It was already dark. But for me, the night was full of a desire to fight against the system and against the savage dictatorship. I had returned in order to take up our common combat. Not all was bleak: it was the beginning of days, months, and years of passion and revolt... Within a short while, "the Doctor" and I began to develop our fraternal affinity and our friendship in a universe of extreme clandestinity. In my mind, all the images I recall are half faded.

> *Through the halls of Sinera I pass grasping scraps of old memories.*[5]

My account is based on "the recollection and the desire" of those of us who refused to lower our heads.

3. Salvador Puig Antich was not a student who revolted, rather he was a part of the revolt of the youth that took place in the '70s. The worker, the head of a family, doesn't have much of a desire to revolt when he sees that the regime or the labor unions hold him back. But the youth have nothing to lose; we don't have families, we don't have to pay off any debt or mortgage and we usually have jobs that are underpaid and unsatisfactory.

Like many of us, he struggled against the Francoist dictatorship and at the same time distanced himself from the left-wing and extreme left political parties. The same thing was happening throughout the rest of Europe. May '68 in France had set us a good example.

When the communist movement split, in Barcelona the

---

5.   Trans: From "Cementiri de Sinera. Poema V" or "Cemetery of Sinera. Poem V" by Salvador Espriu.

response to the PSUC-PCE—which were way too Stalinist and dirigist—arose in the heart of the movements of students and young workers.[6] The Party excluded the insurgents, and the rupture between Communist Party and politicized youth was definitive and concrete.

He and I, like all the other comrades, took up direct action. But at the same time we criticized ETA in the Basque Country, the RAF in Germany (*Rote Armee Fraktion*, or the Baader-Meinhof gang), and the IRA in Ireland. We demanded proletarian autonomy in contrast to the dirigism of legal or clandestine unions. We declared ourselves the heirs of the May Days of 1937 in Barcelona and we criticized the anarchists and the CNT.

In fact, our revolutionary "project" situated itself in the long path stretching from the barricades of the proletarian revolts and revolutions of Europe at the beginning of the twentieth century, to the trenches of the war in Spain and, especially, the Battle of the Ebre, which would lead to the fall of Catalunya, the bastion of the Republic, continuing to the French resistance and the Spanish *maquis* fighting against European fascism. And the activity of the *maquis* in Catalunya did not end until 1963.

Salvador Puig Antich and other comrades constituted the next wave. We were armed, but we also systematically rejected weapons. We organized ourselves as a group, and at the same time we were opposed to political acronyms or party organizations. The fear we sowed in the Francoist dictatorship was minor compared to the influence we had in all the rebellious movements of Western Europe, above all the anti-nuclear and environmental movements. These, in turn, exercised a decisive influence on the popular revolts against the left-wing dictatorships of Eastern Europe. Little by little, the concept of revolt stopped taking the form of an armed insurrection to turn into the force of the will of the people. The era of Puig Antich, our era, was a turning point. To bring dictatorships toppling down, would barricades not be needed, would it be enough for the people, en masse, to desire it?

---

6. Trans: "Dirigism" is a vanguardist and statist tendency in which the government directs the economy and until such time as the Party takes over the government, it closely controls the movement and the workers' organizations.

And I lose myself and I am, with no message, alone,
beyond song, amongst the forgotten.

To rebel is violence, death imposed, war.

4. One midday, together with several comrades, we spoke of the indignity felt by those of us who are familiar with the historical reality of the group that signed its texts and flyers with the names 1,000, MIL, or GAC, the group that put out the magazine *CIA*. We spoke of the repression that aimed to bury us forever. Without the solidarity of our group, without the creation of the Committee for Solidarity with the Prisoners of the MIL, maybe they would have accomplished it.

"The Doctor" and I spoke frequently on how to break out of the obsolete framework of anti-Francoism and how to defend a coherence between theory and action. It was not at all easy to accomplish, due to the contradictions of militancy and daily praxis. What we wanted was a radical social transformation and the abolition of wage labor. We saw clearly how the society of consumerism was turning into the dictatorship of commodities and multinationals.

Two Seat 1430s are driving down Passeig de Maragall. At a red light, the first driver, "the Doctor," pulls up next to the one I am driving. We have just expropriated a bank on Passeig de Valldaura. There are three of us in my car: "Miquel," "Brave," and myself. In his car, there are five. In the mirror I can see his peaceful smile, and one by one I look at the faces of the others. "Sebas," undaunted as always... The other two look a little tense. I don't get to look at the last one, as the light turns green and I accelerate. There is no police alarm. We are calm and we continue to drive parallel until we get to the intersection of carrer de Sant Antoni Maria Claret and Passeig de Sant Joan. There we go our separate ways: he heads into Gràcia and I keep on towards Plaça d'Espanya.

That evening I have an appointment with "the Doctor" next to Plaça d'Espanya and he hands me a bag full of bills. He's wearing a brown bomber jacket, and he's very happy. He's armed, given that he considers this to be a high risk meeting. I'm not, given that we still barely have any weapons.

In the bag is exactly half of our expropriation. He tells me they want to claim the action with a flyer. The next morning, in a meeting with Ignasi Solé, he will seek our agreement and show us a text with the content of the flyer they want to send to the printers and to the police.

We call a group meeting. They win our approval, but with one condition: we don't want to have a name, and we don't want to claim the action but it's okay that they do if they believe it to be necessary and interesting.

One more successful action. This money will allow us to finance the group's first purchase of guns, a few cars, and the rental of three apartments. Another portion of the money will be given to the workers on strike at a small factory. "Brave" takes charge of organizing the delivery and the practical details of our collaboration.

Approximately one year later, on September 25, 1973, "the Doctor" is wounded and arrested in a trap set up at the Funicular Bar on carrer de Girona number 70. "The Doctor" does every-thing he can to escape. He breaks free of the cops who are holding him and fires a single bullet into one of them. He gets shot twice. The cops have dragged him into a doorway, and they are shooting wildly. One of them receives three lethal gunshot wounds. No one will ever know exactly how he died. The foren-sic report in the autopsy does not coincide at all with the obser-vations of the doctors at Hospital Clínic who pronounced him dead. In any case, "the Doctor" had always told me that if they came for him, he would not let himself get taken in.

The Catalan bourgeoisie, the clandestine parties of Marxist obedience, the Franco regime, they all came to an agreement and declared us the gangsters of Barcelona. And not only the ex-MIL, but everyone who spoke of ending the capitalist system instead of replacing Franco with a democratic dictatorship. Everyone who struggled for a different, more just world...

I remember clearly what happened between October 1973 and March 1974, since those of us who formed the Committee for Solidarity with the Prisoners of the MIL decided to send a comrade from the CNT-FAI to the meetings of the Assemblea de Catalunya as an observer for the Committee and to pass on information about the campaign of solidarity with the prisoners of the MIL. We were fully conscious of the possibility that Salvador Puig Antich, Oriol Solé, and Josep Lluís Pons Llobet would get the death penalty.

As the weeks wore on and especially after ETA assassinated Carrero Blanco, I was convinced that they would take revenge and they would kill Salvador. Those were feverish days and the clocks ran faster than we did as we tried to let the world know who the comrades of the MIL were, through our struggles, our texts, our persons, and our actions.

The day of "the Doctor's" trial neared at the pace of a cavalry charge. The Assemblea de Catalunya did not convene any protests. The PCE-PSUC were infuriated by the sabotage and attacks carried out in the name of the Committee.

Amidst it all, there were exceptions that disobeyed the watchwords of the day, as illustrated by the presence of our Committee representative at the Assemblea de Catalunya. The group No Alineats (Lluís Maria Xirinacs, Father Dalmau, Felip Solé Sabarís, who was the uncle of the Solé Sugranyes brothers, and my uncle as well, Damià Escudé, and others) voiced their concern and gave us support with the Assemblea. The latter, finally, sent a petition to the pope in the name of the bishopric of Barcelona and the Abbey of Montserrat, though they waited until the very last moment when "the Doctor"—Salvador to me, by that point—was about to be garroted.

In regards to libertarians, it can be said that in Catalunya, three or four thousand people—militants or simply those with a conscience—were solidaristic and collaborated in the distribution of the three editions of the MIL dossier and the posters and leaflets put out by the Committee for Solidarity.[7]

The sabotage actions and the plans to break "the Doctor" out

---

7.   Trans: Both originally and currently, with the exception of just a few countries, "libertarian" is a synonym for anarchist.

of prison were entirely organized by our group. And it fell upon me to maintain daily contact with the defense lawyers and clandestine communications with "the Doctor" and Oriol.

Miquel, Brave, Olga, Tys, Georgina, Sònia, Gaudí, and all the others—that handful of comrades who constituted our nameless group—were conscious of the fact that the solidarity campaign with "the Doctor" and the other comrades deprived us of our anonymity. We saw how the sabotage actions exposed us to police repression. We were risking our lives. But none of us ever doubted that decision and questioned our solidarity or the complicity some of us had built up with "the Doctor" and his comrades in struggle.

Some of us, like myself, favored a fusion—never completely defined—with the self-dissolved MIL, whereas others, like Miquel, were less in favor of this proposal. In fact, one of the reasons for its dissolution was that we didn't want to act under the MIL initials nor what they represented.

The day of his detention began like any other, even though events had been speeding up since the arrest of Oriol Solé and Pons Llobet in Bellver de Cerdanya.[8]

At ten in the morning, with a pistol under my belt, I met with "the Doctor" like I had every day for weeks. We had a coffee in a bar at the intersection of Avinguda de Madrid and carrer de Brasil. The first topic of discussion was the news about Oriol Solé and Pons Llobet, who had already been transferred to Modelo prison. The other topic was to work out the unification between them and ourselves and the preparation of new actions. They had created the GAC (Grups Autònoms de Combat, or Autonomous Combat Groups). We said yes to "autonomous combat groups," but in lower case, without the initials. "The Doctor" was also in favor of the unification. I informed him of Miquel's reticence, and he told me about the reticence of his own group. I don't remember which of them were in favor and which were not. We spoke for two hours working out details and practical matters. Then half an

---

8. Trans: A Catalan village near the French border and, coincidentally, also the place where Stalinists engineered the assassination of Antonio Martín Escudero in April 1937 as part of their suppression of the revolutionary collectives.

hour just speaking about ourselves, about how we felt, about girls, or music, or problems we each had within our own group.

In parting we exchanged our usual, "Until tomorrow, same time, same place." In the evening after his fatal rendezvous, he was to meet up with Miquel to smooth out the reservations around unifying the two groups.

That very evening, I looked up Miquel to find out how their meeting had gone. He told me Salvador hadn't shown up. With an uncomfortable premonition, we got into the car and listened to the police radio. The voices were very nervous, constantly cutting themselves off when it seemed they were about to say something important. They were under orders to communicate sensitive matters only by telephone. Without learning anything concrete, we went our separate ways convinced something serious had happened. But I never thought that it was "the Doctor" who had fallen...

> When the light risen up from below the sea
> in the East begins to quiver,
> I have looked at this land, I have looked at this land[9]

In those days of unceasing effort, nearly sleepless, ferociously trying to save "the Doctor's" life, my vision of society became more acerbic, but I never got tired of examining the lives of those around me. I looked at everything, I recorded everything, I preserved the memory...

5. It was six in the evening. At the same time nearly every day since the arrest of "the Doctor" and Oriol Solé, I walked into Oriol Arau's office. Before four, also every day, I visited Joan Sardà, Oriol Solé's lawyer. It was a lost battle, since they weren't capable of establishing a political defense. It was already bold of them to mount a technical defense, especially Oriol Arau in "the Doctor's" trial.

Both lawyers passed us all the judicial information they had.

---

9. Trans: From the poem by Salvador Espriu, "He mirat aquesta terra."

They informed us of how the tribunals and the military officers and the judges operated. And they took the risk—not always, and not always graciously—of passing letters to "the Doctor" and Oriol Solé. And they handed me their replies. Sometimes in writing, usually by word of mouth.

Oriol Arau, his face in a grimace, told me that that night the Council of Ministers presided over by Franco would sign off on the execution of "the Doctor's" death sentence. And, if nothing happened to impede it, Salvador would be executed by *"garrot vil"* in the morning.

Fewer than eleven hours remain before his death.

He tells me he is going to Modelo prison, he has just spoken with Salvador's sisters and the four of them will meet inside.

I take charge of informing our comrades. And I have to talk with Joan Sardà, who still doesn't know the execution order has been signed. We decide all three of us will meet in the evening, when Oriol comes back from the prison before nine, at the Hotel Avenida Palace, on Gran Via between Passeig de Gràcia and the Rambla de Catalunya.

At quarter to nine, I walk into the hotel. Joan Sardà has also arrived. He tells me the execution order is inexorable and that night, they are broadcasting a boxing match, Urtain against I-don't-know-whom to keep everyone entranced in front of the television.[10]

He also updates me on the calls from various Catalan figures to the pope in Rome and to European politicians, asking for their intervention to pressure the dictator. Everyone has on their mind the trial of the ETA members in Burgos in 1970 and the last minute commutation of their death sentences. I don't think that will happen this time. I am completely convinced, ever since the death of Carrero Blanco, that they will rub him out in the grossest way possible.

Until now, he hasn't believed it. He still holds out hope. I have a flashback of his response to the two messages sent

---

10.   Trans: José Manuel Urtain was a contemporary boxer from the Basque Country and three-time European heavy weight champion.

through Oriol Arau, proposing two different possibilities of an escape plan. He replied that he was worried they would kill him in the attempt and that it was better to keep fighting in the halls of the military tribunal.

Is it too late now to try something audacious? I think it over again and again, my belly full of rage. Is it really too late?

Oriol Arau walks in the door. His face is even more twisted than before. He comes up to me and tells me that the sisters have stayed with Salvador. And, in response to his request, they have called for a priest, a teacher from his student days. Oriol orders a cheese sandwich. I take a mint and lime blossom tea. Joan reminds us that we have to go quickly to the Bar Association, where there's an urgent meeting. We take a taxi for carrer de Mallorca.

The meeting hall at the Association is full to the brim, or at least it seems so to me.

Oriol Arau takes the floor. He lays out the most recent occurrences at the prison: the disgusting behavior of the guards, the cruelty of the situation, the sisters, alone, with Salvador.

Joan Sardà also speaks. I don't know what he says, because as he speaks I've taken Oriol aside and I tell him he has to ask them to do something, to shake the dust off, to break out of their apathy.

When Joan Sardà finishes, Oriol Arau addresses the room again. More people keep arriving, every time I look up the hall is even fuller. Lawyers, anti-Francoist politicians, left-wing and Catalanist businessmen, well known members of the PSUC... And someone says a comrade of Salvador Puig Antich wants to speak.

A complete, dramatic silence extends though the hall.

Suddenly, all eyes are on me. In the middle of the hall I can see my uncle, the doctor Felip Solé Sabarís.

I go up to the podium and explain that Salvador's death must be prevented. That there is still time to subdue the Francoist regime with bold and resonant actions. I stop to breathe and to get the knot out of my throat.

I begin again! I say: "We must not fall into resignation!" I ask them to organize squads of cars to go to the industrial zones, in front of the factories, to inform the workers coming off their shifts of this latest vindictive murder by Franco. Then these squads should drive through the main streets of the city honking their horns, stopping at every intersection to inform the inhabitants of the crime the Francoists were about to commit.

I asked for more things, things that, in that moment, seemed possible to me.

When I finished, the silence was as heavy as a black fog. In the front rows, everyone was looking down at the ground, their heads lowered.

Someone, from the back, responded: "It's too late to go to the SEAT.[11] The shift has already changed!"

No one else spoke up for one or two long minutes. I looked at them and I didn't understand how anyone could sit there with their head lowered, looking at the ground in the meeting hall.

Were they resigned? Indifferent?

After a while, the murmurs grew. They began speaking about what they would do in the morning when Salvador's corpse was brought to the cemetery.

I felt pain and rage.

Salvador, "the Doctor," was still alive and they were speaking of the flowers they would leave on his grave.

Maybe they were right and there was nothing to be done, but I have never forgiven them.

The slow memory
of the days
that are gone for good.[12]

The time has come to thresh the memories assembled with such passion, joy, and desire...

Barcelona, January 2019

---

11.   Trans: SEAT is the Spanish car company, with major factories in and around Barcelona.

12.   Trans: The final lines of "Cementiri de Sinera" by Salvador Espriu.

6.

Salvador's Memory

(In Mnemosyne's Shadow)
Imma, Montse, Carme, and Merçona Puig Antich

Since that sad 2nd of March, 1974, when the executioner cut short our brother's life, we have sworn, practically without words, that we would defend Salvador's name, as an idealistic youth with a good heart and a great sense of justice, who took responsibility for his convictions and was profoundly committed.[1] We would never let him go down in the history books as a murderer and bandit, which is how the Francoist regime presented him in the media in those treacherous days. That lie only served to cover up their own brutal cruelty.

From the beginning, we encountered people who stood beside us, who encouraged us, and who helped us move forward. With them, over the years, we have discovered the truth in reports and interviews, excellent investigative books, exhibitions, documentaries, conferences, talks, informative events, and even a movie.

From Salvador's execution to the present moment, forty-five years have gone by. For us, the family, it is a fact that hits us day after day, intimately and completely. Many other people as well, personally or as representatives of a public organization, have felt and feel personally affected by Salvador's case. They have given us support and love throughout all of the years that have gone by since that wretched March of 1974. That's why, any chance we get, we express our gratitude for their work and their drive in the struggle for getting the truth recognized and getting justice served.

In our family, and also individually, we have always preserved the memory of our brother. Most of the time we have done so

---

1. Trans: Mnemosyne was the Greek goddess of memory.

naturally and spontaneously, letting ourselves get carried along by the memories that flow through our heads and our hearts again and again. It's not strange that, in the end, we have built a sort of monument out of memories so alive they still make us tremble, alongside others that have crystallized into something like caricatures that, nonetheless, retain their potency. Altogether, it represents for us a way to keep our brother alive. While we live, he will not die.

We can make out different layers in this monument of memory. The first, inevitably, is his life as son and brother until he left home. In many interviews, we have explained what Salvador was like within our family (affectionate, fun, a prankster) and what he was like in the different schools where he completed his primary and high school education (idealist, nonconformist, and rebellious in the face of anything he judged to be unjust).

Another group of memories focus on Salvador as an adolescent, when he began earning a living working in the office of a car dealership and taking economics classes on the side, until it was time to go off and complete his military service in Mallorca and Eivissa. His intellectual preoccupations and his commitment to facing society's problems were already alive and well at that time and it was outside the home where he was able to encounter peers who could better understand and help him.

The period when our brother took the definitive step in his commitment to social transformation, we experienced from a distance, even though for a while he was living in the home of Imma and his brother-in-law. At that point we could guess some things, we interpreted certain behaviors, we lost sleep over the risks he might be running, but we respected him completely, and when we could, we helped him. For his part, he never wanted to involve us, and without breaking off the relation, he kept us on the margins in order to guarantee our safety. Meanwhile, he clarified his doubts, overcame the contradictions that didn't let him sleep for a long time, and his life began to make perfect sense within the activism he carried out in his group, the MIL.

The distance we experienced came to a tragic end on September 26, 1973, when our father read in the newspaper what had happened in the afternoon of the day before: a run-in between the police and a few members of the MIL, the shootout in the doorway on carrer Girona, the death of deputy inspector Anguas Barragán, and our brother, critically injured in the firefight.

From there, our memories accelerate and they pile up vertiginously. Right away we went to Hospital Clínic, where we knew they had taken him. We thought we would be able to see him, but it was impossible; the police wouldn't allow it. All the same, our cries of "Salvador, we're here!" resonated loudly enough that they reached his ears. What we were really afraid of was that Salvador would remain in the hands of the police, who had already tried taking him away and liquidating him, an attempt stopped only by the doctors at Clínic. Afterwards, on October 2, when we learned he had been transferred to Modelo prison, we breathed more easily. At least there they wouldn't torture him...

In cell 443 of the fifth gallery, Salvador was held in isolation and closely watched during all of his visits. Aside from direct family, the lawyer Oriol Arau, who already knew him for a while, visited him almost daily. During the next five months, everything proceeded at a panicked pace. On October 19, they carried out the reconstruction of the crime scene. The prosecutor let it be known that he was asking for two death penalties. On December 20, Admiral Carrero Blanco was assassinated. On January 8, the war tribunal began (and ended) in the office of the Captaincy General of Barcelona, at the end of les Rambles, just next to the Columbus monument. The trial was typical of a totalitarian State: moving quickly, they refused all the defense lawyers' arguments, they refused to carry out ballistics tests, they refused to give Salvador a psychiatric evaluation to assess the state of shock he might have been in during the events on carrer Girona, they did not admit witnesses proposed by the defense, especially not the doctors from Hospital Clínic, etc. At the same time, all the military paraphernalia was resplendent: impeccable uniforms, sabers laid upon the table, brilliant medals... In the morning, *El Noticiero Universal* ran the headline: "Hearing for Sentencing in Six Hours."

The verdict and sentence were dictated in the morning: two death penalties. Quim, the brother who lived in the United States, came home as fast as he could the moment he found out. He thought they might kill him at any moment. He went to see him in prison and Salvador, much calmer than he was, was making jokes about American scientists and doctors. When he came out of the visit, Quim was undone. He didn't go back to see him again.

On January 12, the appeal was presented to the Supreme Tribunal of Military Justice and on February 11, there was a hearing in Madrid. In parallel, petitions for leniency began to circulate among a huge number of groups (journalists, lawyers, religious organizations...) and also attacks on Spanish interests all over Europe (Brussels, Strasbourg, Paris, Rome, Tolosa, Milan...) and in the Spanish state itself (the Monument to the Fallen in Barcelona, in Donostia...). On February 19, a new verdict ratified the death penalty. From then on, there only remained the formality (though not as formal a decision as it might seem) for the Council of Ministers presided by Franco to "*approve*" the order. That happened on Friday, March 1, and in the morning of the next day, the sentence was carried out. The burial happened on the 3rd at the cemetery on Montjuïc.

We have often explained how raw it was to spend the night with Salvador in the chapel. It's engraved in fire in our hearts; we know every minute. We can still see ourselves there, in the prison visiting room, pretending to be strong, making jokes, sharing the latest family gossip, looking at photos, speaking about trivial things... and watching as the possibility of a pardon slipped away with every passing hour. We can still hear the echo of his, "See you later, girls," which was the last thing we heard him say when they were kicking us out of the hall. We left in a rage over not being able to accompany him right up to the final moment. They didn't even allow his lawyer, Oriol Arnau, to be present. Only hostile strangers were there, as spectators, in a final act of cruel, savage revenge—for who could count on decency from a court system that had obeyed the desires of the police and the Francoist State?

At 10:15, we saw the hearse leave for the Montjuïc cemetery. There, for a few minutes, we were able to see the corpse that so recently had been full of life. The next day, at the burial, the police cordoned off the entrances to the cemetery and ended up doling out beatings, as always. The reaction of the public made itself felt, late, but present nonetheless. It was too strong a blow for people's conscience. For days, all the news was about protests, prayers, demonstrations, publications... They shut down the university, overseas they did actions against Spanish embassies, and so forth. From then on, since no one really dies if they're not forgotten, the personal and political memory of Salvador became one of our vital objectives. It was necessary for the truth to come out and for the justice system to recognize the grave error made in Salvador's case.

Right away, we knew we weren't alone in our effort. Individual people, but also journalists all over Europe and even within the Spanish state wanted to know what had happened. And so all sorts of articles in very different media began to appear, and later on, especially on big anniversaries, highly detailed dossiers.

We remember—and here we can only cite a small sample— the articles in the magazine *Arreu* under the title "Puig Antich's Last Night" (February–March 1977); the investigative book by the team coordinated by Ramon Barnils that used the name Carlota Tolosa, entitled *La torna de la torna* (1985); the half-hour report on TV3 (1994), and the related book by Francesc Escribano (*Countdown*, 2001), which served as the basis for the movie *Salvador* (2006), produced by Jaume Roures, directed by Manuel Huerga, and starring Daniel Brühl. In fact, it was the criticism of aspects of this movie that motivated some groups who considered themselves to be the ideological heirs of the MIL to give another vision of the struggle carried out by Salvador and his comrades.[2]

Starting in the '90s, all of these memorials, personal and public, were accompanied by an attempt to reopen the court

---

2. Trans: In fact, as revealed in Chapters 5, 9, and 11, Salvador's comrades never stopped sharing their vision of their common struggle from the moment of his arrest, though his sisters may well not have been in contact with veterans of the MIL and the OLLA until after the release of the criticized film.

case. With the help of solidaristic lawyers, we have attempted two formal appeals, both of which have been unfruitful, despite the Spanish state presuming to be an advanced democracy that has left behind the injustices and arbitrariness of the previous regime.

One of the motives that pushed us to demand a judicial revision was a question of personal dignity. Salvador always assumed responsibility for everything he did. But they portrayed him as a criminal from the moment they arrested him to the moment they executed him, an unscrupulous delinquent who killed in cold blood, who engaged in wanton arson, all the accusations that were printed in the regime's media.

A second reason was a question of collective dignity. In Salvador's case, Francoism made a mockery of the opposition, especially the Catalan opposition, even breaking the rules of their own game. We already know that a trial under the Francoist dictatorship is anything but democratic, but even according to their own criteria they flouted several principal details that left Salvador's lawyers completely defenseless:

First: No ballistics test was carried out, with the members of the jury (military officers every one) alleging that, as men of war, they were competent enough in that regard.

Second: The court neither inquired nor investigated what was done with the shell casings from the shootout. They simply disappeared with the clear intention of avoiding any contradictions in the autopsy of deputy inspector Anguas Barragán.

Third: They put their complete trust in the autopsy carried out at the police station on carrer Enric Granados and not at the Forensic Anatomy Institute of Hospital Clínic, which should have been standard procedure in a case such as this. One must ask if the autopsy were so simple an operation that it could be improvised with hardly any surgical instruments.

Fourth: They rejected all the witnesses proposed by the defense, particularly the doctors who were on duty at Clínic the day of the arrest, who were responsible for inspecting the corpse of the deputy inspector and attending Salvador's wounds.

It was on the initiative of the lawyer Francesc Caminal that we presented our first petition, in 1994, for the reopening of the case, presenting all our arguments. On June 27 of the same year, the Supreme Court denied our petition on the grounds that the defense was not presenting any new evidence nor were there any relevant developments pertaining to the case. We appealed to the International Court of Human Rights in Strasbourg, but that agency claimed it could do nothing, since, at the time of the incident (1974), the Spanish state was not a signatory to the Universal Declaration of Human Rights and, as such, the court had no jurisdiction.

We initiated the second petition in 2002 when the Parliament of Catalunya unanimously approved a motion to provide us with the economic support necessary to file for the reopening of the case. A group of lawyers led by Sebastià Martínez Ramos and Olga de la Cruz, in coordination with Francesc Caminal, got to work and went from A to Z doing everything required by the Spanish justice system to concede the possibility of reopening a military trial: presenting new evidence and new allegations that could be corroborated. They presented the product of this magnificent labor on February 3, 2005, in the Fifth Hall of the Supreme Court of Military Justice, presided over by Ángel Calderón, they entered into record all the irregularities of the 1974 trial (above all the disallowance of any feasible defense on the part of the accused), as well as new evidence:

1) A detailed reconstruction of the different angles of movement of all the actors involved in Salvador's arrest and the subsequent shootout at carrer Girona 70. This was a principal contribution, using a technique that did not exist in 1974 and clarifying a good many things, such as the possible trajectories of bullets fired and the fact that Salvador was not the only one to shoot deputy inspector Anguas. What's more, it highlighted the inexperience and lack of professionalism of a team of police who knew they

were going to confront individuals who might be armed and whom they themselves had characterized as "highly dangerous." On top of it all, they weren't even carrying handcuffs, which is why they had to try to immobilize Salvador with their belts.

2) The minutes from the autopsy performed on deputy inspector Anguas. The notes are typewritten, and one can observe an addition, written later on a different typewriter, regarding the number of bullet wounds in the corpse, and the location of entry wounds and exit wounds. This manipulation changed the number of bullet wounds in the deputy inspector's body to match the number of bullets fired by Salvador. The lawyers proposed to the judges to submit the autopsy minutes to an analysis, but they were overruled given the obviousness of the changes to the document.

3) The lawyers proposed new testimony, primarily from the doctors Barjau and Latorre, who attended to both Anguas and Salvador at Hospital Clínic and who have always maintained that the body of the deputy inspector had more bullet wounds than what was recorded in the autopsy. Other witnesses were also proposed, such as Xavier Garriga, a comrade of Salvador's who was arrested at the same time, and Francesc Caminal, who was Salvador's original lawyer together with Oriol Arau. The magistrates of the Third Hall of the military court heard out the doctors Barjau and Latorre, but they refused the testimony of the other proposed witnesses (including that of a military officer present at the autopsy who agreed to testify).

These and other arguments were presented to the Fifth Hall of the Supreme Court and later, after a debatable and polemic decision by Ángel Calderón, were redirected to the Third Hall. In June 2007, a reduced group of five judges decided there was no cause for reopening the case, voting three against two, almost a tie. The appeal to the Constitutional Court was once again useless, and the appeal to the International Court of Human Rights in Strasbourg was met with the same reply as in 1994: Salvador's case was an internal affair of the Spanish state.

This new refusal by the Spanish justice system, even more arbitrary than the first, incited broader support for Salvador's memory. The journalist Jordi Panyella compiled a brilliant documentation, both new and relevant, in his excellent book on the dark details of our brother's case: *Salvador Puig Antich: Case Not Closed* (Angle Editorial, 2014). Also, a professor in the Contemporary History Department at the Universidad Complutense of Madrid, Gutmaro Gómez Bravo, in his book *Puig Antich: The Unfinished Transition* (Taurus, 2014), carried out a deep and detailed analysis of the circumstances of the 1974 trial and ended with a detailed exploration of the appeal in 2007.

Barcelona City Hall, which had decided to dedicate a plaza to Salvador's memory, solemnly inaugurated the space on March 5, 2016, also erecting a symbolic monument. Even though the plaza was quite distant from the city center, it was a way of recognizing Salvador's honor and that of all the victims of Francoism.

For its part, the Parliament of Catalunya unanimously approved the law 11/2017 on June 29, 2017, in favor of juridical reparations for the victims of Francoism, including declaring null and void all the trials and war tribunals held between April 1938 and December 1978. The total number of those repressed just in Catalunya in those dates is 66,590.

And again, the city of Barcelona, this time in the framework of the Network of Cities Against Francoist Impunity—created among many Spanish cities in 2016 with the manifesto "Truth, Justice, and Reparation"—filed a complaint in 2018 against Carlos Rey, member of the military tribunal and author of our brother's sentence.

The Spanish political world, however, has always followed a different compass. During the democratic transition, they wanted to turn the page on an uncomfortable past, so they used the Amnesty Law (46/1977), approved October 15, 1977. That law, also known as the "full stop" law, amnestied those who had been repressed by the regime (those who hadn't committed any crime from a democratic point of view), but above all it served to protect the Francoist repressors who, from that point on, had the perfect alibi for evading responsibility for all their crimes. There have been many failed attempts to revoke this unjust law, which protects those who have committed crimes against humanity. The Law of Historical Memory, which came into effect on December 26, 2007 and which should have nullified all the sentences passed by Francoist tribunals, also failed to live up to even the minimum expectations.

The disappointment was clear in the first lines of the preamble, given how they insisted that the memory of the victims of Francoism was a personal, family matter and thus denying that the crimes of Francoism were against all society and against humanity itself. In this way, the Spanish state, always careful with the sociological Francoism that still persists, distanced itself from any possible measures that would need to be taken in response to further accusations.

For all these reasons, the victims of repression of the Francoist regime and family members of victims have organized ourselves to achieve the justice and reparations we have a right to. In this context, our brother's case is just one among thousands that demand justice. The refusal of the Spanish state to repeal the Amnesty Law of 1977, despite the petitions of international organizations such as the UN, has pushed the plaintiffs to appeal to tribunals outside of Spain, invoking the concept of Universal Jurisdiction, endorsed by the UN itself, for crimes against humanity, which have no statute of limitations.

This is the basis of the "Argentine Complaint." Involved is a large group of the family members of victims of Francoism who have made declarations and filed complaints with the Argentinian judge Maria Servini, against those responsible for the crimes of Francoism, committed between July 17, 1939 and June 15, 1977 (the date of the first democratic elections). The jurisdiction of an Argentine court is based on the idea of "Universal Justice," which holds that the crime of genocide and other crimes against humanity can be prosecuted by any court system, whether or not it belongs to the country in which the crimes were committed.

Merçona, after an attempt to make a declaration via videoconference at the Argentine Embassy in Madrid, blocked by pressure from the Spanish Foreign Affairs Ministry, traveled to Buenos Aires in December 2014 with thirty other plaintiffs. Their experience was incredible: finally, a judicial authority listened to her statements after years and years of us knowing, impotently, that it could not be proven that Salvador had killed the police officer, as was demonstrated in the petition to reopen the case in 2007. What's more, she could expose many of the irregularities that were committed throughout the trial in 1974 and was able to express her conviction that the death penalty had been the dictatorship's vindictive response for the assassination of Carrero Blanco. As a result of her declaration, the Argentine judge requested the indictment of José Utrera Molina, one of the ministers who signed off on the execution order on March 1, 1974, and that of the previously mentioned Carlos Rey, member of the military tribunal who authored the sentence giving Salvador a double death penalty.

The Argentine Complaint, which already includes four hundred plaintiffs, has given us hope and has already resolved some of the individual petitions, such as that of Timoteo Mendieta's family, who have been able to recover the body of their loved one and bury him with the rest of the family, despite continuous harassment by the Spanish state.[3] Many thousands of other victims of Francoist repression, us among them, are nourished by this hope for justice.

Currently, progress is blocked on two sides: the Spanish state has an obstructionist attitude, ignoring the norms of international organizations regarding crimes that do not expire, and therefore refusing to allow plaintiffs to make declarations and refusing to extradite those who are indicted. And also Argentina today, under the government of Mauricio Macri, is reticent to create more tension in its diplomatic relationship with Spain, and therefore it has ceased to facilitate the labor that Judge Maria Servini has been carrying out up to now.

---

3. Trans: Timoteo Mendieta was a UGT member from Guadalajara, executed by fascist troops in 1939 and buried in a mass grave. Though his story is similar to thousands of others, he became well known due to the efforts of the family to preserve his memory, and to locate and identify his body.

This means that our struggle, and that of so many others beside us, has no expiration date.

March 2019.

7.

Chronology of the Life of Salvador Puig Antich

(1948–1974)

1948-1954

May 30, 1948

Salvador is born in the family home at Pas de l'Ensenyança 1, third floor, second door, in Barcelona. He is the third of six siblings (Joaquim, Imma, Montse, Carme, and Merçona).

June 6, 1948

He is baptized in the parish of Saints Just and Pastor.

He attends the preschool run by the Carmelite nuns on carrer de Lledó until he is six years old.

1954–1958

He attends elementary school at La Salle Bonanova.

At seven, he receives his First Communion at the Carmelites.

1959-1962

He attends high school at La Salle Bonanova.

In his third year, he is expelled for punching a teacher in defense of another student.

He finishes the year at the school of the Caputxins de Pompeia.[1]

---

1. Trans: The *Ordo Fratrum Minorum Capuccinorum* is a branch of the Franciscans and, like the Carmelites, a mendicant order. Under Francoism as before the Second Republic, most education in the Spanish state was controlled by the Catholic Church.

1962–1964

He continues school with the Salesians in Mataró. In his second year, he insists on dropping out or changing schools, threatening to run away if they don't assent. At the end of the year he passes all his classes and, after a conversation with his parents and Father Manero, they agree to let him stop attending the school.

His school performance is adequate, with grades that are low but passing, though he nearly always receives a suspension for behavioral problems, given his restless character and his frequent conflicts with teachers. He prefers sport to school. He is a good footballer (a forward) and a good gymnast, despite his short stature. He wins a few trophies, of which he is quite proud.

He spends most summers with the family at Sant Esteve de Palautordera.

1964–1967

He begins working in the office at Motorsol (a car mechanics on carrer de Mandri). When he finishes his sixth and final year of high school, his parents buy him a wrist watch, which he treasures thereafter.

After school, he continues working at Motorsol and also takes a few private classes. In 1966, he begins night school at the Maragall Institute to prepare for university. There, he meets two future comrades of the MIL: Xavier Garriga and Ignasi Solé Sugranyes.

At the end of 1967, he joins *Comissions Obreres* in the Pi neighborhood. It is the beginning of his political activity.

1968–1969

He finishes night school and begins studying for the university entrance exam. At Maragall, he meets Montse Plaza and the two begin dating for the next two years. He and his friends speak frequently of politics.

In the fall of 1968, he begins studying Economics at the

university, while giving classes on the side in Latin and Greek to high school students.[2]

In January of 1969, the state of exception is declared, and, for security reasons, Salvador leaves his office job and goes to live in the house of a family friend.

July 26 1969

In a photo at his sister Imma's wedding, Salvador appears on his motorcycle, together with Xavier Garriga and Jordi Cortès.

In the fall, he begins his second year of economics, though his focus is elsewhere and he only passes two classes.

He continues giving private classes and, at one point, also works as a driver for his older brother Joaquim, a doctor who works at Sant Climent de Llobregat.

1970

In August, he goes on vacation to Menorca with Mati Muñiz, his sister Imma, and her husband Pep.

September 16

Salvador begins his obligatory military service in Palma. There he writes the following ditty:

"Nights of Palma, / nights in the tent, / I am here, I feel absent. / If the moon is yellow / and the sun resplendent, / I feel turned off, lacking my element. / The earth is dry, / without water it gets sicker / I'll make it through the military with a good helping of liquor."

1971

Assigned to Eivissa with the 48th Teruel Infantry Regiment, Salvador is appointed head of the sick bay (explaining his subsequent *nom de guerre*, "the Doctor").

---

2.   Trans: At this point, Salvador is enrolled as an *"alumne lliure"* or "free student," a designation allowing working class students to pass courses by taking exams only, without the obligation to attend classes.

In February, his father has a heart attack, and he returns to Barcelona.[3] He requests leave through the end of March to fill in at the pharmacy where his father is an employee, Drogas Vita, but they only give him fifteen more days.

In August, his mother comes to visit him in Eivissa. Over the summer, he engages in intensive epistolary activity, writing to family and friends, including some particularly long letters to the latter about the workers' movement and the social revolution.

In September, his mother helps him enroll in Philosophy and Letters at the Universitat Central in Barcelona. At the end of the year, he finishes his military service and moves in with Imma and Pep in their apartment on Via Augusta, where he begins printing clandestine propaganda.

He also begins going to meetings at Santi Soler Amigó's house in Badalona, together with Xavier Garriga and the Solé Sugranyes brothers, Oriol, Ignasi, and Jordi. Together they debate politics. Eventually, his militant activities prevent him from finishing the school year.

1972

In the spring, Salvador goes to Tolosa with Jordi Solé Sugranyes, Jean-Marc Rouillan, and Jean-Claude Torres. They train with guns and learn techniques for stealing cars.

May 29
Oriol Solé Sugranyes is released from prison in France. Quickly the group begins acquiring more guns.

Summer
Salvador goes to Switzerland, thinking to put out a record in homage to Che Guevara. When he returns to Tolosa, he begins to participate fully with the MIL in all its actions. In October, the

---

3.   Trans: After the war, Salvador's father had been up before the firing squad and pardoned at the last moment; his heart never recovered. See the Introduction.

Grups Autònoms de Combat of the MIL are officially created. The group authors the text "On Armed Agitation," published in the first issue of *CIA*.

October 21
First robbery in which Salvador participates: the expropriation of a branch of the Laietana Savings Bank, on Camí del Mig in Mataró (the haul is 990,200 pesetas).[4]

November 18
The MIL and the OLLA act together to expropriate a branch of the Pension Bank on carrer Escorial in Barcelona (169,000 pesetas).

November 23
Salvador's mother writes him a letter, which is smuggled across the border and delivered to him in France. She has leukemia.

November 28
The MIL and the OLLA act together to expropriate a branch of the Central Bank on Passeig de Valldaura in Barcelona (1,000,000 pesetas).

December
The group writes the texts "The Multiplication of the Combat Groups" and "What We Base Our Practice On."

December 14
Robbery (for the second time) of printing material in Tolosa.

December 29
Expropriation of a branch of the Laietana Savings Bank on carrer de Juan Valera in Badalona (764,000 pesetas).

---

4.   Trans: A little over $14,000 at the contemporary exchange rate. In 1967, the peseta is pegged to the dollar at a 70:1 rate.

1973

January
Joaquim visits their dying mother. By that time, he is already living in New York City.

January 19
Expropriation of a branch of the Provincial Bank, on carrer de Benedicto Mateo in Barcelona (658,000).

February 7
His mother dies. Salvador goes home to see her, even though he has been living clandestinely for some time.[5]

March 2
While the group is expropriating the Hispano-American Bank on Passeig de Fabra i Puig in Barcelona, a firefight breaks out with detectives from the Criminal Brigade. Two detectives and one bank employee are wounded (1,500,000 pesetas).

March 8
Trial in Tolosa for the theft of printing materials. Salvador and Jean-Marc Rouillan do not show up.

Spring
He writes the following texts: "Before asking ourselves, what shall we do, it's better to ask, what's going on?"; "Armed Agitation— Real Movement"; a draft of "The emancipation of the workers must be the task of the working class itself, or it will not be"; "On the brilliant idea of dismembering the group"; "We still can't see the horizon"; "Political Military Organization"; "Who can revive a corpse?" and "Point of Discussion."

---

5.   Trans: In fact, he was accompanied by two or three members of the group armed with machine guns, who waited discreetly outside the house, should the police make a raid while he visited.

June

Salvador reestablishes contact with members of the OLLA to coordinate more joint actions and possibly unify the two organizations.[6]

June 6

Expropriation of a branch of the Bank of Bilbao on carrer Major in Sarrià (300,000 pesetas).

June 19

Expropriation of a branch of the Spanish Credit Bank, on Gran Via de Carles III in Barcelona (3,000,000 pesetas).

July

Salvador authors the texts "Terrible History, December '72–July '73" and "To the Central Solidarity Commission."

July 2

Salvador pulls out of a planned expropriation, organized by the OLLA, of the telegraph and postal office on Via Laietana, because he considers it too risky.

July 21

Salvador forgets a bag with falsified documents, keys, money, and a pistol at the Caspolino Bar on Plaça de Gal·la Placídia in Barcelona. With this material, the police locate Montse Plaza, who they detain and interrogate. At her house, they find Salvador's telephone contact number.

Salvador abandons the apartment on Salas i Ferrer and moves into Josep Lluís Pons Llobet's apartment on Avinguda Jordan.

August

The MIL holds a congress in Tolosa where the group decides to dissolve.

---

6. Trans: Contact had waned after their previous collaboration because the OLLA did not approve of the MIL's practice of claiming actions as a formal group.

September 10
Salvador returns to Barcelona and sets hims_lf up in the Vallcarca neighborhood.

September 15
Oriol and Jordi Solé Sugranyes and Josep Lluís Pons rob the Pensions Bank in Bellver de Cerdanya for the second time. The escape goes wrong, as they run into the Guardia Civil and a heavy shootout ensues. The next day, Oriol and Josep Lluís are arrested, while Jordi manages to cross the border and take refuge in France. Salvador and Jean-Marc Rouillan had refused to participate in the robbery.

September 25
Shootout with the police on carrer Girona, resulting in the death of deputy inspector Francisco Jesús Anguas Barragán. Salvador is gravely wounded (shot in the jaw and the shoulder) and arrested.

That very night, a meeting was scheduled to make a definitive decision on the proposed fusion of the MIL and the OLLA.

Salvador's sisters try to visit him at Hospital Clínic, but the police do not allow it.

The OLLA prepares to break Salvador out of the hospital, but they abandon their plan when some sympathetic doctors let the organization know that he is being closely watched.

October 2
Salvador is sent to Modelo prison.

October 19
Police forensics reconstruct the events in the fatal doorway on carrer Girona.

October 23
The military jurisdiction takes over the case.

November 26
The government seeks two death penalties.

1974

January 8
Court martial in the office of the Military Command of Barcelona. The OLLA prepares a plan to rescue Salvador in the evening as he is being transported back to Modelo, but he rejects the proposal, fearing that he or one of the comrades might get killed.

January 9
Salvador is given a death sentence.

January 12
His brother Joaquim arrives in Barcelona and visits him in prison.

February 11
In Madrid, the Supreme Council of Military Justice reviews the case.

February 19
The Supreme Council of Military Justice ratifies the sentence.

March 1
The Council of Ministers signs off on the death sentence. Salvador spends the night in the chapel with his sisters Imma, Carme, and Montse. He has asked them to leave Merçona, the youngest, at home to spare her the experience. The lawyer Oriol Arau works all night to try to win clemency.

March 2
Salvador is executed. The death certificate is signed at 9:40 in the morning.

March 3
Salvador is buried at the cemetery on Montjuïc (Sant Agustí cluster, niche no. 2,737).

Chronology of the Autonomous Workers' Movement in Catalunya and of the MIL and the OLLA

(1962–1976)

1962

Widespread strikes by Asturian miners.

1963

April 20, the Franco regime executes communist leader Julián Grimau.

August 7, the last anarchist guerrilla from the Civil War, Ramon Vila Capdevila, is killed in an ambush by the *Guardia Civil* at Castellnou de Bages.

August 18, the Franco regime executes Francisco Granados Gata and Joaquín Delgado Martínez, members of the anarchist group Defensa Interior.

November 14, the French paper *Le Monde* publishes an interview on the front cover with the abbot of Montserrat. It is the first ecclesiastic voice in the Spanish hierarchy to be raised in a public criticism of the Franco dictatorship.

In December, the State creates the Tribunal de Orden Público (Tribune of Public Order, TOP), a new judicial branch to assist in political repression.

1964

In November, at the Sant Medir church in the Bordeta neighborhood, the Comissió Obrera Central of Barcelona is created at a meeting of three hundred workers representing fifty-nine workplaces. Other Comissions Obreres are also being created in Madrid and the Basque Country.

1965

February 23, three thousand workers protest in front of the Trade Union building on Via Laietana. The previous day, the central committee of the city's Comissions Obreres had been arrested before they could deliver the workers' demands to the CNS. The demands consisted of pay rises, the right to strike, and the right to organize.

The police arrest numerous people at the end of the protest.

March 22, the workers of the Elizalde steel mill go on strike and the very next day, the company agrees to a 30 percent pay raise.

April 30, hundreds of workers participate in a protest convened by the PSUC, MSC, FSF, and FOC. On May 1, three hundred workers participate in another protest on Plaça de Catalunya.[1]

1966

March 9, students of the Sindicat Democràtic d'Estudiants de la Universitat de Barcelona (Democratic Students' Union of the University of Barcelona), convene a meeting at the convent of the Capuchins in Sarrià. Present are thirty-three intellectuals, five hundred students, two priests, three international observers, and seven journalists. The meeting lasts until March 11th, when the police break into the convent and seize the ID cards of everyone present, obliging them to recover their IDs at the Central Police Station on Via Laietana, where they are interrogated, some are arrested, and others given hefty fines. The events become known as the *Caputxinada*.

May 11, 130 priests protest in front of the Central Police Station, presenting a petition of protest against the torture inflicted on a student. They are brutally repressed.

---

1.   Trans: The Moviment Socialista de Catalunya and the Força Socialista Federal, both socialist organizations critical of the Stalinist-controlled PSUC. The other organizations are described in the Glossary.

In October, various meetings are carried out to achieve the reestablishment of Comissions Obreres, with a local coordinating body for Barcelona and the surrounding counties.

In December, an open letter from Comissions Obreres calls for a protest to fight for economic, social, and political demands. In the end, the protest is held on December 7, with three thousand people participating.

December 14, the State holds a fraudulent referendum on the Organic Law of the State to achieve "popular support" and legitimize the Franco regime in the eyes of the democratic world.

1967

At the beginning of the year, repression against workers intensifies in several locales, and in February there is a protest convened by Comissions Obreres and the Sindicat Democràtic d'Estudiants de la Universitat de Barcelona.

In early spring, future members of the MIL make contact with the Juventud Comunista Revolucionaria, the Revolutionary Communist Youth, (a Trotskyist group following Ernest Mandel's line in favor of entryism) but the meeting does not bear fruit.

In August, the PCE(i) (Partido Comunista de España Internacional, or Communist Party of Spain International) is founded out of a schism in the PSUC.

1968

Future members of the MIL establish contact with Raoul Vaneigem of the Situationist International.

The revolts begin in France that will be known as May '68.

In June, the magazine *Metal* appears in Barcelona, expressing a position of workers' autonomy. The print run is five thousand copies. Later the same month, an autonomous and assembly-organized strike breaks out at AEG-Telefunken in Terrassa.

August 2, ETA executes the head of the Political-Social Brigade of the police in Guipuzkoa, Melitón Manzanas, known as *the Butcher of Santoña*.

In November, the workers at the Blansol company autono-
mously organize a strike. Members of Lotta Continua (with the
prominent participation of Bruno Luigi) in Italy publish a book
on the experience, more than seven thousand copies of which are
distributed in Catalunya with the collaboration of future members of the MIL.

1969

In January, the Platforms of the Comissions Obreres are created,
situating themselves strongly to the left of the sector controlled
by the FOC (Front Obrer de Catalunya) and the sector controlled
by the PSUC.

In May, a new autonomous and more radical tendency
appears within CCOO, adding to those that already existed: the
Zones (controlled by Front Obrer de Catalunya) and the majority
tendency, known as the local Coordination (controlled by PSUC).
This new tendency, linked to the Platforms, starts the monthly
publication, *¿Qué Hacer?* (What is to Be Done?).

May 15, a conflict begins at the Helados Camy factory, leading to a long, radical strike in the summer.

In the summer, future members of the MIL make contact
with Jean Barrot, of the *Vieille Taupe* bookstore in Paris.

In October, the Exterior Team appears.

In December, *¿Qué Hacer?* disappears, replaced by *Nuestra
Clase* (Our Class), with the participation of the Exterior Team.
The Circles for the Training of Cadres are organized. The same
month, the Commission of Political Forces of Catalunya is created in clandestinity.

1970

In February, the Theoretical Team (TT) publishes *The Workers'
Movement in Barcelona* and makes contact for the first time with
the Exterior Team (ET) and the Workers' Team (WT).[2]

---

2.   Trans: The three teams mentioned throughout the chronology are in

In March, the TT enters into contact with the Circles for the Training of Cadres.

In August, *Nuestra Clase* publishes the *Dictionary of the Militant Worker*, printed in Tolosa and authored by workers from the autonomous movement and members of the TT.

In October, the TT publish *Revolution All the Way*.

In November, the Circles for the Training of Cadres are dissolved.

December 3, the Trial of Burgos begins, with sixteen detainees accused of being members of ETA and Melitón Manzanas executed.

December 15, a "state of exception" or martial law is declared throughout the entire Spanish territory. It will last for months.

December 17, a strike begins at the Harry Walker factory that will last until February 15, 1971.[3] The three teams (ET, TT, and WT) participate in the sixty-two day strike. The TT publishes the text, *What Are We Selling? Nothing. What Do We Want? Everything!*

1971

In January, the TT translates *Savage Europe*, which is released along with *The Struggle against Repression* and *Proletariat and Workers' Organization* by Paul Cardan.[4]

In March, *Boycott the Union Elections,* distributed by the ET, becomes the first text signed by the MIL, though at this point the name is written as a numeral: 1,000.

The Grupos Obreros Autónomos (GOA, or Autonomous Workers' Groups) are created.

October 18, amidst the strike in the SEAT car factory, the police kill worker Antonio Ruiz Villalba.

November 7, the Assemblea de Catalunya is created in the Sant Agustí church in the Raval neighborhood of Barcelona, an initiative of the Coordinadora de Forces Polítiques de Catalunya.

---

large part the predecessors of the MIL.

    3.   Trans: An important automotive factory in Nou Barris, Barcelona.

    4.   Trans: One of the early pseudonyms of autonomous anticapitalist theorist Cornelius Castoriadis.

Its character is democratic and anti-Francoist, essentially formed by the PSUC together with several minority organizations like PSAN, FNC, UDC, MSC, and progressive sectors of the Church.

At the end of the year, the action group of the Partit Socialista d'Alliberament Nacional (PSAN, or Socialist Party for National Liberation) breaks off to constitute itself as an autonomous group.

In December, the Exterior Team and the Theoretical Team rupture with the Workers' Team.

1972

In the first months of the year, other autonomous groups arise, following the example of the first group that had broken off from the PSAN. They are primarily created in different neighborhoods of Barcelona, Badalona, Santa Coloma de Gramenet, Mataró, and Terrassa.[5]

In January and February, the TT sets up its library. In February, the Grupos Autónomos de Combate (GAC, or Autonomous Combat Groups) are formed, connected to the MIL.

July 1, the GAC carry out their first expropriation, at the offices of Habilitación de Clases Pasivas in Barcelona.[6] By September 1973, the GAC will have carried out more than thirty expropriations in Barcelona, Badalona, and Mataró, for a total value of twenty-four million pesetas.[7]

In August, a printing press is expropriated in Tolosa and put to use printing the texts of the autonomous movement.

In the summer, the first contact occurs between the MIL and the OLLA (the name given by the police to a close network of autonomous groups in Catalunya) on the mountain of Moixeró, in Cerdanya. The two parts come to an agreement to share information, weapons, material, and logistical support.

In September, growing tensions appear in the GOA between

---

5.   Trans: All primarily industrial cities in central Catalunya.
6.   Trans: A social welfare office of the Franco regime.
7.   Trans: Approximately $343,000 at the contemporary exchange rate. In 1967, the peseta is pegged to the dollar at a 70:1 rate.

the increasingly anarchistic tendency that publishes *El loro indiscreto* (The Indiscreet Parrot), and the Marxist tendency that publishes Ruedo Ibérico (Iberian Arena).

In October, the Barnuruntz group, a breakaway from ETA's military wing with more autonomous, anti-authoritarian positions, begins to collaborate with the TT's library.

October 21, the MIL-GAC, with the collaboration of the OLLA, expropriate a branch of the Caixa bank on carrer Escorial in the Gràcia neighborhood of Barcelona. During the action they distribute a political communiqué.

November 28, the second and final joint expropriation carried out by the GAC and the OLLA takes place at the Central Bank on Passeig de Valldaura. By the end of 1974, the OLLA will have carried out seventeen actions, including six expropriations that net a total of thirteen million pesetas.

In December, the TT publishes *Capital y trabajo* (Capital and Labor).

The GAC expropriate printing material to be used distributing texts from the autonomous workers' movement written by the workers themselves.

December 29, during the expropriation carried out at the Laietana Savings Bank in Badalona, a communiqué is released in memory of the anarchist guerrilla Quico Sabaté, coinciding with the anniversary of his final voyage, a few days before he was killed.[8]

1973

In January, the Theoretical Team and the Exterior Team create the publishing group Ediciones Mayo del 37 (May '37 Editions). Their first publication is *Entre la Revolución y las trincheras* (*Between the Revolution and the Trenches*) by Camilo Berneri.[9]

---

8. Trans: Sabaté was the most famous of the *maquis*, the anarchist guerrillas who fought the Nazis in WWII and then continued their fight against the Franco regime. The MIL and the *maquis* often used the same paths to cross the Pyrenees from France.

9. Trans: Berneri was an Italian anarchist critical of CNT collaborationism, assassinated by Communists in Barcelona during the May Days of 1937.

January 24, in an official bulletin, the police announce the existence of an armed group with a communist tendency, referring to the MIL-GAC.

In February, the action group of the OLLA divides in two cells or rings. The women comrades decide not to create a third action group of exclusively women and instead three other groups are created, specializing in study, contacts, and creating audiovisual material in support of the anticapitalist struggle. Throughout the year, the OLLA carries out various expropriations (the Central Post Office, an armored car of the Catalan Bank...) while also creating a significant structure for intelligence, safe houses, armaments, documentation, and logistics.

In March, the MIL-GAC and Ediciones Mayo del 37 hold a congress in Tolosa de Llenguadoc.

In April, the first issue of *CIA (Conspiración Internacional Anarquista)* is published. Intended to be the mouthpiece of the MIL-GAC, it is the first time the organization is named under these initials. The issue includes the text "Agitación armada," or "Armed Agitation."

April 3, during a strike at the power plant in Sant Adrià del Besòs, police kill the worker Manuel Fernández Márquez, sparking a violent protest and continued strikes by two thousand workers, reaching a level of class combativeness not seen since the Civil War.

Subsequently, wildcat general strikes break out in Cerdanyola and Ripollet.

In the spring, the OLLA expropriates three tons of explosives (ammonium nitrate), detonators, and thousands of boosters from a stone quarry on the Collserola mountain range.

June 11, a new Francoist government is formed under the presidency of Luis Carrero Blanco.

In August, the MIL-GAC dissolve themselves as a political-military organization. Shortly thereafter, they publish the second issue of *CIA*.

September 15, in the aftermath of an expropriation carried out by former members of the MIL-GAC at the Savings Bank in Bellver de Cerdanya, Oriol Solé Sugranyes and Josep Lluís

Pons Llobet are arrested by the *Guardia Civil*, while Jordi Solé Sugranyes manages to escape and cross the border. Over the next few days, various members of the MIL-GAC are arrested, and the organization is effectively dismantled.

September 25, Salvador Puig Antich is ambushed at a meeting, wounded and arrested, while one cop is killed.

September 30, the autonomous groups of the OLLA create the Committee for Solidarity with the Prisoners of the MIL, which will publish three dossiers.

In October, they will push for the creation of other solidarity committees, which will spread to Paris, Brussels, Perpinyà, Genève, Torino, Zürich...

Also in October, members of the ex-MIL write the text, *1,000 or 10,000?* and the next month, *¿Gángsters o revolucionarios?*

In November, the autonomous groups of the OLLA hold a congress where they decide to boost the solidarity with the ex-MIL prisoners even more, to propel the creation of more autonomous groups, and spread the terrain of armed agitation against the repression.

December 20, Carrero Blanco, president of the government and Franco's favorite, is killed in an *attentat* by ETA.

Fifteen minutes later, *Proceso 1001* begins, a trial against ten leading members of CCOO. The sentences, handed down a week later, will be extremely heavy: between twelve and twenty years for illegal association.

1974

January 8, in a military trial, Salvador Puig Antich is given two death sentences.

Starting in January, the OLLA make two attempts to break Puig Antich out of prison. Sabotage actions multiply in Barcelona, Badalona, and Mataró. Three monuments to the Fallen are blown up, various police stations are machine-gunned, and explosives are placed at a number of bank offices.[10]

---

10.   Trans: *Los Caídos*, the Fallen in defense of the Fatherland, are those

January 19, the autonomous groups of the OLLA hold a second congress. Three different tendencies become manifest: the anarcho-Catalanist (the Mataró group), the council communist tendency, and the majority tendency, which is influenced by Situationism and anti-authoritarianism. Nonetheless, the differences are sidetracked in favor of an effective joint struggle against repression and solidarity with the prisoners of the ex-MIL. They sketch out a strategy to encourage autonomous groups within the workers' movement.

March 2, Salvador Puig Antich is executed by *garrot vil* at the Modelo prison in Barcelona. The same day, the prisoner George Michael Welzel, alias Heinz Ches, is executed at the prison in Tarragona.[11]

The OLLA consider attacking the Central Police Station on Via Laietana. Instead, they blow up the electrical substation in Sant Andreu, leaving several Barcelona neighborhoods in the dark. The day after the execution, a strike breaks out in the university and several factories, along with significant protests resulting in hundreds of detentions.

Throughout the month of March, the OLLA carries out sabotage actions and protests occur in cities throughout Catalunya, including Barcelona, Terrassa, Girona, Tarragona, Sant Cugat del Vallès, Cerdanyola, and Sabadell. There are also acts of solidarity and protest in other cities of the Spanish state, in Madrid, Zaragoza, València, and Iruña, as well as in France, Switzerland, Belgium, and Italy.

Forty members of autonomous, libertarian groups involved in solidarity actions with the MIL are arrested in Catalunya and France.

March 22, twenty-two members of various libertarian groups

---

who fought and died on the fascist side during the Civil War, and a main patriotic fixture during the Franco regime.

11.   Trans: A refugee from East Germany who had killed a Guardia Civil. As he had no connection with local movements and no one knew his story, it was much easier for the regime to portray him as a deranged murderer. They killed him the same day as Puig Antich so as to put the photos of both, side by side, in the newspapers the next day.

are arrested in Barcelona. Two of them are connected to the OLLA.

April 7, three members of the OLLA are arrested at Estació de França in Barcelona, where they were awaiting the delivery of anti-tank mines from Switzerland. Twelve vehicles and thirteen apartments full of military hardware and documentary archives fall into the hands of the police.

April 25, the Carnation Revolution breaks out in Portugal, consisting of a military coup and subsequent popular democratic mobilization that puts an end to the Salazar dictatorship and begins a revolutionary process.

May 1, the OLLA attacks police stations and banks in the Barcelona neighborhoods of Sant Andreu, Poblenou, and Nou Barris.

May 3, the OLLA expropriates an agency belonging to the Commercial Transatlantic bank on carrer Girona, with the participation of a libertarian group from Zürich.

May 4, eight members of the autonomous groups of the OLLA go into exile in France.

The director of the Bank of Bilbao in Paris is kidnapped by the Grupos de Acción Revolucionaria Internacionalista (GARI, or Internationalist Revolutionary Action Groups), to demand the release of the prisoners of the MIL.

May 7, the GARI release their first communiqué demanding the release of Santiago Soler Amigó, member of the ex-MIL who is extremely sick, along with other revolutionary demands.

July 19, Juan Carlos de Borbón takes over as provisional head of state until September 2, due to the declining health of the dictator.[12]

July 24, the Junta Democrática de España (Democratic Council of Spain) is created as an initiative of the PCE.

October 30, the final arrest of members of the OLLA takes place. In total, there are now sixteen members of the group in prison.

---

12.   Trans: A noble named by Franco as king and head of state to succeed him, a position reaffirmed in the Spanish Constitution and referendum of 1978. He ruled until 2014. His son is the current King of Spain.

1975

The number of strikes rises considerably this year. Some of the most important are the strikes at Laforsa, in the construction sector, and the general strike of the Baix Llobregat region.[13]

June 11, the *Plataforma de Convergència Socialista* is created.

September 27, two members of ETA are executed by firing squad—one in Cerdanyola del Vallès and the other in Burgos. Also, three members of the FRAP are executed in Madrid. These executions take place amidst strong international and internal protest against the regime.

November 20, Franco dies.

1976

In January, the dockworkers in the port of Barcelona begin a wildcat strike, which will last twenty-one days, and break out again several times more until 1988.

April 5, a wildcat strikes lasting forty-nine days breaks out at the Bultaco factory.

The same day, twenty-nine prisoners break out of Segovia prison.

April 6, Oriol Solé Sugranyes, one of those who broke out of prison in Segovia, is shot down by the *Guardia Civil* one hundred meters from the French border.

---

13.   Trans: A steel mill in Cornellà, a city in Baix Llobregat county and part of metropolitan Barcelona. The wildcat strike there, lasting 106 days, was the longest strike of the Transition. It also sparked off a ten-day general strike throughout Baix Llobregat in which ninety-five thousand workers participated.

9.

The MIL and the OLLA

Ricard de Vargas Golarons

> "Until they become conscious they will never rebel, and until
> after they have rebelled they cannot become conscious."
>
> George Orwell, *Down and Out in Paris and London* (1933)

This text is based on the article "1,000 / MIL / Movimiento
Ibérico de Liberación and OLLA / Organització de Lluita
Armada" (published by Klinamen), which in turn was an
edited version of my presentation, titled "The anticapitalist
and autonomous workers' movement: the political experience of the MIL and the OLLA," in the Seminary of Workers'
Autonomy and Antagonism, held in the Enclave de Libros
bookstore in Madrid in April 2010.

Good evening to all. I'm grateful to be here in a bookstore to
give this talk, because those of us in the MIL were especially
interested in books. If the MIL arose, it was in large part to
create a collection of revolutionary texts—we called it "the
library"—which is to say we are meeting in the most appropriate of places.

As the comrade who introduced me noted, the MIL is well
known and has been the object of various studies. A dozen
important monographs on the topic exist in Catalan, Spanish,
and French; on the other hand, at the moment, there isn't a single one about the OLLA.

I believe my personal experience can help recover an episode of the workers' movement that has vanished from popular
memory. I began collaborating with the MIL in 1972. As a worker

in graphic arts and in hotels, I entered the collective in the very
year the MIL began to exist as such: the publishing of revolutionary texts increased and the first expropriations were carried
out. I joined the theoretical team, but I didn't limit myself to
intellectual tasks. I also carried out logistical and infrastructural
functions and contacts with the neighborhoods, workshops, and
factories. I translated nearly all the texts distributed as MIL publications by Ediciones Mayo del 37, a duty that required me to
perfect my French, a tongue which up to that point I was familiar
with but did not dominate. In those days, the very best literature
that came to us was in that language, unlike today when English
is the *lingua franca*.

The MIL was broken up in September 1973 and the majority
of members were imprisoned, among them Puig Antich. Only
a few managed to escape into exile. I also managed to slip the
police; after being holed up for fifteen days in an apartment in
Gràcia, I fled clandestinely to Italy, where we had the support of,
among others, the comrades of Lotta Continua and Autonomia
Operaia. Two months later, in November 1973, I return to
Barcelona and immediately joined the autonomous groups that
the police subsequently label OLLA. I was arrested on October
30, 1974, and after nine days of interrogation at the central station on Via Laietana, I was locked up in Modelo prison until the
first wave of amnesties for political prisoners.

I've referred to the MIL and the OLLA just so we're on
the same page. In fact, many who were members of either of
these collectives consider that they never existed. It's a contradiction that should be cleared up. In the beginning, the MIL
defined itself as a support group for the most combative and
radical part of the working class in the Comissions Obreres
of that period, and just as they rejected any protagonism,
they also refused to brand themselves with any initials, even
though, later, they would name themselves Grupo Autónomo
de Combate (Autonomous Combat Group, GAC). In the beginning, in January of 1971, the MIL presented itself with the number 1,000. From the start, the quantity referred to the group's
anonymous character: a thousand, ten thousand, a million... We

would have considered opportune any large number that could express the immense mass of the exploited and the oppressed. This is how we signed the pamphlets against participation in the election of delegates for the CNS (Central Nacional Sindicalista, or National Labor Central), the obligatory and vertical unions under Francoism.

In April 1973, CIA (*Conspiración Internacional Anarquista*, or International Anarchist Conspiracy) appeared, with the pretension of becoming the organic publication of the MIL, and the figure 1,000 was transformed into Movimiento Ibérico de Liberación, Iberian Liberation Movement, or MIL. This change was quite a surprise: many of us didn't agree with the innovation, we believed it clashed with the nature of our collective, which should be characterized as an affinity group and not a proper organization.

With regards to the OLLA (Organització de Lluita Armada, or Armed Struggle Organization), it never existed under that explicit name. While it was active, it developed as an autonomous group with no name, and to allude to it within the subversive world, it was referred to interchangeably as "Resistance," "Socialist Resistance," "the Basque's group or Genet's group," both of these being aliases of Felip Solé Sabaté, the group's best known member. Actually, only members of the MIL referred to us with the name OLLA, and only occasionally, as a humorous antiphrasis, since the group, in the letter of introduction it sent to the MIL, forcefully affirmed that it was not "an armed struggle organization... but rather we define ourselves as an autonomous group in favor of the autonomy of the working class."

This document remained in the hands of the MIL, and when several members fell, the police found it and, lacking any other identifier, saddled them with that label. Once they managed to arrest militants from the group, they accused them of belonging to an organization with those initials. The name that has been preserved in the history books was nothing but police clumsiness, naming a group that had refused the protagonism the initials and names entail.

Precursors

The oldest precursors of the MIL, as regards armed action, are the direct action groups. Examples would be the group of Durruti and Ascaso in the 1920s, and the anarchist guerrilla groups of the '40s and '50s, like those of Facerías and Quico Sabaté.

But our historical references were not only the revolutionary conquests, like the anarchist-inspired collectivizations in Catalunya and Aragón during the Civil War, an experience that led us to attach a great historical significance to the accomplishments suppressed by the counterrevolution of 1937.[1] They also included workers' resistance under the dictatorship. In 1939, when Barcelona was occupied by Franco's troops, the workers at La Maquinista Terrestre y Marítima maintained the Republican flag on the front of the factory. Two years later, workers there went on strike for almost ten days, organizing with the CNT, leading to the militarization of the factory and the summary execution of several workers.[2] And in August 1945, the workers of the same factory carried out a political strike to celebrate the defeat of the Japanese Army and the end of World War II.

Also in 1945, once the Nazis were defeated, the working class in Catalunya began organizing clandestinely with the CNT, which came to have—according to the sources—between sixty thousand and two-hundred thousand members. A year later, strikes broke out in several cities in Catalunya, led by the textile sector in Barcelona, Sabadell, Terrassa, and Mataró. The

1. As is widely known, in May 1937 during the Civil War, the USSR and the Republican government tried to liquidate the revolutionary drive that had exploded as a result of the fascist coup attempt. With fatuous excuses, the Stalinists sent the Guardia de Asalto police guards to take over the central telephone exchange in Barcelona, self-organized by the employees, who were affiliated with the Confederació Nacional del Treball (CNT) and who refused to give the building up. From May 3–7, revolutionaries and the institutional left clashed, until the "anarchist" ministers called on them to put down their weapons and go back to work.

2. Sanz Oller, Julio (pseudonym of Santiago López Petit), *Entre el fraude y la esperanza. Las comisiones obreras de Barcelona* (Paris: Ruedo Ibérico, 1972), 264. Paul Preston confirms these events in the compilation, *La República asediada* (Barcelona: Ediciones Península, 2015).

dictatorship was forced to militarize the Hispano-Suiza factory, and the strike reached its apogee in February 1951 with the tram strike that paralyzed Barcelona, followed by a First of May strike organized by the CNT that mobilized fifty thousand workers in Barcelona, Mataró, Manresa, and other industrial centers.[3] In 1957, there was another tram strike in Barcelona, though not as strong as the first.

As regards armed resistance, between 1939 and 1963, various guerrilla groups were organized; I have documented more than five hundred combatants killed, though some of these were not guerrillas, properly speaking, but contact people or family members.

But the MIL did not only adopt the history of the Iberian class struggle, but also incorporated international experiences. For example, we recovered the memory of the Revolution of 333 Days in Hungary (1919),[4] the *Rätebewegung* (council movement) and the November Revolution in Germany (1918–1919),[5] the Bavarian Council Republic (1919)… A whole ensemble of struggles self-organized by the working class and unknown in the Spanish state. At the same time, we would analyze and adopt other workers' struggles, such as Berlin 1953, Hungary 1956, Belgium 1960–1961, and of course we cannot forget the force of the rupture constituted by May '68 in Paris.

Starting in the '60s, a radical change takes place in the class struggle. The new generation replaces the old one: the generation that fought in the Civil War is dying out and the youth is stepping up. Daily life is being transformed. There is a rapid economic

---

3. Trans: Readers should keep in mind that the figures of 200,000 union members or 50,000 strike participants are extremely impressive in a fascist dictatorship that murdered 400,000–500,000 people during and immediately after the Civil War.

4. Ivan Völgyes (Hrsg.), *Hungary in Revolution, 1918–19: Nine Essays* (Lincoln, NE: University of Nebraska Press, 1971). Rudolk Tökés, *Béla Kun and the Hungarian Soviet Republic: The Origins and Role of the Communist Party of Hungary in the Revolutions of 1918–1919* (New York: F.A. Praeger, 1967).

5. André Prudhommeaux and Dori Prudhommeaux, *Spartacus en la Commune de Berlin 1918–1919* (Paris: Spartacus, 1977). Pierre Broué, *Révolution en Allemagne (1917–1923)* (Paris: Minuit, 1971).

development, propelled by the technocrats of Opus Dei and their Development Plans, and by the subsequent investment of foreign capital, which causes a general emigration of the population especially from the south of the peninsula to Catalunya. Between 1960 and 1975, Catalunya grows from 3.9 to 5.6 million inhabitants, a 45 percent rise felt most in the colossal growth of the working class and the exorbitant expansion of the industrial cities.

In 1962, some of the first workers commissions are created in Asturias in the middle of a struggle self-organized through assemblies. It is an autonomous movement, with permanent revocable delegates, and as such, completely unlike the current sclerotic structure of the CCOO.[6] In 1964, there is an important strike in La Maquinista and other major Catalan factories, especially in the steel sector, in solidarity with Asturias. I myself was present in the refounding of the *comissions obreres* of Catalunya that took place in a church in the Bordeta neighborhood in 1966, a year in which the struggles were shaping up.

In the *comissions obreres* in Barcelona and the city's industrial belt, there is a clash between three milieus at the end of the decade. The first, which has a majority at that time, appears under the dominion of the Front Obrer de Catalunya (FOC, or Workers' Front of Catalunya), the local version of the Frente de Liberación Popular (FLP, or Popular Liberation Front), which is a dissident group to the official communist line. The second is under the control of the local coordinating body, which is monopolized by the Partit Socialista Unificat de Catalunya (PSUC, or Unified Socialist Party of Catalunya), itself a sister organization of the Partit Comunista de España (PCE, or Communist Party of Spain). This is the milieu that would achieve a definitive hegemony and maintain control of the organization from that point forward.

Nonetheless, in July 1968, a third milieu appears, anti-authoritarian and pro-autonomy, that expresses itself in the magazine *Metal*, five thousand copies of which are distributed—a considerable print run at the time. This group, directly opposed

---

6.   Since the end of the '70s, the CCOO has been a completely bureaucratic, "yellow" labor union like the UGT.

to the dirigism of the PSUC, manages to initiate, for example, a major strike at the AEG-Telefunken factory in Terrassa free of the leadership of any party and always controlled by its own assembly. In this way, the most conscious part of the working class opposes any outside interference.

In this same line half a year later, in January of 1969, *Metal* is replaced by the monthly, *¿Qué hacer?*, which disbands in September, just over half a year later. That is when the Platforms of *comissions obreres* are formed, independent of all political parties. Three months later, in November, the Platforms begins to publish the magazine *Nuestra Clase: Comisiones Obreras*, which is printed in Tolosa and distributed throughout the red belt of Barcelona with the participation of future members of the MIL. Additionally, the Circles for the Training of Cadres, which are formed in the same month as the Platforms, September 1969, as a wager on the importance of reflection, last a little more than a year before disbanding. Amidst this alphabet soup of acronyms, the hasty, fluid existence of these groups stands out, as does the radicality of their positions. Under the conditions imposed by clandestinity, one could not choose one's militancy according to ideological unity. You went to a meeting, not because you had selected it *a priori*, but via the invitation of a friend, a classmate, or a family member who had told you about it, sometimes without any idea what would be articulated, only the desire to get a grasp of something you understood only vaguely. There is nothing strange about the fact that people were jumping from Catalan independentism to workers' autonomy or vice versa. In clandestinity, there was a greater exchange of people and ideas from one organization to another than under formal democracy. In a matter of weeks, a faction could be created, distance itself from the mother organization, split off, and then fuse with another more or less like-minded group.

The most radical sector was gradually forging an openly anticapitalist consciousness, critical of any type of manipulation and in favor of workers' autonomy starting in struggles in the factories and neighborhoods and in response to a growing repression. Without this background, the MIL never would have arisen, given that this was their ideological foundation, and that their human component were the people who were already participating, directly or indirectly, in these struggles. The MIL is, therefore, a consequence of the radicalization of the class struggle.

A final methodological warning: the MIL acted from two centers, Barcelona and Tolosa; initially from both of them with a similar intensity, even though it is evident the focus of their strategy and action was Catalunya. With the intention of being as lucid as possible, I will focus on the most significant details and speak as little as possible of the affairs in Tolosa.

The MIL, therefore, did not appear out of thin air. Many of its members were wrapped up in workers' struggles in Barcelona. In those days, being revolutionary was presented as being inseparable from Marxism-Leninism, in the factories as well as in education, particularly in the universities. With the historical continuity of anarchism cut short—despite its deep roots in Catalunya and other regions of the Iberian Peninsula—moving towards anti-authoritarian positions could only occur with Marxism as a starting point.

Some future members of the MIL even started out in Leninist parties until, swayed by the radicality of the workers' struggles, they began joining the autonomous movement and combating the dirigism and authoritarianism of those parties. Very early on, in 1967, future members of the MIL established contact with the Juventud Comunista Revolucionaria, a Trotskyist youth group following Mandel's line in favor of entryism, though nothing came of it.

Oriol Solé, for example, collaborated with the Sindicat Democràtic d'Estudiants de la Universitat de Barcelona (SDEUB), the anti-Francoist student union; joined the Joventuts Comunistes de Catalunya youth group, a subsidiary of the PSUC; jumped over to the Maoist and as such Marxist-Leninist-Stalinist Partido Comunista de España (internacional) (PCE(i)); then he found a home with the magazine *¿Qué hacer?*—during the period of the Camy ice cream strike, in which, under cover of night, he threw some molotov cocktails at the ice cream kiosks and was surprised in the act by the police—and then he landed with Acción Comunista—a splinter group of the exterior section of the FLP, which started in the '70s and had grown to establish bases inside the country—and which affirmed a heterodox Marxism in open conflict with Leninism.

In December of 1969 he participated together with other future members of the MIL in the Acción Comunista congress in Frankfurt am Main, an event that led to the dismantling of the Barcelona cell of the organization, which motivated Solé Sugranyes to enlist in the Platforms and, finally, to militate with the MIL.

Though he was not a traditional leader in any way, he exercised a powerful influence over the other comrades, since he was older, had more experience, had the status of a political refugee, and, above all, for his innate ability to project, energize, and organize. He is one more example of the radicalization of the committed youth in that era—the members of the MIL and the OLLA were all around 20–25 years old—which synchronized with the workers' struggles occurring all over the continent.

A basic component of the pre-MIL was its eagerness to confer a theoretical link to the revolutionary movement. In December 1969, future comrades of the collective published a very important text in Tolosa, *The Worker's Movement in Barcelona,* authored by Ignasi Solé Sugranyes and Santi Soler Amigó, alias "Little Guy" or "Fede," who would become the most prolific and influential author in the MIL.[7]

Before translating texts from other countries, Ignasi Solé and Santi Soler had established the urgency of critically examining the multitude of factions representing the different political tendencies that swarmed Barcelona, which they referred to as "a cocktail of acronyms" or an alphabet soup. Duplicated on the worst quality paper, the pamphlet criticized the manipulation carried out by reformist communists and by all the leftist groups. It was so well received that two months later it was reprinted in Barcelona, with higher quality. Previously that same year, in

---

7. After his participation in the MIL, he published the books *Lucha de clases y clases de lucha* (Barcelona: Anagrama, 1978) and *Marxismo: señas de identidad* (Barcelona: Libertarias, 1981). He died in April, 1999.

response to an important wildcat strike at the Blansol company, Lotta Continua in Italy organized the printing of a book written by the workers who participated in the strike. At a run of eight thousand copies, it was smuggled into Catalunya by members of the Platforms and future members of the MIL, and distributed in multiple factories.

In August, 1970, various workers from the Grupos Obreros Autónomos (GOA) and from Platforms launched a suggestive project, *Dictionary of the Militant Worker*. When the project was already well underway, they invited Santi Soler to contribute. He respected the initial authorship and limited himself to adding recently coined terms like "Situationism," "Bordigism," or "auto-gestion." In the definitive edition, the credits page stated the book was published in Tolosa by the "Exterior Team—*Nuestra Clase.*"

A third text from that era was *Revolution All the Way* (October 1970), requested by Platforms, which we called "the brick" and which presents, in fifty pages, a serious attempt at a manual for the political education of workers, with a crystalline critique of Leninism. We lost countless hours of sleep preparing it, even though it was never widely distributed in the workers' move-ment, given its excessively theoretical character; in the end it was largely for internal use.[8]

Aside from expressing the autonomous movement in Barcelona's industrial zone, the pre-MIL also served as a mirror for all the international theorization that found its ultimate artic-ulation in May 1968 in Paris (where several future members par-ticipated, for example Emili Pardiñas, alias "Pedrals," who passed on in October, 2011), and in the hot Italian autumn of 1969 (the MIL maintained various contacts with revolutionaries in that country).

There was also a particularly intense relationship with Le Vielle Taupe, a leftist bookstore on rue Odéon in Paris. It was the only place to stock up on the new texts published by the Situationist International, the Bordiguists, Pouvoir Ouvrier,

---

8. Republished in 2015 by Ediciones Reapropiación, Xixon, *Revolución hasta el fin*. The text mentions topics that had barely been discussed at that time within the Spanish state, like consumer society.

and so forth.[9] And Santi Soler had solid contacts there, through which he could acquire plenty of texts that would immediately be translated and distributed by the future MIL. Personal relations were also established with Bordiguists and council communists, heirs of the thinking of Anton Pannekoek (1873–1960). Among the living authors, it is necessary to mention Gilles Dauvé (1947), who then wrote under the pen name Jean Barrot, and with whom a personal contact began in August 1969; and the Situationists— the confluence of a non-authoritarian Marxism and revolutionary anarchism—whose works were distributed on the Peninsula by the MIL.

The meeting with Raoul Vaneigem (1934), one of the principal theorists of the Situationists, occurred in March 1968 (two months before May '68, which the Situationists, together with the *enragés*, will lend ideological substance).[10] To sum up, relationships were established with a series of tendencies that, though diverse, shared the common denominator of understanding that Leninism served as the extreme left of Capital and of the bourgeoisie, and as such did not deserve to be qualified as revolutionary.

Imminence of the Revolution

At the time, the revolution seemed to be just around the corner. There was a confluence of radical changes in daily life, in the family, in society. It became clear that alienation cannot be fought from alienated positions, including the alienation implicated in docilely obeying the Party. The world was boiling over. To take the pulse of the world in that era, we can dispense with precise dates and simply name the geography of revolt. Between 1971 and 1973, Chile attempts to take a peaceful road to socialism, but the

9. Though it seems impossible to believe, starting in 1979, Le Vielle Taupe drifted into negationism, denying the genocide perpetrated by the Nazis, and abandoning all its leftist traits. But that is another story.

10. *Enragés et situationnistes dans le mouvement des occupations* (Paris: Galimard, 1968); Jean-Pierre Duteuil, *Nanterre 1965–66–67–68—Vers le Mouvement du 22 Mars* (Paris: Acratie, 1988).

general tone in Latin America was one of armed struggle. From Argentina to El Salvador, guerrilla movements enter into combat, from rural guerrillas in Central America to urban guerrillas, less well known but more interesting for us: the guerrillas of Carlos Marighela in several Brazilian cities, the Montoneros and the Ejército Revolucionario del Pueblo (ERP) in Buenos Aires, or the Tupamaros in Montevideo.

In the Near East, Black September, the Popular Front for the Liberation of Palestine (FPLP), the Organization for the Liberation of Palestine (OLP), and Fatah. The yankees suffer a total defeat in Vietnam, Cambodia, and Laos. In Africa, Portuguese imperialism is corralled by the Frente de Libertação de Moçambique (FRELIMO), the Partido Africano para a Independência da Guiné e Cabo Verde (PAIGC), and the Movimento Popular de Libertação de Angola (MPLA). In South Africa, the African National Congress (ANC), South African Communist Party (SACPO), and Umkhonto we Sizwe are engaged in armed struggle. Yemen and Ethiopia become States that proclaim socialism.

Also the very center of capitalism is struck by revolt. In the US, black inner city neighborhoods rise up, and groups like the Symbionese Liberation Army (SLA), the Black Panther Party (BPP), the Weather Underground, and Venceremos enter the fray. In Canada, the leftist Front de Libération du Quebec (FLQ) is active. In Poland, Italy, and France there are wildcat strikes that displace the reformist unions, following the same line as the one that resulted in the movement of workers' councils that momentarily triumphed at the collapse of the Great War in Europe.

The flame of armed struggle rises higher than ever. Throughout the '60s and '70s in Italy, as many as sixteen armed groups become active, which I will merely name: Brigate Comuniste (BC), Brigate Rosse (BR), Collettivi Politici Venetti (CPV), Comitati Comunisti Rivoluzionari (CiCoRi), Formazioni Comuniste Armate (FCA), Gruppi d'Azione Partigiana (GAP), Gruppo XXII Ottobre (XXII Ottobre), Volante Rossa Martiri Partigiani (Volante Rossa), Movimento Comunista Rivoluzionario (MCR), Nuclei Armati Proletari (NAP), Nuclei Comunisti Territoriali (NCT), Fronte Armato Rivoluzionario Operaio

(FARO), Panthere Rosse (PR), Giustizia Proletaria (GP), Nuclei Operai di Resistenza Armata (NORA)... In Germany, armed groups include the Rote Armee Fraktion, Bewegung 2. Juni, Tupamaros München, Tupamaros West Berlin, Revolutionären Zellen, Sozialistisches Patientenkollektiv... In England, there are the Angry Brigades, in France, Groupe d'Action Révolutionnaire Internationaliste (GARI), Noyaux Armés pour l'Autonomie Populair (NAPAP), Action Directe (AD), Mouvement du 22 Mars, Gauche Prolétarienne and Nouvelle Résistence Populaire (NRP).

In the Spanish state, there are the Grupos de Resistencia Antifascista Primero de Octubre (GRAPO), the Frente Revolucionario Antifascista y Patriota (FRAP), and Acción Revolucionaria Unida (ARU), a group that broke off from the PCE(ml) in Madrid.

This list gives a sense of how common armed struggle had become, but we were different from all those groupuscules, many of them Leninist and vanguardist. It must be the workers themselves who arm and organize themselves, not a specialized group.

Across the Spanish state, the situation was becoming ripe for such a process. Workers' struggles grew, particularly in Catalunya, Madrid, Euskadi, and Asturias. A neighborhood movement emerged, also impelled by comissions obreres. There were solidarity associations. It seemed that everything was possible, that capitalism was breaking apart like a shipwreck. The 1973 oil crisis intensified capitalism's structural problems: the stock exchange became lethargic, companies began laying off workers, inflation was glorified as a good thing. Series of events began to occur that until that moment we had not even dared to dream.

Collective bargaining was a novelty of the moment, and from this arose shop-floor employees' committees, and, as a culmination, in some factories they even dared to create self-defense groups. In the most conscious circles of the proletariat, people debated the role of class violence. The repression contributed decisively to the radicalization of the struggles. The workers armed themselves with whatever they had at hand and even attacked police stations, as occurred in April 1973 in Sant Adrià del Besòs. The working class went on the offensive for the first time under the dictatorship.

The dead also belonged to the working class. In 1971, in Zona Franca in Barcelona, the police killed Ruiz Villalba, a SEAT laborer, in a context of brutal repression in which the helicopters swooped overhead and the police broke into the factory with machine guns blazing. In response to the murder, they created the Self-Defense Group Ruiz Villalba, which would take action beyond the factory grounds and in 1977 would lead to the creation of the Ejército Revolucionario de Ayuda a los Trabajadores (ERAT, or Revolutionary Army of Workers' Aid).

The victims keep piling up. A neighbor of Erandio (1969), three construction workers in Granada (1970), another in Madrid (1971), the SEAT steelworker just mentioned (1971), two more steelworkers in El Ferrol (1972). In April 1973, there is another killing at the Besòs power plant: Fernández Márquez is killed during an impressive strike of more than two thousand workers who carry out occupations and battle with the police. In August of 1973, the police in Reus torture Cipriano Martos, bricklayer and FRAP militant, whom they force to drink a molotov cocktail, leading to his death. The lives cut short do not belong to the anti-Francoist petty bourgeoisie, but to workers of all ages. For the first time since the Civil War, the working class again becomes the motor of history.

A panorama of the moment bogs us down in an alphabet soup of Trotskyists, Maoists, Stalinists, and so many other tendencies and nuances, but all of them were united by the ambition of directing the working class. At the twilight of the dictatorship, it seemed obvious that in short order, one of the parties would have to assume the leadership of the people and serve as a privileged interlocutor for the bourgeoisie, playing the same role as the Communist Party in France or in Italy, controlling the working class and impeding steps towards rupture with the capitalist system.

At a sociocultural level, it also must be emphasized that in the '60s, a countercultural youth erupted onto the scene, breaking with the earlier generation in everything from musical tastes to sexual relations, their conception of the family, and their preference for communal life.

Origin

The MIL is born from the local workers' movement, which is moving in the same direction as the international workers' movement, although here it takes on specific characteristics given the dictatorship and the inherent repression.

The MIL starts to take action in December 1971, even though most of its members had been participating in the autonomous movement for a long time already. The catalyst should be identified as the most important conflict of the era: the Harry Walker strike. This 470 employee company was a subsidiary of Solex, which had factories in France, Italy, the United Kingdom, and Brazil. A strike broke out at their Barcelona factory, and lasted for sixty-two days, from December 1970 to February 1971. A unified committee was created, representing all the workers, and with a preponderance of workers with a clear class consciousness, anticapitalist and autonomous, who neutralized the Party attempts to push them into reformism or to slow them down. The strike ended up being very fierce, as we can see when, on the third day, the bosses fired four workers, their co-workers occupied the whole factory floor, and the police violently evicted them. At the subsequent daily assemblies, 160–200 workers participated, while the pickets kept the scabs from getting in, scattered the managers, and smashed the office windows.

In the Harry Walker strike, some of the members of the three future "teams" of the MIL were already active, with Oriol Solé Sugranyes serving as a nexus between them.

1. The Exterior Team organizes international solidarity and communicates their experiences directly to Solex workers in Lyon and Milano, a contact that allows them to raise solidarity money and that motivates a French committee to travel to Barcelona and participate in the general assembly (February 1971). Later, the Exterior Team, filled out with Barcelona youth and the children

of anarchist exiles in Tolosa, will take charge of expropriations by forming the GAC (Grupos Autónomos de Combate).

2. The Workers' Team comes in large part from the Platforms of comissions obreres and the Circles for the Training of Cadres. They are workers who spread propaganda and energize the struggles.

3. The Theoretical Team writes a text that synthesizes the meaning of the strike: "What are we selling? Nothing. What do we want? Everything." Later, the Theoretical Team will take responsibility for Ediciones Mayo del 37.

The Harry Walker strikers, despite the high price of thirty-three workers fired (of whom six spend several days in jail), achieve almost all their demands. They are no longer forced to work overtime, and the environmental conditions improve substantially. The strike becomes an example, and other workplaces in the steel sector enter into what the official euphemism calls "labor disputes." Probably the one with the greatest reach was the SEAT strike (December 1971). They are all wildcat strikes that constitute a head-on confrontation with statism, dirigism, and Leninism. The MIL did not represent a leap of faith, rather it arose from a real class struggle, a concrete and convulsive reality.

The MIL attempted to lend the workers' movement theoretical tools that would aid in its political and class self-education. This included creating a revolutionary library named Ediciones Mayo del 37 (in February 1972). Its objective was to make available to the workers the accumulated experience of the global workers' movement, past and present, which had been extirpated from the popular memory through repression and alienation. This included everything from the critique of Leninism, to subversive experiences evaluated by those who lived them, to educational introductions. To print the written materials, we needed money, and to get money the most efficient instrument was expropriation. Consequently, these expropriations constituted an instrumental means, though they also served as a form of agitation. In that framework, the MIL arose by combining theory and praxis, though always—even in their writings—putting praxis first, that which we called "real movement."

> Those who know the functioning and the character of the MIL know that it could not have a mastermind. All of us were inside and outside, practice and theory, connected to the workers' struggle and distanced from it.[11]

Ideology

Up until that moment, all the subversive organizations defined themselves as anti-Francoist, but the MIL assumed an anticapitalism with no masks. We were not fighting to overthrow the fascist regime; rather, we went a step further. We were in combat against capitalism, though, obviously, we recognized the difference between dictatorship and bourgeois democracy. We wanted to put an end to class society and wage labor in order to achieve social emancipation. It might seem like an excessive position, but it felt like we were living at the beginning of the end.

The MIL was very critical of the sea of acronyms, where every little chapel had its guru. We fought for the unity and autonomy of the class in the face of external saviors. We were against all permanent structures, that just ended up as bureaucracies: we fought against the parties and the unions. In opposing permanent organization, we proposed an "organization of the tasks," the logical consequence of the maxim, "from each according to their possibilities, to each according to their needs." We insisted in remembering how the bureaucratized organizations had betrayed the class throughout the twentieth century, especially after World War II.

We were familiar with all the great struggles of the workers' movement. It is worth noting that the armed anarchist resistance

---

11. Statement by Santi Soler Amigó, transcribed in Jean Claude Duhourcq and Antoine Madrigal, *Mouvement Iberique de Liberation: mémoires de rebelles* (Tolosa de Llenguadoc: CRAS, 2007), 123.

of the Catalan *maquis* over the prior decades was probably decisive in our determination to arm ourselves. We knew of this tradition through oral histories, spoken memories, and the contacts that some comrades—Oriol and Jean-Marc—had with survivors of that guerrilla war in the south of France. So it was a fitting homage to that cause that we expropriated a savings bank in Badalona in December 1972, where we claimed the memory of the guerrilla Quico Sabaté on the anniversary of his final voyage into Catalunya.

Though a great value was placed on anarchism and there were comrades who claimed this ideology, Marxism predominated in the milieu of the MIL, though with an emphasis on Marxism's most anti-statist facets and against any form of exploitation or oppression, favoring libertarian positions in every aspect of existence. We weren't living for a future revolution, we wanted to make the revolution present in our daily lives.

"Live as you think, or you'll end up thinking the same as those who live like you," warned the comrades of '68. Situationism was a major influence on the MIL. We rejected living for the future revolution.

The Situationists said you cannot fight against alienation with alienated means, and we wanted to break with capitalism, with exploitation, with domination. We proposed liberation on every front: social, cultural, sexual, familial, and political.

> The MIL was an anticapitalist movement that fought against capital in all its forms, that fostered self-organization and workers' autonomy, beyond the division between manual labor and intellectual labor; that promoted direct action and the autogestion of struggle; and that angrily criticized Leninism, bureaucratization, and all the vanguardist tendencies and professional militancy that reproduced the class domination of the prevailing oppressive system.[12]

12. This paragraph reproduces my introductory text in *Antologia poètica popular a la memòria de Salvador Puig Antich*. Edited by Ricard de Vargas Golarons, Barcelona, 1996.

We criticized and overcame the hierarchical conception of social and individual life, and highlighted syndicalism as an instrument of integration and control of the working class within capitalist society. We rejected and combated the division between leaders and followers and made a great effort in favor of the transformation of daily life.

Direct Actions

The MIL adopted the discourse of the GOA and the Platforms against the proliferation of factions and in favor of the non-transferable protagonism of the workers themselves.[13] We identified with the slogan of the First International, the emancipation of the workers must be the task of the workers themselves. We simply offered a support group that served as a catalyst for self-organization. As an organization, we had our agreements and disagreements with the GOA and the Platforms. In April 1971, José Antonio Díaz and Manolo Murcia, charismatic delegates of these groups, distanced themselves from what would become the MIL, until the following year in which relations improved, especially with Platforms. Altogether, there were many factory workers who collaborated actively during the brief history of the MIL, two examples being Marcelo López and Ernesto Núñez, alias "el Chato."

The MIL tried to consolidate the nascent subversion and radicalize it, combining armed action and agitation in an

---

13.   The Autonomous Workers' Groups. The Circles for the Training of Cadres had arisen in comissions obreres as an expression of the autonomist tendency, with the intention of theorizing the autonomous practice and stealing back from the intellectuals their central role in educating the workers, returning this protagonism to the workers themselves. They disappeared in November 1970, fragmenting into groupuscules of the extreme left. Gathering the experience of the Circles, the GOA arose to coordinate groups in the workplaces and in the neighborhoods with the goal of aiding in the spreading and publishing of texts, some written by the GOA themselves (their publishing project was called Editorial Obrera Clandestina). One of the most innovative aspects of the GOA, in regards to the tools they offered to the class struggle, was to start a library of prohibited books that grew to three thousand copies, stored clandestinely in an apartment in the Clot neighborhood of Barcelona, and available to workers in struggle.

indissociable whole. In that era, armed combat encompassed a broad ideological spectrum: aside from all the leftist organizations we have already cited, there were the movements of a nationalist character: ETA (with all its schisms: ETA Político-Militar, ETA V Asamblea, ETA VI Asamblea...), the Irish Republican Army (IRA), the Fronte Paisanu Corsu de Liberazione (FPLC), Ghjustizia Paolina, Front de Libération de la Bretagne (FLB-ARB), Front de Libération Jurassien (FJL)... In Catalunya itself, the Exèrcit Popular Català (EPOCA) and the Front d'Alliberament de Catalunya (FAC) struggled with weapons in hand.

All of these groups shared the tendency to disassociate armed struggle and social agitation. Our position was categorically original, which does not necessarily imply that it was realistic, given the immense difficulties we faced. We believed in armed agitation, which is to say that the armed struggle had to germinate below, in the very bosom of the working class. It was not about fighting in the name of the proletariat, but rather getting the proletariat itself to take up armed combat. Far from a vanguardist, authoritarian position, we proposed armed agitation from the grassroots and from within the class struggle.

In summary, armed agitation considers itself to be, and effectively constitutes, one of the facets or aspects of the class struggle of the proletariat from the current level to the general insurrection towards which it tends. Via the practice of necessarily limited actions, armed agitation demonstrates that the level of violence with which one can act here and now, and as such the level with which one ought to act, is significantly superior to what is generally believed. Armed agitation, as with all forms of agitation, indicates the purpose of the class struggle of the broad masses, helping them orient themselves, radicalize, and advance with an increasing robustness. At the same time, the concrete objectives of said agitation also fulfill a function of support for the class struggle.[14]

---

14.   Extract from "On Armed Agitation," *CIA* no.1 (April 1973).

In May of 1972, the GAC are created—which, as we have seen, were an expansion on the old Exterior Team—and these set themselves the task of carrying out expropriations, moving their operations between Barcelona and Tolosa, facilitating the adherence of quite a few libertarian youths from families of exiles who have settled in the French city. Some of the members are Catalans, including Josep Lluís Pons Llobet, the four Solé Sugranyes brothers, Puig Antich, Santi Soler, and others are French, like Jean Claude Torres, alias "Cri-Cri," and Jean-Marc Rouillan. Their common objective was to acquire money to be able to publish revolutionary texts, set up a war chest (to cover the expenses of strikers and fired workers), and create an infrastructure of apartments, weapons, printing machinery, and so forth, all of it for the militant use of the working class.

The first guns we had came from Tolosa and Andorra, from old anarchist militants who had fought the Nazis and still held onto them. In contrast with the CNT in exile, which washed its hands of the struggle in the interior, some veteran anarchists, when they found out we wanted to reinitiate the urban guerrilla movement (it should be remembered, nonetheless, that we were in favor of "armed agitation" but against "armed struggle"), were thrilled, and they dusted off their arsenals, which they had very carefully hidden: Sten machine guns, .22 carbines with sawed off barrels, 8mm revolvers, hand grenades, two *naranjero* machine guns... all kinds of weapons.

Aside from these supplies, we acquired new model hunting rifles and two Cetmes—the assault rifle used by the Guardia Civil—on the black market. At the same time, ETA provided us with some 7.65mm Ruby pistols. Of them all, the most emblematic and mythical guns were the Stens, which came from the resistance against the Nazis during the 2nd World War. In fact, for a while, the police called the MIL "the Sten gang" before we had a name for ourselves.

It was a weapon that the Allies had dropped by parachute to give the Resistance, particularly in the south of France, more firepower. These same weapons had been used in the '40s and '50s by the anarchist guerrilla movement in Catalunya. It would

not be until 1973 that the police identified—and then clumsily—
the specific ideology of the "Sten gang," as a result of the armed
clash on the border at Cerdanya, in which two strangers opened
fire on the Guardia Civil and the Gendarmerie at the same time,
leaving behind a machine gun, 250,000 pesetas, and—the most
important in this case—abundant propaganda.[15] From the seized
material, the Spanish police finally were able to publish an official bulletin in which they announced the existence of "armed
groups of a communist tendency."

In February of 1971, the first expropriation (or bank robbery, from the police perspective) was carried out. More exactly,
that was the first frustrated attempt. Then there were a series of
unimportant actions, all in Tolosa, until July 1972, in which the
welfare offices on carrer Mallorca in Barcelona were expropriated, with a haul of 800,000 pesetas.[16]

The following are the group's main interventions, leaving unspoken those that occurred in the south of France. In
September, two months after the first socialization of bank
wealth, we took action in Salou, stopping a Savings Bank
employee in the middle of the street, but it turned out the only
thing in the bag he was carrying was his sandwich.

The same day, we failed to expropriate the Savings Bank in
Igualada, in this case going off information from—as unbeliev-
able as it sounds—future Nobel Peace Prize nominee, Lluís Maria
Xirinacs.[17] We quickly recovered from these two fiascoes and, on
the 15th of September, expropriated a million pesetas from the
Savings Bank in Bellver de Cerdanya. (As we shall see, there was
an attraction to Cerdanya, as this was the region where the Solé
Sugranyes brothers had spent their summers as children.)

The next month we recovered 990,200 pesetas (this according to the prosecutor) from the Laietana Savings Bank in Mataró.
During the action, a leaflet was distributed underscoring the

---

15.   Trans: The Gendarmerie were military police guarding, respectively,
the Spanish and French sides of the border.

16.   Trans: In 1967, the peseta is pegged to the dollar at a 70:1 rate.

17.   Trans: Priest, philosopher, author, proponent of nonviolence, and
politician active in the '70s movement against the dictatorship.

political character of the action. In November, we debuted the Stens, expropriating 169,000 pesetas from the Pensions Bank on carrer Escorial in Barcelona. A few days later, with the collaboration of three members of the OLLA—which had access to good information—four members of the MIL walked into the Central Bank on Passeig de Valldaura in Barcelona, to recover a million pesetas. We explained the purpose of the actions, stuffing flyers into the pockets of the bank employees.

A month later, on December 29, 764,000 pesetas were recovered from the Laietana Savings Bank in Badalona. From that moment on—coincidence or not, but probably not—the majority of financial offices were under the guard of the *greys* (agents of the Policía Armada), who would take up posts on the sidewalk, next to the front entrances. This helped spread the rumor that there was an armed struggle group knocking off banks. In the first month of 1973, we collected 658,000 pesetas from the Provincial Savings Bank in the Sarrià neighborhood, located on the same block as the headquarters of the Brigada Político-Social (Franco's political police).

A comrade from the OLLA had informed us that the bank branch was in charge of depositing the Brigade's salaries, so as we exited the bank, we left a mocking note for them. Two months later, we took action at the Hispano-American Bank on Avinguda de Fabra i Puig in Barcelona. Though there was an exchange of shots with two detectives from the Criminal Investigation Brigade and one of the bank employees resisted and was injured, the four members of the commando managed to flee. Although, of the six million pesetas that might have been expropriated, only one and a half million could be socialized.

In June, 300,000 pesetas were stolen from the Bilbao Bank on carrer Major in Sarrià. In this action, an explicit communiqué was left behind, obliging the press to acknowledge the political motivation of the action; they compared us to the Tupamaros. A few days later, thanks to a tip from the OLLA, there was a successful expropriation at the Spanish Credit Bank on Gran Via (linked to Banesto, the State Bank), with a haul of 3,724,000 pesetas. The pamphlets left behind proclaimed: "Armed agitation demands action from the workers' movement." The press imputed responsibility to a clandestine anarchist group that passed the stolen money to strikers.

Three months later, when the MIL had officially been dissolved, there was an expropriation in Bellver de Cerdanya that provoked sweeping consequences, which we shall discuss in more depth.

We also seized printing material on several occasions to be able to duplicate our texts. In August of 1972, we carried out an action in Tolosa that allowed us to confiscate a Linotype valued at 76,000 francs. Unfortunately, less than a week later the Gendarmerie located it in a farmhouse rented by a member of the MIL, thirty kilometers outside Tolosa. To replace what the police had snatched away from us, in December we executed another socialization of printing equipment in the same workshop where we had confiscated the earlier machine, and this one remained definitively in our hands. We installed it in a secret room that could only be accessed by way of a pivoting bookshelf that hid the entrance.

As regards the tactic of the political *attentat*, in the MIL we had proposed executing the police commissioner Antonio Juan Creix, a notorious torturer and so extreme a case, he was the only political police commander in the Franco regime to be purged, before the dictator's death, in a disciplinary action resulting in a three year unpaid suspension. He had behaved with brutality in Euskadi, he had tormented the defendants in the Trial of Burgos (1970) and, stationed in Granada, he was the instigator of the murder of three workers. What's more, it was also a question of personal vengeance: Creix had personally beat Oriol Solé with a live electrical wire. We had a plan half sketched out, but we left it hanging. It was under discussion when the repression accelerated and we were dismantled. We didn't have time. In general, though, and as a principle, our intention was to never kill anyone, and even less so in cold blood. We only accepted it in self-defense.

Independently of the expropriations, the MIL anticipated carrying out sabotage actions, but it never jelled. We also proposed kidnapping Johan Cruyff, the popular player with Futbol Club Barcelona starting in the 1973–74 season.[18] We had a little prison cell prepared in a village on the mountain of Moixeró, in Cerdanya. We never finalized the plan, because all actions had to be debated by everyone, and some members dissented, considering that such an action would bring heavy repression not only within the Spanish state but also internationally when, until that moment, the police had not managed to unearth any solid leads.

What's more, the kidnapping would have been unpopular, since Cruyff led Barça to astounding victories, the club had subtle connotations contrary to the Franco regime, and the fans were legion, particularly implanted among the popular classes. We also imagined kidnapping Duran Farell, a fat cat of the managerial class with a reputation for being a liberal, a confidant of the Urquijo Bank group in Catalunya, with executive or representative positions in the Catalunya Hydroelectric Company, La Maquinista Terrestre y Marítima factory, and also Catalan Gas and Electric. In the end we realized the plan was not fully prepared, and we left it pending until we acquired more intelligence or infrastructure.

Publishing

The principal justification of our armed actions was for the publishing. Printing was our obsession, putting out flyers, distributing propaganda. We named our imprint Ediciones Mayo del 37 (founded in January 1973) as a way to claim the workers' uprising in defense of the collectivizations and the rest of the revolutionary labor undertaken in Catalunya at the beginning of the Civil War.[19] As our letter of introduction, we wrote the following paragraph:

---

18. Trans: Hendrik Johannes Cruijff, voted the second best footballer of the century after Pelé, transferred from Ajax to FC Barcelona in 1973 upon being offered a world record transfer fee.

19. The chronology of this section is approximate, since to throw off the repression our texts were given older dates, and the various chronologies in circulation, including those made in the 1970s, contradict one another.

Ediciones Mayo del 37 sets itself the task of demonstrating the purpose and mechanisms of the struggles of the
proletariat in their communist practice past, present, and
future. We understand that to annihilate all of Capital's
mystifications, whether they come from the State, from
the Communist Party, or from the factions, is a communist practice. Whether this is accomplished in word or in
deed corresponds to the necessities of each moment and
each circumstance. To participate in the agitation and in
the unification that the social movements undertake from
their different places is a communist practice. In its own
way, communism has gone on the offensive.

The selection of texts followed pragmatic criteria: they had
to be comprehensible, but not superficial, long, or confusing,
and it should be emphasized that they came from different origins and tendencies: anarchism, acracy, council communism,
Luxemburgism, Bordiguism, heterodox Marxism, Situationism...
The MIL did not have a theoretical line, properly speaking.

Ediciones Mayo del 37 should not be confused with a project of dissemination or theory; rather it is a theoretical
practice in direct relation with the other practice.[20]

Theoretical publications do not give the masses some book-
ish truth, they are more than a simple "theoretical practice";
the publications constitute an act of provocation and agitation that favors the struggle of the masses, which already
possess the truth of their own situation and of the opening
of new situations. The provocation–agitation advances this
opening up and points to the new situations, not only indi-
cating them as possible but even sometimes helping bring
them about.[21]

---

20.   MIL-GAC, *Entre Mayo 37 y la agitación armada*, March 1973, a debate
text distributed among all the sectors that were in contact.
21.   Sergi Rosés Cordovilla, *El MIL: una historia política* (Barcelona:
Alikornio, 2002), 135.

Even so, it should be made clear that between the library and the other part of the collective—particularly the Tolosa nucleus—there was a gap. This explains how in Barcelona, all the comrades were well familiar with the Situationists, while a comrade in the city of Llenguadoc could claim without any theatricality that he had never even heard of them.[22]

Paradoxically, the pamphlets—they must be categorized as such, given how few of our texts exceeded fifty pages—were printed in Tolosa with a run of between one- and two thousand copies, they arrived in the Barcelona region by car, and they were freely distributed amongst workers' groups, political organizations, and a few bookstores that secretly sold prohibited books.

But even before they began appearing under the name Ediciones Mayo del 37, we had published a long list of texts. We have already mentioned some of the publications put out by the pre-MIL through December 1970, now we will pick up where we left off. In January of 1971, we published a Spanish version of *Wild Europe: Study on the Wildcat Strike Movement in Europe in the Second Half of the 20th Century*, translating the pamphlet by ICO (Information et Correspondance Ouvrieres), which recorded the principal wildcat strikes: of the miners in Belgium, in Poland, in Italy, where the situation became so extreme that the bosses of some companies did not even dare go to work. We published these without any name or logo and, given their favorable reception, they were republished by the GOA under their own label, which struck us as magnificent, since it increased the distribution. In *Workers Councils in Hungary* (published in July 1971), we updated the message of the revolution that Béla Kun led in 1919 to also include the workers' councils in 1956.

Since pure theory can't stand up on its own two feet, let's not forget the practical manuals, distributed for immediate use. In this light we printed *How to Fight the Stopwatch* (April 1971), written and edited by Platforms, and *The Struggle against Repression* (February–March 1971), printed in Perpinyà. One front that was

---

22. Carlota Tolosa, *La torna de la torna: Salvador Puig Antich i MIL* (Barcelona: Empúries, 1985).

beginning to open up in those moments was the neighborhood struggle, so we published *The Struggle in the Neighborhoods* in two volumes (July–August 1973). The original had appeared in the magazine *Komuna 2*. We also wrote and distributed pamphlets connected to other contemporary conflicts. A few examples are *Boycott the Union Elections: No to Bourgeois Legality* (March 1971), written by Oriol Solé and the only time the "1,000" logo appears on a text; two months later the GOA were born and together with future members of the MIL they published *The Struggle of Santa Coloma*, though it appears with Platforms' logo. There was a pamphlet distributed at the Bultaco factory. Later on, and thanks to the expropriations, we could donate a printing machine to the workers at that factory, and they used it to publish *El loro indiscreto* (September 1972), a magazine of an anarchistic tendency that would cause tension in the GOA with those of a Marxist tendency who published in Ruedo Ibérico, the famous publishing house of exiled Republicans headquartered in Paris. As a final example, we can cite the *Dosier San Adriá del Besós* (April 1973), edited by Ediciones Mayo el 37, about the already mentioned conflict at the power plant.

Our ideological positions were highly flexible and we distributed materials from very different tendencies, only requiring that they reinforced the practices of self-organization, autogestion, and workers' autonomy. Under this assumption, we published texts by the Dutch theorist Anton Pannekoek, like *Party and Working Class* (April 1971) and *The Workers' Councils in Germany* (March 1973), the first Spanish translations of the most important theorist of council communism. The second text was originally written in English, translated to French by the publisher Bélibaste, which had a reputation for being anarchist, and then republished by *Éditions Spartacus*, who were anti-Leninist Marxist revolutionaries. Of the previously mentioned Jean Barrot, who at the time defined himself as a supporter of council communism—a subtle counterposition to councilism—we translated *Notes for an Analysis of the Russian Revolution* (September 1971). We also put out in Spanish pamphlets previously distributed by ICO, like *The Strikes in Poland, The German Revolution* (both in January 1972), and *On Class Organization in the German Revolution 1920–1921* (April 1973). Regarding this last text, out of ignorance we attributed it to ICO, when in reality it was by Henk Canne-Meijer (1890–1962), one of the founders of the Gruppe Internationale Kommunisten (GIK), an interwar Dutch councilist association. All of these were writings that expressed a strong desire for rupture and that exalted the revolution.

In a completely divergent line, we translated *Are We Heading for a New 1929?* (February 1973), which originally came out in the magazine *Revolution Internationale*, published in Tolosa by a group of the same name that postulated that a party was needed to map out the political orientation of the proletariat, but taking precautions against leading it.[23] By Marx's son-in-law, Paul Lafargue (1842–1911), we published *The Right to Be Lazy* (February 1972), basing ourselves on Maspéro's edition. It is a work that, as expressed in its title, destroys the absurd glorification of hard labor that characterizes almost the totality of revolutionary literature. To consider just one quote:

> A strange delusion possesses the working classes of the nations where capitalist civilization holds its sway. This delusion drags in its train the individual and social woes which for two centuries have tortured sad humanity. This delusion is the love of work, the furious passion for work, pushed even to the exhaustion of the vital force of the individual and his progeny...[24]

Regarding a completely different theme and with a focus in perfect disagreement, we put out *On the Poverty of Student Life* (June 1973), a Situationist text very popular in Paris in May '68, written by Mustapha Khayati. In another direction, again completely different, we published *The Commune: Paris 1871, Kronstadt 1921, or Poland 1970–1971* (February 1972), an original

---

23. Organisation communiste et conscience de clase (CCI). fr.internationalism.org/brochures/organisation_communiste.

24. Trans: 1883. I have used Charles H. Kerr's translation, Charles H. Kerr and Co., Co-operative, 1883.

by *Cahiers Spartacus*, a monthly publication put out continuously since 1934, though censored during World War II. As with earlier works, it came out unsigned by author or editor.

Finally, to show clearly our theoretical malleability, the texts by heterodox, anti-authoritarian Marxists must be mentioned. These definitively demonstrate our inclination towards heterodoxy and free and independent reflection. From Paul Cardan, one of many pseudonyms of Cornelius Castoriadis (1922–1997), Frenchman of Hellenic origins, we published "Proletariat and Organization" (April 1971), distributed by Platforms, though without any specific mention of them. It consisted of an article from *Socialisme ou barbarie*.[25]

By the Croat Ante Ciliga (1896–1992), we published *Lenin and the Revolution* (May 1973). From the Frenchman of Hungarian origins, Balázs István (1905–1963)—which we surprisingly mangled as "Esteban Balazs"—an ex-Trotskyist Sinologist, we published *What Comes After Capitalism?* (January 1973), in which he takes on capitalism both in its decentralized or occidental modality and in its statist modality, while also auguring the imminent triumph of libertarian socialism.

Completely exempt from a toll on Marxism would be *Between the Revolution and the Trenches* (January 1973), a posthumous text by Camillo Berneri (1893–1937), an Italian anarchist assassinated during the May Days of '37 in Barcelona. Though we invented the title ourselves, it corresponds to the edition of *Class War in Spain* published by *Cahiers Spartacus* in 1946. The text directs a strong criticism against the leaders of the CNT-FAI who took government posts in the Popular Front during the war, crossing to the other side of the barricades and betraying the cause. For our edition we translated from the original (we did not realize that it had already been translated to Spanish in 1946 by Tierra y Libertad, the publishing group of anarchists in exile in Bordeaux), and as a prologue we wrote "Class War in '37—Class War in '73," a dissertation we will discuss presently.

In our circle, debate was continuous: action and theory set

---

25.   No. 27, April/May, 1959, and no. 28, July/August, 1959.

the pace and they materialized in texts that we distributed as widely as we were able, only taking precautions to uphold the most basic norms of security. Some references are "Economic Analysis of Spain" (April 1972), an attempt to avail ourselves of an analytical instrument that went further than the short-sighted democratism of Ramón Tamames, an author who at the time had been elevated to cult status. There was "Capital and Work" (December 1972) and "On Class Organization: Barcelona 1973" (June 1973). The latter in particular, written by Ernesto Núñez, a militant from Platforms, reflects on class organization as a unitary political-workers' organization. "Between May '37 and Armed Agitation" (March 1973) was where we definitively distilled the already mentioned theory of armed agitation. "Notes for an analysis of our tendency" (April 1973) was an internal letter illuminating the contradictions that over the coming summer led to our disbandment. "Contribution to the Critique of the Present Situation and Its Immediate Overcoming" (August 1974) was a pamphlet written by comrades of the ex-MIL under the collective pseudonym "The Ghost of Fu Manchu and the Black Hand, Inc." Finally, "History Will Absolve Us" provides a chronology of the collective, elaborated when some of the comrades were in prison. The original version still has not been published, but it has served as a reference for various chronologies about the group that are in circulation.

CIA (Conspiración Internacional Anarquista) deserves a special mention; it was presented as a periodical publication of the collective (April 1973), when in fact it was the unilateral initiative of the Tolosa group of the MIL.[26] This was the first appearance of the acronym MIL, for Movimiento Ibérico de Liberación, to the great consternation of those of us who organized the library and

---

26.   Articles included "On the 50 Year Anniversary of the FAI," "Anarchist Resisters After 1945," "Police Stations Are Also Erotic Sites," "The Angry Brigade," "The Stoke Newington 8," "The Final Morning of Antonio Juan Creix," "The 'Freak Brothers': execution by firing squad in Carabanchel." As a supplement it included "Revolutionary violence, on the Baader-Meinhof Gang," an extract from Émile Marensin's *La "Bande à Baader" ou la violence révolucionarraire*. Paris: Éditions Champ Libre, 1972.

of the workers in the milieu of the Barcelona group. The most interesting article in the magazine related to armed agitation. Another article to highlight was "Evaluation and perspectives of the workers' struggle," developed from a sketch by Santi Soler, "Anti-authoritarianism in the workers' struggle in Barcelona," prepared the previous year. On the whole, the issue exalted anarchist armed actions and neglected the role of the library, a posture that contrasted sharply with its ludic style, with illustrations and comics profusely altered in Situationist *detournement*.[27]

The most serious matter was that the article "Chronology of the MIL-GAC" allowed the police to connect actions that had previously seemed unrelated, and provided names of comrades who already had files with the French Gendarmerie but not yet with the Brigada Político-Social. Between two- and three hundred copies of the first issue were printed, though only a dozen copies arrived in Catalunya, since the comrades in Barcelona refused to distribute it.

The second issue of *CIA* included essential political texts, like "Dissolution of the politico-military organization the MIL. Conclusions from the MIL congress. August 1973."[28] Here the discrepancy between the library and the sector in favor of strengthening the armed actions was expressed. Though we will later explore this confrontation in more detail, for now we should note that one thousand copies were printed and distributed in Tolosa, Barcelona, Madrid, and Euskadi.

Among the authors we were planning on adding to our catalogue but we never got around to publishing, were Karl Marx (1818–1883), Lev Trotsky (1879–1940), the French surrealist and

---

27.   *Detournement* is defined as "the liberating 'inversion' of capitalist infrastructure towards playful ends." Guy Debord, "Detournement as Negation and Prelude," in *Internationale Situationniste*, no. 3 (Dec. 1959), republished in *Situationist International: An Anthology*, ed. by Ken Knabb (Berkeley: Bureau of Public Secrets, 1981), 55. Put simply, *detournement* consists in altering a "work of art" with a capitalist message, giving it instead a socialist one.

28.   Other articles from the second issue include "Italy, the Red Brigades," "Against the National-Socialism of the IRA," "The Civil War, communist movement?" and "Outline of the workers' movement in Barcelona in June, 1973."

Trotskyist Benjamin Péret (1899–1959), the German councilist Otto Rühle (1874–1943), the British Trotskyist born in Palestine of Jewish origin, Tony Cliff, pseudonym for Yigael Gluckstein (1917–2000), the French councilist of Ukrainian origins Maximilien Rubel (1905–1996), the quasi-Trotskyist Catalan Andreu Nin (1892–1937), the anarchist Gaston Leval, pseudonym of Pierre Rober (1895–1978), and the Austrian/North American psychoanalyst Wilhelm Reich (1897–1957). A whole garden of revolutionaries, speaking diverse dictions.

Without counting re-editions, the last text published by Ediciones Mayo del 37 was *Milestones of Defeat: The Promise of Victory. The May Days,* by Grandizo Munis, pseudonym of Manuel Fernández Grandizo (1912–1989), a member of Izquierda Comunista de España and of the 4th International who, over time, grew closer to the positions of council communism. The full version of the work, such as that published in Bilbao by Zeta (1977), has the expressive subtitle, "Critique and Theory of the Spanish Revolution: 1930–1939," an objective it completes to perfection over the course of its 517 pages. Our edition, circumscribed to the pamphlet format, was limited to Chapter VI of the second part, dedicated specifically to May 1937. Ediciones Mayo del 37 closed the same year the dictator died.

Tactics

The police never managed to infiltrate our organization. For meeting points we used bars, a different every time. If you had arranged to meet at five in the afternoon, and the other person had not shown up at one minute past five, the meeting was considered canceled. You could not wait any longer. That is not how they dismantled us.

A delicate topic was how to act with workers who tried to impede an expropriation at their place of work. In fact, it had never been proposed as a topic for debate *a priori*, but we came face to face with the dilemma on March 2, 1973, in a branch of the Hispano-American Bank, near the metro station Fabra i Puig, when an accountant tried to close the safe with a comrade still inside, and we had to act forcefully: he was shot in the head, wounded but not killed. This provoked an internal debate. Not exactly in moral terms, because he had behaved objectively as an ally of Capital, but because of the counter-propaganda they could spread under the headline "Bandits Injure Worker." Either way, the spilling of blood left an indelible mark on us.

The expropriated funds were not destined to specific causes before the cash was already in hand. Thanks to Manolo Murcia and José Antonio Díaz, who closely followed the conflicts in the factories, an evaluation was made as to whether the money should go to a particular strike fund, like for the Bultaco strike, to the library, or to infrastructure (typewriters, duplicators...). The decision was made according to whatever need seemed most urgent. We also acted on our own initiative. We never carried out an expropriation "to order" with the money already earmarked for a specific cause.

If we did not even speak with the militants of the PSUC, our relation with the local extreme left was fluid and cordial, whether they were Catalanists or internationalists, Maoists or Trotskyists. We shared printed materials. We made our first contacts with ETA and with Lotta Continua in the Cuixà monastery in North Catalunya, where Oriol Solé hid out after being identified by the police as the agitator who burned down Camy ice cream kiosks. Later, contacts were renewed with ETA V Asamblea (in January 1971), even though we were separated by clear ideological differences: they were anticapitalists but authoritarians. They passed us some pistols, 13,000 francs—a huge sum at the time—and we exchanged views of our political projects as well as printed materials. In October 1972 in Euskadi we also contacted a group close to ETA, Barnuruntz—also called The Block—through Txus Larrenea, who would join the MIL though his activity was exclusive to Tolosa de Llenguadoc. Barnuruntz, a split from ETA V Asamblea, was half Luxemburgist and half libertarian and, as such, was more compatible with our own positions. Eventually they would distribute our subversive literature in Euskal Herria.

In Asturias we had a relationship with Comunas Revolucionarias de Acción Socialista (CRAS, or Revolutionary

Communes of Socialist Action) and in Madrid with the dissidents of the Organización Revolucionaria de Trabajadores (ORT, or Revolutionary Organization of Workers), a party with a Maoist tendency.[29] The members of CRAS and the dissidents of ORT supported workers' autonomy, though we only had sporadic contact, given that the dismantling of the MIL (in September 1973) did not leave us time for anything else.

In Italy we maintained contact with Lotta Continua starting in 1968. Through Paris, we had direct or indirect contact with all of Europe: we maintained a close relationship with the Situationist International, with Pierre Guillaume, the owner of the bookstore La Vieille Taupe (1965–1972), and with Gilles Dauvé-Jean Barrot, who was closely linked to the bookstore and in that era had published *Le mouvement communiste* (Champ Libre, 1972) and *Communisme et question russe* (La Tête de feuilles, 1972).[30] In Paris we also maintained relations with the Organisation Révolutionnaire Anarchiste (ORA), at that moment following a completely councilist line, with René Lefeuvre, *Éditions Spartacus*, responsible for Cahiers Spartacus, and with various libertarian groups.

Both the Spanish CNT and the French one—with more than five thousand paying members in the region of Tolosa de Llenguadoc, although only 150 went to the meetings—disowned the MIL from the beginning, inevitably, saying we weren't anarchists and that the armed actions compromised their (in) activity. On July 19, 1973, the anniversary of the insurrection against fascism, the CNT organized an event at the Halle aux Grains stadium in Tolosa, and some comrades from the MIL wanted to set up a table with books we had published. The CNT bureaucrats did not waste any time in kicking us out rudely. But the bad blood was only with the leaders of the Intercontinental

29.   Valentín Brugos Salas, "La izquierda revolucionaria en Asturias: los diferentes intentos de construcción de un proyecto alternativo al PCE." In: Francisco Erice (Coord.), *Los Comunistas en Asturias (1920–1982)* (Gijón: Trea, 1996), 459–502.

30.   Christophe Bourseiller, *Histoire générale de l'ultra-gauche* (Paris: Denoël, 2003); Richard Gombin, *Les origines du gauchisme* (Paris: Seuil, 1971).

Secretariat; many of the rank and file helped us out a thousand different ways.

Dissolution

The dissolution of the MIL is the consequence of a flagrant contradiction that originated in the very genesis of the collective. The ideology did not mesh with the practice.

Ideologically, we were opposed to the dissociation between armed agitation and the workers' movement, but we ourselves contravened this axiom. The contrast between one and the other became more and more evident. We were against specialization, but the solitude imposed by armed action obliged us to specialize and to isolate ourselves more and more. All the progress in our political analysis, by the very nature of the organization, impeded a congruous praxis. Despite our aversion, the MIL had degraded into what it had presumed to combat: another faction, definitely not vanguardist, but self-satisfied and distanced from the Movement. We fought the proliferation of acronyms, but we used them and spread them ourselves.

Practically, the Exterior Team (or the comrades of the GAC, which are basically the same) was in favor of making a qualitative leap and initiating a second, more intense phase against the repression, with sabotage actions, kidnappings, and assassinations. With the MIL obstinately dedicated to carrying out expropriations, distance grew with the workers who collaborated with us at the same time as we began to neglect our publishing activities. The police had created a brigade especially assigned to wiping us out (June 1973), under the direction of Inspector Santiago Bocigas.[31] We should remember that, in the same month, Carrero Blanco was named president, a position reserved until that moment exclusively for Franco: the regime had to reassemble itself to not show any signs of weakness. We understood that the expropriations followed an ever rising slope going nowhere.

31.   Matelo Rello, *Puig Antich en el laberinto*, www.soliobrera.org/actualidad /laberinto.html.

We could not continue to follow that path. In the MIL congress, it was agreed that the expropriations would have to be intermittent and that the tendency in favor of the qualitative leap in armed agitation and the tendency in favor of the publishing of texts would have to work separately. The organizational divorce constituted, definitively, the group's dissolution.

In March 1973, the MIL authored "Between May of '37 and Armed Agitation" for internal distribution, and it ended up serving as a sort of forum for these issues in which, for the first time, the dissolution of the MIL was considered, though the text ends by rejecting that option. In April, "Notes for an analysis of our tendency" was distributed to our internal circle as an expression of the internal unease caused by these unresolved contradictions. In August, after being postponed several times, the MIL congress was convened in Tolosa and agreed on disbanding the organization. Issue 2 of *CIA* includes the notes from the meeting. (In an irony of history, it is after the dissolution of the group that the repression grew and the group's revolutionary project was liquidated.)

The MIL disbanded not to curb the struggle, but because it had not succeeded in encouraging the appearance of new armed groups within the movement, and as such had to continue the fight, through propaganda for instance, and at a greater intensity if possible, with eyes on an indeterminate horizon when armed agitation would arise as a practice in effective solidarity with the movement. And there were certainly attempts. At the SEAT factory there were workers' self-defense groups. For its part, the library wanted to distance itself from the armed agitation and the acronyms so that the books—exempt of excessively tarnished connotations—could achieve a wider distribution and spread their message further. This failed, however, to resolve the contradiction that their printing required money and this could only be gotten in large enough quantities through expropriations.

The "definitive conclusions" of the congress were explicit and deserve to be reproduced:

> Terrorism and sabotage are weapons that are currently usable by every revolutionary. Terrorism by word and

by deed. Attacking Capital and its faithful guardians—whether they belong to left or right—is the current purpose of the *GRUPOS AUTÓNOMOS DE COMBATE* that have broken with all the old workers' movements and promote new criteria for precise action. Organization is the organization of tasks: for this reason, the grassroots groups coordinate to carry out actions. On the basis of these certainties, organization, politics, militancy, moralism, martyrs, acronyms, our own labels, have passed into the old world.

As such, each individual will assume their personal responsibilities in the revolutionary struggle. There are no individuals who dissolve themselves, it is the politico-military organization MIL that is dissolved: it is this going down in history that makes us definitively leave the prehistory of class struggle.

The groupuscules found it more viable to set up a separate, closed, and sealed military apparatus, than to do so from the movement itself and connected to it.[32] The dissolution occurred because the group's failure had been confirmed, it had become one more groupuscule. In fact, once it had been eclipsed, the MIL continued its armed agitation on the margins of the movement. But this practice lost touch with our philosophy. We refused to climb the rungs of power. We were against *putsches*. Revolution did not consist in seizing power in the name of the class, but in the class itself conquering and holding power. Revolution delegated can elevate one clique to power that might happen to be better than the last one, but it will invariably degenerate.

The GAC, once separated from the library, resumed their plan for immediate action for that coming autumn: Black

---

32.   Trans: To clarify this point, Ricard adds that it was necessary for the different parts of the group to enjoy autonomy, so that the military sector would not be dictating to the library, for example, but that the separation also accelerated the self-isolation of the military sector. And though the needs of clandestinity and security make isolation a likelihood, the OLLA's method of avoiding specialization, with the same members continuing to struggle in the workplace and also carry out other actions, was perhaps more viable for maintaining a connection to the movement.

September–Red October, a polysemic allusion to the Bolshevik's October Revolution, to the Black September of the Palestinian movement, and to the red and black flag. Their objectives included the assassination of Commissioner Creix and of the chief of the police unit who murdered the worker Manuel Fernández Márquez, and the kidnapping of the Venezuelan console's wife; they would hold her in their little prison on the mountain of Moixeró. Since the GAC at that point only had three members, they sought the collaboration of the OLLA, which did not agree to carry out any of the plans, considering them to be excessive.

Self-Criticism

The MIL committed errors of diverse kinds:

> Ideological errors. One highly important mistake was the adoption of the Marxist theory that the contradictions of capitalism, once they reached the phase of monopolies, would culminate in its end. And since the wildcat strikes multiplied like never before and the oil crisis brought about a recession, it was assumed that the situation was already ripe: that capitalism was at the point of breaking apart, as the workers' movement in Catalunya, across the Peninsula, and throughout the world, was ascendant. We believed we were at the beginning of a new world. It is reflected in a pamphlet, *Are We Heading for a New 1929?*, which answers in the affirmative. But this did not correspond at all with reality.

In the introduction to the book by Camillo Berneri, playing with the inversion of '37 and '73, it was affirmed that the May Days of 1937 were absolutely current, as though we were in an open war with the forces of the reformist left. In 1937, the Catalan working class all had Mausers in their hands; in 1973, they didn't. That parts of the working class were armed with Kalashnikovs on distant points of the globe did not help us in the least.

While it is certain that there was a radicalization of the workers' movement in Barcelona's industrial belt, the struggles were
isolated, they never fully coordinated or came into synergy. The
decisive moment in these conflicts was between 1969 and 1971.
Starting in 1973, the GOA are eclipsed and Platforms lose steam.
We were never a majority. More than an autonomous movement,
we should speak of scattered autonomous struggles. It was a class
in training. Afterwards, a new stage arrived, that of the Transition,
during which, though protests and strikes proliferated, they were
not in favor of the proletariat but in favor of formal democracy.
The assemblies in factories were nothing like workers' councils.
It's true, in the assemblies everyone participates, but often there is
a manipulation from the shadows orchestrated by the Communist
Party, Bandera Roja, and other parties, who were constantly on the
hunt against autonomists and anticapitalists.

It is not true—as López Petit or Miguel Amorós erroneously
affirm—that we would have achieved such a tremendous force
as to be able to defy the State and even take power. The literature of the era, to the extent it had to inflate our courage, systematically glorified the deeds, which could lead unadvised readers
today to confuse that which was announced with that which
occurred. There were autonomous tendencies and struggles of
the same color, but they lacked a coordination of strategy and a
strategy of coordination. We faced two enemies: the bourgeoisie
and the members of the PCE. We could find the first—or, more
accurately, their lackeys—in the workshops, but we ran into the
second all over. We were forced to fight them. We did not relate
with them like comrades, all the contrary.

Until 1939, there was a vibrant popular culture that had
taken off at the end of the nineteenth century, a tradition of
struggle through the CNT, the FAI, the Anarchist Social Centers,
Houses of the People...[33] The proletariat was training itself. The

---

33.   Trans: *Ateneus Llibertaris* literally renders as Libertarian Aetheneums,
but as one word, has fallen into disuse and the other has been co-opted by
its exact opposite, I have decided to give the term an up-to-date rendition to
Anarchist Social Centers. Such a place today could be called simultaneously
ateneu llibertari and *centre social anarquista*.

government could function without the CNT, but not against it. It had so much strength in all the working-class neighborhoods of Barcelona that it could not be avoided, to such an extent that they operated like independent republics. The process was interrupted after the Civil War. Despite it all, under the Francoist occupation, in the '40s there arose a significant level of proletarian activity and anarchist guerrilla resistance, but in the 1950s, due to exhaustion, the intensification of repression, and international isolation, with a dictatorship endorsed by the USA, many surviving anarchist militants only wished to spare their own children the battles they had fought and which had proved sterile.

What's more, the anarchist movement did not know how to adapt to the new situation. The lack of adaptation was total. Until the 1960s, the CNT distributed pamphlets from the '40s, which, in turn, were reprints from the '20s, as though they were perfectly up-to-date. A gap of four decades! In this way, they entered the final phase of Francoism having passed through an abysmal generational desert. The libertarian movement, as an organization, had been annihilated by the repression. Despite it all, we should highlight that, at the beginning of the '70s, the fishermen of Barceloneta and the theater and cinema workers continued paying dues to the CNT. Some of us sympathized with this revolutionary anarchist tradition, but we were a minority who searched for the creation of new paths of libertarian practice. The first explicitly anarchist group in the Spanish state I can find reference to is an assembly in the county of Vallès Oriental, and it appears at such a late date as 1974: Tribuna Libertaria, created by young people who had broken with the official CNT, headquartered in exile in Tolosa.[34]

The new proletariat mostly came from the countryside, above all from Andalucía, where they had suffered a cruel degree of poverty. What's more, the new workers' movement only had six or seven years of experience and it was mutilated by repression and alienation. People with a political education were a minority. The vast majority could not even understand

---

34.   Trans: Vallès Oriental is contiguous with Barcelona.

our pamphlets. When we distributed them, many copies ended up in the trash. They did not have a revolutionary consciousness, but on the other hand they did have a consciousness of mutual aid, self-organization, and solidarity. The GOA had around forty members at most, but the industrial working class in Catalunya numbered one and a half million. For the masses, the revolution boiled down to what they wanted in their day to day life: buying a television, having a car, getting a plot of land where they could build a vacation house. It would be enough just to gain better pay, even if it was at the expense of long hours. The slogans of the Communist Party, clearly accommodating, only demanded formal, bourgeois democracy, and only aspired to economic improvements, positions that satisfied the greater part of the proletariat.

The PCE slogan, "With democracy, rising wages" discouraged combativity. There were very few of us committed to intensifying the contradictions. Because of this, the radical strikes were localized, temporary, and isolated. From 1970–71 there was the Harry Walker strike, but a year later it hadn't even left a residue. They were stagnant struggles. In 1973, there was the strike in Sant Adrià del Besòs, and in 1974 in Ripollet, Viladecans, Montcada i Reixac, where there was a vigorous autonomous movement; in 1976, the strike in la Roca, in Gavà... but there was no thread that stitched them together. A new stage had begun.

Errors in our activist practice. The group was always running like hell, with haste and without pause, and quickly ran headlong into the consequences. Outright imprudence was not the general rule, but the two definite cases of such behavior had grave consequences. In June of 1973, Puig Antich left a bag with 100,000 pesetas, a pistol, ammunition, information about a rented apartment, falsified documents, and his real ID in the bar Caspolino on plaça Gal·la Placídia. Salvador managed to evade arrest, but the documents allowed the police to locate a safe house and seize everything stored there: munitions, propaganda, masks, detonators, etc. The second case of excessive haste led to even graver consequences. As already mentioned, on September 15, 1972, we carried out an expropriation at a bank in Bellver de Cerdanya, a small village in the Pyrenees. Short on resources, exactly one year later, on the same month and day, a second expropriation is attempted at the same bank. The three members who carry it out are intercepted by the Guardia Civil during the getaway, there is an intense firefight, and for two days the Guardia comb the forest of Alp in search of them, finally grabbing Oriol Solé and Pons Llobet, while only Jordi Solé manages to evade them and cross the border. The detainees are interrogated for three days; subsequently, and given the rush of events, one member after another fall prisoner in Barcelona. A few days after the arrests near the border, in the apartment of the Pons Llobet family, they grab María Angustias Mateos, sixteen years old, partner of Josep Lluís Pons. Next to go is Emili Pardiñas and his partner, Maria Lluïsa Piguillén, Manuel Antonio Canestro, Santi Soler Amigó, Puig Antich, and Francesc Xavier Garriga.[35]

OLLA

There is no book or monograph about the OLLA, and they only appear obliquely in texts dedicated to other organizations; furthermore, these references make categorical assertions that also happen to be incorrect, given that they never consulted with any old militant from the OLLA. Sergi Rosés, author of the most erudite study on the MIL, qualifies them as nationalists, which he puts forward as the reason why the fusion between the MIL and the OLLA did not come to fruition as, according to him, the

---

35.   Trans: Santi Soler was arrested when he returned to Barcelona by airplane, after French police had passed his information on to their Spanish counterparts. After three days of torture, Soler gave the Spanish police the time and location of the meeting, thinking that no one would show up amidst the wave of arrests. Unfortunately, Garriga and Puig Antich decided to go.

former were suspicious of the latter.[36] For his part, in one of his recent books, *De Memoria I: Los comienzos: otoño de 1970 en Tolosa de Llenguadoc*, in which he relates his experiences, Jean-Marc Rouillan affirms the opposite, presenting the OLLA as an autonomous group that did not in any way want to join with the MIL.[37]

The fact is, there is no history of the OLLA worthy of the name, and it should be written before all the protagonists disappear—among them, myself. Carl Einstein (1885–1940), a German and Jewish anarchist, avant-garde art critic who fought in the Durruti Column and took his own life in France before falling into Nazi hands, declared that revolutionaries are anonymous.[38] But this has a flipside. Since actual names are not preserved, neither is reliable memory, and inaccuracies get repeated.

The OLLA began to act in 1971 (though some of its members had already collaborated with the pre-MIL years back). It arose when the three members who constituted the recently created action group of the Partit Socialista d'Alliberament Nacional (PSAN) split off.[39] In those days, many of the subversive formations had an action group, a collective prepared to carry out actions of collective self-defense when the situation demanded it. PSAN was a Catalan independence formation that had come from the Front Nacional de Catalunya (FNC), from which it split in 1969.[40] The FNC was a movement with vintage that began in 1940, independentist, with basically petit-bourgeois positions, while all sorts of political and social sensibilities came together in the PSAN: Leninists, Stalinists, heterodox Marxists, libertarians, autonomists... It was a conglomeration with one common

36.   Salvador López Arnal, "El MIL, tal como era: entrevista con Sergi Rosés Cordovila," *El Viejo Topo* 222–23 (July 2006), 27–29.

37.   *De Memoria I: Los comienzos: otoño de 1970 en Tolosa de Llenguadoc* (Barcelona: Virus, 2009).

38.   From his radio address from Barcelona after the death of Durruti.

39.   Fermí Rubiralta i Casa, *Origen i desenvolupament del PSAN, 1969–1974* (Barcelona: La Magrana, 1989 and *El nuevo nacionalismo radical: los casos gallego, catalán y vasco (1959–1973)* (San Sebastián: Gakoa, 1977).

40.   Daniel Díaz i Esculies, *El Front Nacional de Catalunya (1939–1947)* (Barcelona: La Magrana, 1983); Robert Surroca i Tallaferro, *Memòries del Front Nacional de Catalunya: cavalcant damunt l'estel* (Barcelona: Arrels, 2006); Ferran Dalmau and Pau Juvillà, *EPOCA, l'exèrcit a l'ombra* (Lleida: Edicions el Jonc, 2010).

denominator, a new generation with a swerve to the left. At the end of 1971, PSAN's action group, made up of radicalized workers, breaks off and forms an autonomous, anti-dogmatic, anti-authoritarian, anti-party group. Despite its genesis as the splinter of a nationalist party, the national question was never brought up in the two congresses of the OLLA (the first in November 1973 and the second in January 1974).

In particular, each of us, whether we were natives or immigrants, could have the same ideas: many of us were not opposed to independence and some were even supporters, but always subordinating that concern to the social revolution. The only positions that we put in common were anticapitalist struggle and solidarity with the oppressed everywhere in the world. We were revolutionaries with an anarchist practice.

An original element of our group was the position of equality that the women comrades assumed. Ours is the generation that began to tear down traditional masculinity. When I was an adolescent, I got the idea to clean the house, but my mother warned me as long as she had her health, not to try it again. There were many women workers. My grandmother worked in a textile factory. Until the 1960s, women had a double shift, whereas when the men got out of the factory, they headed to the bar to talk until supper time. But in the middle of the '60s, the most conscious ones began proposing a change. It is impossible to fight against capitalism and oppression and remain blind to the exploitation of women. In the MIL, with one exception, the women maintained a passive attitude: they were the companions of the members. In the second expropriation at Bellver de Cerdanya, the participation of a woman comrade was proposed, but in the end it was rejected.

In the OLLA, there were seven women active who had come from the labor struggles, workers who assumed the same roles as the men. The women acted the same as the men in the actions, with machine guns, blowing up monuments; they were equal in the debates, equal in everything. In the first half of 1973, some of them even formed a group—today we would consider them feminists—to deal with their specific problems, taking on the topic of free abortions, among others. This group began planning their own expropriation, but in the end the project was scrapped.

Relation with the MIL

In order to situate the MIL and the OLLA within an adequate historical perspective, we have to compare the chronologies of the two organizations. The first, as we have seen, was born at the end of 1971, and the second was as well: the same time, just a few days apart. In the summer of 1972, the two organizations held formal talks on the mountain of Moixeró. On one side, Oriol Solé and Jean-Marc Rouillan, and on the other, Felip Solé, Joan Jordi Vinyoles, accompanied by Ignasi Solé. The MIL gave the OLLA a .38 revolver without ammunition, and they exchanged logistical information and revolutionary texts, and agreed on joint actions.

As Sergi Rosés is obliged to recognize, "the group in the interior with which [the MIL] collaborated most was the OLLA [...], with whom they carried out some expropriations, exchanged information, etc."[41] But more than collaboration, the word that defines the relation between both collectives is "coordination,"[42] above all "at the military level, [at which they had] constant and effective contact."[43] Cooperating in armed socialization actions—with all the risk they entail—requires a very high degree of rapport. The two organizations carried out some joint expropriations in the autumn of 1972. For example, on October 21, they went into action at the Savings and Pensions Bank on carrer Escorial, in the Gràcia neighborhood, where they left explicitly political communiqués. What's more, this coordination was on the rise, such that "in the moments preceding the dissolution of the MIL, agreements of a technical and tactical type were established with [the OLLA]."[44]

The positions of the two groups were largely overlapping. In

41.   López Arnal, "El MIL, tal como era," 20–21.

42.   Rosés, *El MIL*, 152.

43.   López Arnal, "El MIL, tal como era," 22.

44.   Cortade, André, *Le 1000: histoire désordonné du MIL. Barcelona 1967– 1974.* Paris: Dérive, 1985.

terms of ideology, the communion was complete: the OLLA and the MIL shared "autonomous conceptions on the organizational plane."[45] According to Rosés, the OLLA had "a more anticapitalist discourse than [the PSAN],"[46] which at the time defined itself as Marxist-Leninist, and "little by little was seduced by positions similar to those [of the MIL]."[47] And the OLLA was "anxious to acquire [sic] the library of Ediciones Mayo del 37." Discarding the sentence's mercantile connotation, the meaning can only be interpreted as proposing an identical ideology.[48]

More to this effect: the OLLA wished for "unification" with the MIL.[49] "The OLLA made [disbandment of the MIL] a requirement to begin the debate on moving [the two collectives] closer together" (note that, according to this source, the OLLA sets the conditions and the MIL has to fold to meet them).[50] On the whole, both the MIL and the OLLA were in favor of fusion. Taking into account the latter's origins, we might suspect that the principal divergence was the national question, but as we have already explained, the OLLA subordinated that topic to a strictly social struggle. On the other hand, "it is true that within the MIL, two people defended nationalist [sic] positions, the brothers Ignasi and Oriol Solé (also, though years after the MIL, Santi Soler...)."[51] To finish, we should also remember their dialogue with ETA, which shows that the MIL did not demonize nationalism.

Finally, there were also transfers in their membership: Puig Antich thought of going over to the OLLA. And after the dissolution, "contacts [...] multiplied [...] when [the MIL] considered the possibility of proposing a meeting to open up to other collectives." In the fall of 1973, three members of the collective, the brothers Ignasi and Raimon Solé Sugranyes, and myself, joined the OLLA, staying until it was dismantled a year later, in 1974.

---

45.   López Arnal, "El MIL, tal como era," 120.
46.   Duhourcq and Madrigal, *Mouvement Iberique de Liberation*, 20; compare Rosés, *El MIL,*129.
47.   Duhourcq and Madrigal, *Mouvement Iberique de Liberation*, 208.
48.   Rosés, *El MIL*, 173.
49.   López Arnal, "El MIL, tal como era," 25.
50.   Duhourcq and Madrigal, *Mouvement Iberique de Liberation*, 227.
51.   Ibid., 243.

With the great affinity between the two groups established, it is not necessary to minimize the differences that separated them. The MIL wanted to stamp their logo on all the actions it carried out, while the OLLA believed in anonymity as a formula to allow the protagonism to fall upon the whole of the working class, while also avoiding giving the police free clues. It was precisely this divergence that explains why the MIL became well known, whereas the OLLA, consistent with its beliefs, has not left the slightest mark on history. Despite the greater theoretical preparation of the MIL, demonstrated by all its publications, this did not prevent the workers of the OLLA putting in quarantine some of the MIL's ways of acting.

The OLLA, thanks to being made up of wage earners, operated with privileged information. If they prepared an action at the Central Post Office, they did so with the help of someone among the personnel who had previously tipped them off. If they expropriated the Catalan Bank, it's because two employees had given them highly detailed intelligence. The MIL did not dispose of important details. They became experts in expropriations because they were free of the need to earn wages, and their need for money was urgent, because they had no way of acquiring it other than the path of armed action.[52] The OLLA represents, in some ways, the inverse of the MIL. The operation at the Central Post Office (June 1973), for example, should have been carried out with the participation of one member of the MIL who backed out, so in the end it was done with three comrades from the OLLA. They went up to the second floor of the building, which was restricted access, employees only, and they left a fake bomb made of a bar of soap, a sort of homage to the techniques Quico Sabaté used to cover his escapes.

The OLLA made use of a good infrastructure, much superior

---

52. Trans: The word in the original is *alliberats*, the same word used to describe union officials who receive a paycheck from the union or the State and no longer need to earn wages. The CNT was the only major union to not accept the practice of having such bureaucrats, arguing that once "liberated" they would no longer have the same perspective or interests as the rest of the class. A similar argument could be made in this case.

to the MIL's. The strikes carried out by the latter were on the basis of minimal information, whereas the OLLA had a solid network of collaborators who passed on information. As far as armament is concerned, the OLLA acquired good weaponry on the Swiss market, an operation that was repeated several times. And from the storehouse of a stone quarry at Santa Creu d'Olorda, in the Collserola mountains that rise just above Barcelona, we extracted three tons of ammonium nitrate explosives, also known as ANFO, but since there was so much, we had to make more than one trip to the storehouse to get it all.

Actions

The OLLA carried out fewer expropriations than the MIL, but with greater gains in strictly economic terms. Perhaps the proportion was two to one. In January of 1973, a week after the MIL struck in the neighborhood of Sarrià, the OLLA expropriated the Vizcaya Bank, number 96 on Passeig de Manuel Girona, close to a military residence. Three comrades—the same who had helped the MIL in an action in November 1972—armed with revolvers and machine guns collected two and a half million pesetas. The technique was especially original. One or two weeks before the action, a collaborator cased the bank to get a clear picture of the target. Then on the day of the action, two of the three comrades entered the bank brandished Sten guns and shouted threats in Catalan and, the third, hands raised, held a grenade and threatened to pull the pin. The media that reported the occurrence mused that to encounter bank robbers who spoke in Catalan, one had to go back to the days of the *maquis*, two decades earlier.

For the escape, three or four cars were required. One, with a driver waiting at the wheel for the three who had gone in; another nearby, with three or four additional comrades ready to spring into action should the first group need help, and one or two more an appropriate distance away to change vehicles. According to my count, the MIL carried out more than thirty socializations through September of 1973, for a total value of 24 million pesetas. For its part, the OLLA carried out seventeen expropriations for a total of 50 million. This calculation is not perfect, as some actions were carried out jointly and I don't have any of the accounting at hand.

We compiled information on the barracks of the Guardia Civil and the stations of the Policía Armada, on key figures in the regime, on the city network of sewage tunnels; we had a multitude of contacts.[53] We were preparing ourselves just like the MIL, but more thoroughly, creating an infrastructure little by little that had as its final objective the arming of the whole working class.

To get passports, the MIL went to an agency and took the blank passports at gunpoint (March 1973). The OLLA, on the other hand, went to the street market at *els Encants*, bought a huge sample of all kinds of keys, and entered an agency to grab a few without anyone noticing the theft.

To get Spanish IDs, we used a different method: a comrade went to work under a false name at the official print shop that produced the IDs and she managed to smuggle out five thousand of them. We also worked out a method to intercept the driver's licenses mailed out by the Provincial Traffic Police. We worked the same way—with perseverance and astuteness—in other fields.

In April 1973, when they murdered Fernández Márquez and gravely wounded two other workers in Sant Adrià del Besòs, in the struggle at the power plant, we proposed blowing up one of the huge smokestacks on the compound, given as how we possessed explosives, the blueprints and a map of the routes and schedules of the security patrols. It should also be mentioned that the power plant was decried by the local population as a major source of pollution and a blight on the landscape. Everything was ready, but in the end the plan was canceled because of the technical difficulties involved: the explosion would have to have been immense, and there was no way we could guarantee not harming the night maintenance workers.

We also began plans to blow up the barracks of the Policía

---

53.   Trans: The Guardia Civil, in a tacit admission of their function as an occupying force, traditionally live with their families in restricted blocks that are a cross between barracks, base, and gated community.

Armada in la Verneda, but we rejected plunging into a spiral of terrorist actions that might further isolate us. However, we had a map of the sewer network, and using that to place the explosives unseen, the plan was to set off an alarm and when all the police agents had evacuated, blow up the building, and in that way avoid a total massacre. It was doubtful that killings would be well received by the popular classes.

Our project was centered on the multiplication of autonomous groups. With this intention, in the first half of 1973, we formed a team dedicated to creating audiovisual material, as we assigned great significance to images, considering them the language of modernity. A second group transformed into the theoretical team, which, along with shorter texts, wrote *Theory of the Offensive*, still unpublished. It was mostly written by Jordi Bañeres, alias "Parides," taking up an old position of August Thalheimer (1884–1948).[54] A third group were the two units or "rings" responsible for armed agitation, some of whose members would have been "liberated" from wage work to focus on armed activities only after the decision of the first congress (November 1973), and with whom the MIL-GAC probably would have fused, had they lasted longer.

Each group was autonomous, and we coordinated in a pattern like a spiderweb, such that in each nucleus there was only one person who served as the contact with the other nuclei. And once a week these representatives met up to take stock of the situation and sketch out short-term perspectives.

Starting with the initial group of three people who broke off from the PSAN, in the summer–fall of 1972, the OLLA had forty activists, as many as the GOA, operating in the popular neighborhoods of Barcelona, as well as Badalona, Santa Coloma de Gramenet, Terrassa, and Mataró. The groups grew slowly, but what caused our fall was the dismantling of the MIL. The entire organizational effort that had been in progress was sacrificed in support of solidarity with the MIL, in an attempt to save our

---

54. "Some Tactical Problems of the War in the Ruhr," *The Communist International*, No. 25 (1923): 99–103.

comrades, Puig Antich and the others who were in prison and in danger of receiving long sentences or even the death penalty. This shows the extent to which the MIL and the OLLA shared the same beliefs and considered one another comrades. We created—together with the FAI and CNT-Informa, among others—the Solidarity Committee. As this had to act in the open, it hastened our fall.

Apogee and Collapse

The figure of Salvador Puig Antich has been magnified. He was just another member of the movement. From prison, a first text was released in this line, titled "Neither Martyrs, Nor Trials, Nor Prisons, Nor Salaries! Long Live Communism!" (October 1973). The point is, we were radically opposed to martyrs and their manipulation. Puig Antich was a revolutionary from head to toe, a person who assumed the consequences of his ideas. Yet he became a personality others tried to capitalize on, because he attained a great deal of popularity. Anonymous writers dedicated poems to him.[55] He is spoken about without mention of his origins, his ideology, the what and how of his struggle. For example, presenting him as a good boy in the petitions for overturning his conviction. If he were alive, he would be indignant at that.

We cannot beg for anything from the bourgeois State he fought against. There have been requests to overturn the convictions of Puig Antich, Lluís Companys, Joan Peiró...[56] The promoters of such foolishness should be blushing with shame. Faced with a fascist, military dictatorship that murdered thousands and thousands of workers, above all anarchists, begging for a small handful to be rehabilitated, forgetting the immense majority, is senseless. To do so would legitimize the fascist regime. At the

---

55.   See *Antologia poètica*.
56.   Trans: Lluís Companys was the President of the Generalitat during the Civil War, leader of ERC, executed by the fascists at the end of the war. Joan Peiró was the General Secretary of the CNT in the 1920s and Minister of Industry for the CNT in the Republican government during the Civil War, executed by fascists at the end of the war.

very least, one should ask the nullification of every single military trial.

Puig Antich clashed with the police in an ambush and he opened fire in self-defense with the goal of escaping. It does seem to have been demonstrated, however, that the fatal bullets in the gun fight were friendly fire, which is to say, fired by the police themselves.

When Puig Antich fell, the OLLA threw itself into solidarity work and left on standby the organizational tasks on which it had been focused. The very September that the MIL is dismantled, we constituted the Committee for Solidarity with the Prisoners of the MIL and published an informational dossier with materials selected by Joan Vinyoles, Ignasi Solé, and Felip Solé. On a little press the latter built by hand in his apartment in Barcelona, the dossiers were printed at runs of two hundred, five hundred, and seven hundred copies, engraving the MIL's image. Copying these dossiers word for word, the French comrades with *Libération* and *Politique-hebdo* became the first media in the world to report on what had occurred.

A large part of the funds the OLLA had expropriated were invested in the labors of the solidarity committee, to pay for the defense lawyers and organize local support committees all over Europe. We had to save him, and it was vital to spread the word about his struggle, which was our struggle as well. In November in Barcelona, we organized the first congress of the OLLA, which we called the Congress of the Autonomous Groups, where we decided to fortify even more our solidarity with the prisoners of the ex-MIL, as well as to initiate the consolidation of new autonomous groups and extend the field of armed agitation against the repression.

To fulfill this program, through December of 1973 we published three dossiers to inform people about the MIL and counter the distortions transmitted by the ideological apparatuses of the State and the Communist Party. We encouraged the creation of solidarity committees in Brussels, Geneva, Torino, Tolosa, Perpinyà. In Paris, two committees were created, one by Front Libertaire and the other presided over by Vidal-Naquet, but they quickly joined together. In a matter of days, the proofreaders union of the French CGT demanded that everything possible be done to save the Barcelona prisoners.

At the request of comrades in Tolosa, Jean Barrot wrote "Gangsters or Revolutionaries?" which was rapidly translated. From the Modelo prison, members of the ex-MIL wrote "1,000 or 10,000" and asserted that imprisonment had not silenced them. The solidarity committee in Barcelona took charge of distributing both texts. Over the following months, the reactions multiplied without interruption. In Paris, under the auspices of Amnesty International, a petition for a pardon signed by hundreds of public figures was released. Two protests were held, the first with one and a half thousand people, the second with four thousand. There was a rally at la Mutualité and thirty members of the Parti Socialiste Unifé (PSU) occupied the Spanish tourism offices.[57] François Mitterand, head of the opposition, sent a telegram to the Spanish government. The French Communist Party (PCF) sent a telegram to Pompidou and to Franco in favor of Puig Antich. At the Ivry airport, four people unsuccessfully tried to divert an Iberia airplane and were arrested.[58]

In Tolosa, the Centro Español was occupied, a Spanish bank branch was attacked, and three protests occurred in front of the Spanish consulate, with high participation and clashes with the Gendarmerie.[59] Anonymous people ransacked the offices of Iberia and machine gunned the consul's automobile. In Brussels, people occupied the offices of Iberia, the Spanish embassy, and the headquarters of the Belgian radio and television company. In Torino, someone threw a bomb at the consulate. In Zürich, the Iberia offices were spray painted and someone placed a bomb at the Spanish consulate. In Geneva, there was a large protest. In Buenos Aires, they occupied the offices of Iberia and flooded them with tar.

---

57. Trans: La Mutualité is a famous conference center in Paris, headquarters of a non-profit mutual insurance federation.

58. Trans: The Spanish airline company.

59. Trans: Centro Español is a cultural center connected to the exile community.

In contrast to this wide spectrum of mobilizations, in the Spanish state, in Catalunya even, the acts of resistance are scarce. In Barcelona, there are two protests, both of them very violent. In January 1974, Puig Antich and Pons Llobet are handed two death penalties and thirty years in prison, respectively. In Madrid, various bombs go off on the same day.

The OLLA prepared two attempts to rescue Puig Antich. (In this context, it is necessary to remember that Oriol Solé had escaped from prison in Perpinyà in August of 1971—Operation Anita—which is to say that our expectations did arise from a certain factual basis.) The first attempt was at Hospital Clínic, where Puig Antich was recovering from the injuries caused by the police. When it was ascertained that he was heavily guarded, the plan was aborted. The second attempt was to exploit the fact that the trial was held at the Captaincy General and he was transported in a van between there and the Modelo prison; the idea was to assault the van. Puig Antich opposed the plan and he let us know through the lawyer. He did not believe he would be sentenced to death and he did not want his comrades to risk their own lives.

Months later, after Salvador Puig Antich had already been executed, there was an attempt to liberate Oriol Solé Sugranyes and the other comrades locked up with him, organized by one of their brothers, who was arrested with me in 1974. Oriol Solé, who was already familiar with Modelo, and some other comrades interned there had informed us of the possibility of escaping through the network of sewer tunnels, and this comrade spent twenty hours exploring the network under the prison, but he got lost in the labyrinth of sewers and culverts, so we abandoned the plan.

It seems incredible but in June 1978, fours years later, forty-five prisoners—including fourteen from the COPEL (Coordinadora de Presos en Lucha, or Coordinator of Prisoners in Struggle)—escaped through a tunnel that connected the infirmary with the sewer network.[60] Which is to say, we were on the right track, though we had bad luck.

---

60.   Obra Colectiva, *La cárcel Modelo de Barcelona: 1904–2004: Cien años bastan, derribemos la Modelo para no levantar otra* (Barcelona: Ateneo Libertario Al Margen, etc., 2004), 68.

Unable to liberate our comrade, between January and February the OLLA blew up three monuments to "the Fallen" in Barcelona, Badalona, and Mataró. Infuriated, the fascists convened a protest for reparations and the restoration of the statue in Barcelona. Coinciding with their demonstration, we set off bombs at the Sant Andreu police station and at two banks.

The first of March, the Council of Ministers confirmed the sentences. The Committee for Solidarity in Barcelona redoubled their efforts to achieve a general mobilization, which did not materialize. The next morning, March 2, 1974, they killed Puig Antich by *garrot vil* in Modelo prison (and in Tarragona, also by *garrot vil*, they kill Georg Michael Welzel, alias Heinz Ches). Military officers and the colleagues of the dead cop are present in the hall where the execution takes place, savoring their vengeance, whereas the defense lawyer Oriol Arau is prohibited from attending; in both cases a violation of their own regulations.

After the execution, the OLLA spent the whole night discussing what action we wanted to carry out. There was a proposal to assault the provincial headquarters of the Policía Armada on Via Laietana, but our final decision was to not do that, not for fear of injuries or deaths, but because we ran the risk of undermining all the work we had carried out to create more autonomous groups.

Elsewhere, actions multiplied. There were protests in Perpinyà, Tolosa, Lyon, Baiona, Montpellier, Paris, Geneva, Brussels, Liège, Luxembourg, Rome, Milano, Genova, etc. There were also numerous *attentats* in southern France, such as the arson that the "Commando Puig Antich" carried out against the newspaper *L'Est républicain*. In Barcelona, there was a call for a strike in the universities, though participation was low, and a protest of some two- or three hundred people on les Rambles, ending with a few clashes. The participants who regrouped at the Montjuïc cemetery for Puig Antich's burial were assaulted by the police. There was also a relatively successful strike at the SEAT factory, Pegaso, La Maquinista, and some others. The police arrested more than two hundred strikers. The OLLA attacked an electrical substation very close to the Artillery School in Sant

Andreu, leaving several Barcelona neighborhoods without electricity for ten hours.

In Catalunya, there were protests in Sant Cugat del Vallès, Cerdanyola, Terrassa, Sabadell, Girona, and Tarragona. In the rest of the Spanish state, actions were also carried out in Madrid, Zaragoza, València, and Pamplona. It's a shame; all of this should have been organized before the execution. But everything has its reason.

When they killed Puig Antich, Santiago Carrillo was already participating in negotiations with the regime technocrats regarding a "national reconciliation," which the Communist Party had been advocating since 1956.[61] In the Assemblea de Catalunya, the PSUC had been maneuvering purposefully to prevent any movement of solidarity with Puig Antich, whom they labeled a criminal and gangster. Salvador was condemned from the very first day. In Hospital Clínic, agents from the Politico-Social Brigade tried to lynch him, and they didn't succeed because the municipal police got in their way. Later, the mayor of Barcelona, Joaquim Viola, assured the officers that Franco had personally confirmed to him that he would be executed within six months.

But the battle continued. Between February and March, two comrades were arrested who maintained contacts with local anarchist groups, though a heavier hammer would fall in April. We had a relationship with anarchists in Zürich who passed us explosives expropriated from the Swiss army, mines and grenades in particular. They had arranged to send us some anti-tank mines they had acquired from the arsenals scattered throughout the Helvetic territory. They were to arrive in a suitcase from Geneva in the Talgo train to Barcelona, via Perpinyà. On April 7, in Portbou, on the border, the Guardia Civil noticed the suitcase, and when the comrades went to pick it up at Estació de França in Barcelona, they sprang the trap. One managed to escape, but the other three were arrested: Ramon Carrión, Georgina Nicolau, and Joan Vinyoles. Those three comrades coordinated the greater

---

61.   Trans: Santiago Carrillo is the Secretary General of the PCE from 1956 to 1982.

part of the autonomous groups and their arrest led police to locate thirteen safe houses in Barcelona, full of documents, money, weapons, and 2,500 kilos of explosives, as well as the loss of twelve cars. The press filled up pages on the dismantling of the group with bloodcurdling details.

Despite it all, at the end of April, we had planned an expropriation, and the Swiss comrades were unflagging in their desire to participate. It happened on April 27, at a branch of the Central Bank on carrer Girona. Everything went according to plan, a complete success. Three days later, on the 1st of May, we attacked various police stations and banks with incendiary devices in the neighborhoods of Sant Andreu, Poblenou, and Nou Barris. A few days later, seven of our comrades left by car, going into exile in Perpinyà. Every now and then, they returned to Barcelona to follow up on the mobilizations, but the police were alerted. What's more, some militants from Terrassa and Santa Coloma de Gramenet were wary of continuing, though others of us thought we had to carry on against all odds, despite everything, and independent of any consideration of the risks. On October 30, the police carried out more raids targeting the OLLA, and the total number of prisoners rose to sixteen.

From that point on, the struggle south of the Pyrenees passes the torch to the northern side. The moment belongs to the Grupos de Acción Revolucionaria Internacionalista (GARI, or Internationalist Revolutionary Action Groups), a series of autonomous groups with an anti-authoritarian ideology that had coordinated to carry out actions of armed agitation and propaganda in solidarity with the prisoners of the ex-MIL. After the execution of Puig Antich, the GARI take action to avoid a possible death sentence against other members of the MIL, like Oriol Solé Sugranyes and Josep Lluís Pons Llobet, who are at that moment locked up awaiting trial. Though the acronym first appears the day after the kidnapping of the director of the Parisian branch of the Bank of Bilbao, March 3, 1974, they have already acted anonymously: in February, machine-gunning the car of the Spanish consul in Tolosa; in March, blowing up the railroad near the Spanish border and derailing a train; and in April, expropriating the Courtois Bank at a location near Tolosa. The group's trajectory will continue through August 1974—or possibly January 1975, with a rather muddled epilogue in the summer of 1977—but telling that story distances us substantially from our own narration.

Attempts have been made to dress Puig Antich up as a Catalanist. It is possible that he considered himself very Catalan, but as a personal identity. They have perpetrated the same manipulation against Oriol Solé, killed by the Guardia Civil on April 6, 1975, at the border between Navarra and France, after he had escaped from the Segovia prison together with Josep Pons Llobet and members of ETA and the FAC. A journalist from *La Vanguardia*,[62] with an unquestionable zeal for profit, dedicated a book to Oriol Solé, *The Catalan Che*,[63] which from the very title distorts the significance of his struggle down to the very root. Salvador and Oriol always fought in favor of the liberation of their class, never to achieve an interclassist Catalan state. Their entire lives were dedicated to the social struggle and the workers' struggle. The media wanted to repeat the same manipulation they had perpetrated against Quico Sabaté.[64]

---

62.   Trans: The principal newspaper of Barcelona, created in 1881, founded by and to this day the property of the Count of Godó. It goes without saying that the paper is a mouthpiece of the establishment and well practiced in spreading all manner of lies against social movements and in favor of the violence of the police and government institutions.

63.   Joaquim Roglan, *Oriol Solé, el Che català: vida, fugida i mort d'un revolucionari* (Barcelona: Edicions 62, 2006).

64.   The first book about Quico Sabaté was written by my excellent friend and comrade, Antoni Téllez Solà (1921–2005) in Paris in 1972 (Éditions Bélibaste). I should remark that this book exercised a great influence on us, and we considered it an exemplary book. In the 1990s, he expanded the work and wanted to publish it in Catalan, because he considered the guerrilla to be very much rooted in his country. He contacted several publishing houses, but all of them turned the project down even though Sabaté was highly popular among the peasants and factory workers, regardless of the ideological framing. In that decade, the Catalan publishing houses were either in PSUC's orbit or that of right-wing Catalanists. All of them concurred in boycotting the book. Now, nearly twenty years later, the book has been released: *Sabaté: Quinze anys de guerrilla urbana antifranquista (1945–1960)* (Barcelona: Virus Editorial, 2011). Incredibly, it was released earlier in English, as *Sabaté: Guerrilla Extraordinary* by Elephant Editions and AK Press, 2000.

In the '80s, Jordi Pujol prohibited any mention of the *maquis*.[65] Until TVE dedicated a documentary series to him at the end of that decade, no Catalan institution mentioned him.[66]

The workers' autonomy movement returned to the ring with the 2006 movie *Salvador*.[67] When the film was released to theaters, many of those who had personally experienced the whole episode remained silent, despite the shameless manipulations the film is full of. A good documentary would be necessary to restore a truthful telling. There is a documentary in circulation, *MIL: The History of a Family with History* (2006), directed by Martina Loher Rodríguez, which, as the title suggests, only provides information about the numerous Solé Sugranyes family.

The Autonomous Movement after the MIL and the OLLA

The authorities dismantle the ex-MIL in September 1973, but Ediciones Mayo del 37 continue publishing—or, more precisely, reprinting—over the following years, until 1975, printing in Tolosa and distributing across the Peninsula. The MIL had isolated itself from the autonomous movement, and the OLLA followed the same path, though not to an equal extent. On January 19, 1974, at the 2nd Congress of the Grups Autònoms—a more appropriate name for the OLLA—three different tendencies were made manifest: the anarcho-Catalanist (the Mataró group), the council communist

65.   Trans: Jordi Pujol (1930–), banker, a founder of the CDC, the main political party of the Catalanist right, supporter of the Transition and President of the Generalitat from 1980 to 2003, implicated in a major corruption scandal after leaving office.

66.   *El maquis a Catalunya 1939–1963*, script by Ricard de Vargas Golarons, co-directed with Jaume Serra. Broadcast on TV-1 (December 1988–February 1989).

67.   Directed by Manuel Huerga, produced by Jaume Roures (MEDIA-PRO), the movie is based on the novel by Francesc Escribano, *Compte enrere: la història de Salvador Puig Antich* (Barcelona: Edicions 62, 2001). For a detailed study on the cinematographic manipulation, see Ana Domínguez Rama, "Salvador (Puig Antich) en el viejo mundo: Algunas consideraciones históricas respecto a su recuperación mediática." In *Hispania nova: revista de historia contemporánea*, 7 (2007) hispanianova.rediris.es. And, in a tone of self-glorification, Manuel Huerga, "Memoria del Director," in the movie's "Dosier de Prensa," www.salvadorfilm.com/prensa/media/salvador-castellano-pdf.

(with Ignasi Solé Sugranyes at the head), and the majority current, influenced by Situationism and anti-authoritarianism. They sketch out a strategy to strengthen the autonomous groups within the workers' movement, but the Congress represents a swan song. In the whirlwind produced by Francoism's evident decline, the autonomous movement was losing steam. There were a few spearheads, but the masses were not behind them.

After the end of the MIL, autonomous groups for armed agitation were created in Catalunya and the Valencian country that tried to follow the same path, but they held different positions. They lost their organic connection with the movement and became disconnected.

The OLLA was made up of workers who organized sensibly, without haste but also without pause, reinforcing workers' autonomy step by step. We carried out the expropriations and sabotage actions after the workday had ended. Some groups had been successful with the specialized formula of armed struggle, like ETA in the Basque Country. They radicalized the national question with weapons in hand, though they entered into a feedback loop that has been called a spiral of violence. But in, Catalunya, the situation was more difficult, and it was difficult to gain popular approval for armed attacks. During the Transition, there was the constant blackmail of a coup d'etat, a threat the PCE played with expertly, terrifying people constantly with the idea that if they were too radical, the military would take power again, an anachronistic reference to 1936.

In the Transition, the struggles for Catalan autonomy, for amnesty, for formal democracy, all came together. The workers' struggle shrank, but it did not disappear. There was the Roca strike (1976), the Barcelona port strike (1981–82), and others. On one occasion, I was in the street with comrades, clashing with the police, when someone from the Communist Party came up and told us not to use violence against them, since they were wage workers and comrades just like us. The police, who beat us, who shot to kill, were wage workers "like us." But even the extreme left allied with the reformists, helping the latter retain their hegemony. The workers' movement was uncoordinated. The GOA tried to reorganize the autonomous groups fighting in Santa Coloma, in Vallés, in Baix Llobregat, but they had nothing but an ember left of their former flames. They faded away.

There always have been and always will be autonomous struggles. But the autonomous movement vanished, at least until further notice.

There was one final hope: the reconstruction of the CNT. During the Transition, the CNT recovered thanks to the fact that the majority of the autonomous movement, especially the steel and graphic arts sectors, swelled its ranks. The Confederation justified itself with the affirmation that we had to join the unions to take the daily pulse of the working class. It was an even more flagrant contradiction, because the CNT did not update its way of functioning, but rather maintained the same structure from the 1920s and '30s that clashed with the present socioeconomic reality. If the autonomous movement had been strong at that moment, it would have continued with its own dynamic. The fact that it flocked to the CNT demonstrates its weakness in this period, contrary to the insistence of some other participants in the movement.

All told, the MIL and the OLLA constitute a thwarted history. They did not have the time they needed to mature. The OLLA had a little more than the MIL; but everything fell apart when they were still in development. And with the Transition, a new stage opened up. It was evident that the Franco regime was passing away, and everything seemed like it could change.

The Present Moment

The day they killed Puig Antich, Oriol Solé wrote the following text in Catalan from the Modelo prison:

Utopia demolished?

Died building a better life, March 2, 1974
Humanity will be happy the day the last capitalist is hanged with the guts of the last bureaucrat.

*I don't know, but a prophetic wind blows up and down this
mountainous terrain*

*I don't know when, but a day will come when the Pyrenees
reign* (J. Maragall)

In the United States, in Europe, under the rule of the
superpowers, the proletariat has disappeared. Society has
engendered a new social class that creates surplus, accu-
mulates capital, and at the same time grows bloated on the
surplus generated by millions of wage workers in the poor
countries. A new class that builds itself a paradise paid for
with the blood of the exploited poor of Africa, Asia, and
Latin America.

Capital has created an insolidaristic salaried being, a
blood-sucker, and it has let this being loose into a world
of total solitude to wander in anxiety over its condition as
exploited and simultaneously exploiter. This being must
obviate their neighbor, their coworker on the production
line, the humanity of the Eastern bloc, rituals and absences,
globalities, processes, terms, and words.

Word-destroying managers have cast man into solitude,
they have believed that it would be enough to rip out the
meaning of the words "love" and "freedom." But it was
necessary to invent new words for every process, every
cadence.

In solitude there is no room for the word "love,"
there is no freedom. Your paradise, your utopia, has been
demolished.

I am from a different neighborhood, a different caste, a
different planet than you.

Listen to this youth, listen to this lyric in the Odéon. It
is May, it is Paris, the shouts rise above the sterile discussions of intellect. It is a shout arising from your solitude.

It is a shocking text, as the immense majority of texts by
the MIL transmit optimism. It provides, however, a premonitory
message. The working class as a historical subject has been fro-
zen. The clock is reset to zero, as regards objectives, the struggle,

the militants themselves. Many young people adopt anticapitalist beliefs, but at the same time they all compete with one another, and they are all cloistered in their respective rooms, left incommunicado within the social networks. In Catalunya, in the last elections for the legislature, not even half the population participated. Discontentment dilutes into passivity, resignation. In another epoch, the events of the last years would have provoked, at the least, mutinies and riots. Power is so accustomed to trampling us that it accelerates without restraint. But many things have changed, some traditional forms of struggle have become obsolete and insufficient, and new ones need to be activated. For example, using social networks to boycott mortgages and organize rent strikes, or carrying out actions to disrupt the nerves and nodes of capitalism.[68]

What to do, then? That is what we asked ourselves in the eponymous magazine of the 1960s. But as Antonio Machado said, *the path is made by walking*. There are no magical solutions. The MIL carried out an economic study of the situation we inhabited and deduced that the crisis of '73 was not peninsular, but unequivocally international, and therefore the revolution had to be global or it would not be. We must act, but also study reality to know how to act. To do so in our present context, we would need to hold at least twenty days' worth of talks and debates about the last forty years, from the Transition—or better yet, from the Development Plans, which already began preparing for post-Francoism—until the present day, to understand the whole process from a historical perspective on all levels, local, statewide, and international; and to understand its endogenous and exogenous aspects, as well as the dialectic between unions, parties, and superpowers.[69]

In 1982, I was traveling through Andalucía during the

---

68. Trans: The present text was written when neighborhood eviction defense was becoming more widespread, and some months before Catalunya was shut down with a wave of airport, train, and highway blockades and sabotage actions, as well as the heaviest rioting since the Transition.

69. Trans: The Development Plans were three successive social and economic plans instituted by the Franco regime between 1964 and 1975.

hangover from the first "democratic" elections, in which the PSOE, the PCE, and the Partido Socialista de Andalucía (Socialist Party of Andalucía, which identified as autonomous socialist) claimed victory. The common people in the villages believed that it was their people who had won, and the agricultural workers were preparing to occupy estates, like the prologue to a revolution. Of course, it was not their people who had won, and nothing changed. The hope deposited in the parties transformed into a tremendous frustration.

We would have to analyze a multitude of factors to understand society and the workers' movement that sprang from it. For example, we would have to explain how the PSOE of late Francoism, which could only count on a few intellectuals in the Basque Country and Asturias, became the most voted-for party in a few years, with a powerful union in its pocket. The explanation resides in the huge amount of money funneled into it from the German social democrats and the Trilateral Commission.

Before the death of the dictator, the PCE had already renounced its struggle and joined its path with the monarchy in exchange for the meager alms of being able to set up a union and enjoying a quota of positions in municipal governments. During the Transition, there were combative neighborhood associations, but then the socialists and communists came from the respective Town Halls, took them over and slammed on the brakes. In order to enter the European Union, Felipe González sacrificed the Catalan textile industry, the Basque steelworks, and the Galician shipyards.[70] These are the necessary points of departure for understanding the present moment. We are currently suffering an economic crisis and immersed in a sort of neo-Francoism. By making such a study of the historical roots of this moment, we could develop the tools to intervene in this reality with greater force.

The MIL and the OLLA left behind a legacy. Not creating power structures, being consequential with our beliefs, not

---

70. Trans: González was Secretary General of the PSOE from 1974 and President from 1982 to 1996.

accepting a transactional strategy—for example rejecting any government financing, a sure way to turn subversion into subsidies—and completely refusing entryism, the basic plank of Trotskyism. If you play with the behemoth, it will swallow you whole and spit you out. There is no escape.

In that era, Die Grünen, the German Green Party, began to throw their weight around. They presented themselves as firmly anticapitalist, but they compromised and entered Parliament and they made deals with the ever astute public powers. They are currently further to the right than Angela Merkel.

Autonomy must be preserved, always: autonomy of the group, of the class, of our ideologies. This is a lesson to be retained that many do not want to learn, and even justify rejecting. But it is a perennially valid lesson.

"What to do?" is not the pertinent question, but rather, "What not to do?" We should not waste our accumulated experience. "There is no duty to remember; on the contrary, we have the duty to do something with memory: to create a project."[71]

---

71. Declaration of Boris Cyrulnik, collected by Esther Benbassa in *La soufrance comme identité* (Paris: Fayard: 2007), 251.

10.

Salvador Puig Antich in the MIL-GAC: A Brief Political Biography

Sergi Rosés Cordovilla

> "Armed agitation, a direct, non-dependent relation, anti-Leninism, anti-groupusculism, self-defense, insurrectional strikes, proletarian-revolutionary violence, anti-authoritarianism, etc.; these are the concepts that, though they may be insufficiently explained, constitute the focus, to say the least, of our political practice."
>
> Salvador Puig Antich, "'Terrible' History, December 1972–July 1973"

Salvador Puig Antich began his political journey in the Comissions Obreres local of his neighborhood and, especially, at the Maragall Institute in Barcelona, where he was enrolled in the pre-university course at the end of the 1960s, while also hold-ing down a job.[1] There, he became friends with Xavier Garriga i Paitüví and Ignasi Solé Sugranyes. The latter, already highly politicized (he had militated in Acción Comunista, where he befriended Santi Soler i Amigó), introduced his two friends to dis-sident Marxism—critical of the classical postulates of Leninism and contrary to Party organization, opting instead for a council

---

1. Trans: Sergi Rosés is a Marxist historian who became active long after the dissolution of the MIL. He authored an "erudite" study on the group, in the words of Ricard de Vargas, but readers should also be aware that his is a project to claim the MIL exclusively as a part of the Marxist tradition. And while Marxism was an integral part of the MIL, it is largely a testament to the anti-dogmatism and pluralism of anarchists like Ricard de Vargas that this text is included, in keeping with the anti-dogmatism and pluralism of the MIL themselves, who belong firmly and intractably to both the anarchist and Marxist traditions.

communist tendency with Situationist influences. Garriga, who came from the Forces Socialistes Federals, quickly got involved and joined the study group Ignasi Solé formed with Santi Soler and Puig Antich. For his part, Puig Antich shared their criticisms of the anti-Francoist Left (especially the Partit Socialista Unificat de Catalunya, or PSUC [Unified Socialist Party of Catalunya]), but he had doubts, and though he maintained interest, stayed in contact, and kept up with his reading, he didn't develop a revolutionary commitment until November 1971, when he returned to civilian life after completing his obligatory military service.

At the beginning of that year, in Tolosa, one of Ignasi's older brothers, Oriol, founded the group 1,000 (mil), together with other comrades, including Jean-Marc Rouillan, whose nom de guerre was "Sebas." The 1,000 quickly linked up with the group in Barcelona organized by Santi Soler, Ignasi Solé, and Garriga, and together they carried out several expropriations in Tolosa. In March, Oriol Solé was arrested by the French police and sentenced to a year and a half in prison. With him in prison, the 1,000's armed practice deteriorated, and was practically suspended until his release. Ignasi Solé recruited one of his younger brothers, Jordi, whose nom de guerre was "Sancho," and then in November Puig Antich, who went by "the Doctor" (because of his work in the infirmary during his military service).

While Oriol Solé was in prison, the 1,000 discussed plans for an "anti-tourism campaign" that never got off the ground, and they carried out some actions between the summer and October to acquire some IBM typewriters and printing material (which were passed on to autonomous activists connected to Platforms), and they tried to coordinate with the Front d'Alliberament de Catalunya in November. The most important development in this period was the 1,000's decision to change their theater of operations from Tolosa to Barcelona and its industrial belt, though in the period between December 1971 and April 1972, they did not carry out any robberies, having decided first to go through a training period in Tolosa.

The life of the group underwent a transcendental shift in the spring of 1972, when Oriol Solé was released from prison on May 29, which led to a reorganization of the 1,000, and the adoption of the name MIL (Movimiento Ibérico de Liberación). With Oriol Solé on the street, the activist members of the group (Puig Antich, Rouillan, Jordi Solé, and Jean Claude Torres) came face to face again with their prime mover, who immediately proposed a first phase of robberies that would provide them with the infrastructure they needed to proceed to the phase of "military action" (the "Black September–Red October" plan). The reasons given to justify taking up arms were twofold: the fight against repression and support for the proletarian struggle. Both actions would be achieved carrying out sabotage on the one hand—though this never materialized—and on the other, expropriations, which served to finance the group as well as to finance other groups of workers in struggle, contributing to the objective of radicalizing these struggles and preparing for a revolutionary insurrection.

From the perspective of the MIL, what was most important was the self-organization of the workers, and the group argued that the workers became radicalized and adopted an assembly-based practice when they found themselves in the most critical moments of class struggle, during the strikes. It was a matter, then, of acquiring money for the anti-repression funds and enabling the strikes to last as long and spread as far as possible. On the basis of a logic that united the struggle against Capital's repressive forces with support for workers' struggles and the attempt to radicalize them, the expropriation actions became the order of the day, as is expressed in one of the first flyers by the group, distributed during a robbery at the Central Bank branch on Passeig de Valldaura on November 20, 1972:

> This expropriation, together with earlier ones, has as its objective to support the struggle of the proletariat against the bourgeoisie and the capitalist State. For their struggle, revolutionaries appropriate money stolen by capitalists from the working class.
>
> The daily struggle of the proletariat against exploitation obliges revolutionary combat groups to carry out the

actions imperative for this struggle to meet its revolutionary objectives.

While repression from the capitalists beats down the working class, the proletariat and all its revolutionaries will continue to attack Capital and its lackeys ...[2]

The group—and above all Santi Soler—theorized about the necessity of "armed agitation" (as opposed to "armed struggle") and included in their foundation of council communist Marxism the debate about armed practice: for that reason, the name GAC, Grupos Autónomos de Combate, was added to the name MIL (MIL-GAC). The actions that were proposed and prepared, then, generated serious doubts for Puig Antich, who temporarily distanced himself from the group. In reference to this period, amidst a scarcity of facts, some authors have written that, supposedly at Oriol Solé's suggestion, the group agreed that Puig Antich should go to Switzerland to record a record in homage to Che Guevara for the fifth anniversary of his assassination (which would be that October), as a way of raising money. It has also been asserted that Puig Antich lived for a short time in London, aiding in anarchist tours, but that is highly improbable and has never been documented.

---

2.   "Esta expropiación..." Flyer, 1972. Reproduced in *CIA* no.1. I have kept in my possession the printed version and the original composition of all the cited documents, without corrections. A later flyer repeats the same idea:

"The situation demands the completion of a whole series of vital labors for the consolidation of the autonomous class struggle. But it is evident that these tasks (recovery of material, strengthening of solidarity funds, etc.) cannot be completed by militarist petty bourgeois groups .... It is necessary to combat police repression with armed proletarian violence.... The generalization of struggle and a simultaneous growth in repression bring with them the indispensable appearance of numerous autonomous combat groups, which carry out robberies and other violent actions, situating themselves in a general framework of armed agitation. It is not a gratuitous fact, therefore, or a strategy estranged from the working class (like petty bourgeois military groups that redirect the daily violence of the workers' struggle towards nationalist aims, for example). It is about a tactical requirement of the workers' movement corresponding to the current situation of class struggle, with its own objectives: the self-organization of the class that will usher in the INSURRECTIONAL STRIKE." (MIL-GAC. "The workers' movement's tactical requirement for armed agitation." Flyer. CDHS-AEP.)

In August of that year, 1972, the MIL-GAC broke into a print-shop in Tolosa and seized a printing press and other materials; however, one month later, the police arrested Oriol Solé and Jean Claude Torres (Rouillan was able to escape). Torres was released a few days later, but Oriol Solé was imprisoned again, this time for nine months. And once again, as had happened a year before, Ignasi Solé called on Puig Antich to actively rejoin the group. His assent that September would mark his total and definitive association with the MIL-GAC. Two months later, in November, Josep Lluís Pons Llobet joined (recruited straight from high school by Raimon Solé Sugranyes, another of the Solé Sugranyes family who, though not a member of the group, maintained contact). Shortly thereafter, Ignasi Solé acquired two new comrades: Emili Pardiñas Viladrich ("Pedrals") and Nicole Entremont ("Aurora").

Starting in the winter of 1972–73, the expropriations accelerated, with the main participants being Pons, Puig Antich, Rouillan, Jordi Solé, and Torres. Puig Antich started off driving the vehicles used in the actions, but within a few months he was also going into the banks. Garriga began to distance himself, basically over his disagreement with the plan for "justice in the street" (which included plans to execute notorious cops, but which was never fully prepared, much less carried out). Ignasi Solé began to cease his theoretical labors to focus on organizing infrastructure, locating possible targets, making contact with other groups, etc. The rest of the group dedicated themselves to the infrastructure, and so the library fell to Santi Soler, who was aided by Ernest Núñez and Marcelo López, activist workers in Platforms who maintained contacts with the rest of the workers' movement and saw to the distribution of publications (what would become Ediciones Mayo del 37).

On March 2, 1973, during the expropriation of a bank on Passeig de Fabra i Puig, an employee was wounded while trying to stymie the action by the MIL-GAC, and shortly thereafter part of the activist sector decided to leave for Tolosa to avoid repression. Puig Antich saw it as the beginning of a new stage, not for its repressive implications, but for its political ones:

Nonetheless, our practice was more radical than our proposals. The action at [Fabra i Puig] is simultaneously the
burial of the previous stage and a clash with political and
military reality.[3]

With the retreat of part of the group to Tolosa after that robbery, the fulmination of tensions that accumulated during the
months of the winter and spring of 1973 accelerated.

A first result was the expulsion of Ignasi Solé from the group:
it seems this act was not motivated by any political disagreement,
but by a question of proper function (incoordination between the
activist sector and Ignasi Solé), with a deterioration of personal
relations between him and the majority of the activists, though it
is evident that the step towards continuous expropriation actions
fostered this deterioration.[4] Puig Antich, who believed that the
dismemberment of the group constituted a failure and that,
what's more, with the expulsion they would lose contact with the
other groups, tried to intervene in the conflict and adopt, in his
own words, not the attitude of an intermediary or counterweight,
but of political concretion, conscious that his position was located
between the two tendencies and trying to center the debate, not
so much in past political differences as in the formulation of a
political solution tailored to the moment in which the group
found itself:

Everyone has something to say, and wants to say it because
there is no room for temporary solutions. My position,
halfway between two tendencies (or more precisely, individuals), puts me in a situation of contradictory aspects: a)
counterweight b) intermediary c) concretion.

---

3.   Salvador Puig Antich, "'Terrible' History, December '72–July '73"
[draft], July 1973 (copy in the CDHS-AEP).

4.   Trans: The group adopted the term "activists" instead of the more
common choice at the time, "militants," which conveyed to them too much of
the obedience of the Party member carrying out orders. A dispute would arise,
though, as to whether all the group participants were "activists" or only those
carrying out the armed actions. Throughout this chapter it is used primarily in
the latter sense.

Neither counterweights nor intermediaries are valid [...]

Concretion: there is such a pile of personal shit that any proposals, if there actually are any, can be boycotted by one side or the other. How can one or the other personal position become decisive, when only personal arguments are advanced in order not to accept, or at least to argue against, a particular proposal? [...]

We will not find a solution (a super optimist word in this situation) in the past, but on the other side of the fog [...] We cannot forget all the personal problems we have had, but it is on a political level and only on a political level that our arguments will become useful means for continuing onward. This, therefore, is my task over the next few days.

The current state of the group is unsustainable. As such, we can be rid of all this burden and on the basis of individual decisions, form a new group on a new foundation, even if we are the same individuals. What is failing to function now are not the individuals but the principles, that should spell out clearly what we are doing and why[...]

It is immoral to remain so nonchalant as we hear affirmations, that I wish would be unwarranted, like: "I don't give a damn about political problems, I am leaving because I don't want to work with a certain individual." Or, "I might understand better what you think, but I am leaving for personal shit." Are we crazy? Blind?

We are dirtying ourselves and using up the greater part of our strength on internal conflicts, such that a comrade becomes more of an enemy than the true enemy. What romantics we are that with such a panorama, we still want to continue! [...]

The general exhaustion is accentuated when I can barely trust in my ability to offer an alternative. The connection that theoretically united us has died and everyone is preparing to take away the biggest chunk of the inheritance.[5]

---

5. Salvador Puig Antich, "We Still Can't See the Horizon" (draft), March 1973 (Copy in the CDHS-AEP).

This text shows the greater implication Puig Antich had in the political life of the group, looking for political solutions to the crisis and proposing a reinforcement of the political apparatus rather than the military one, and also proposing better planning for future armed actions. While he situated himself critically with regards to how actions had been carried out up to that point—and, as such, was openly critical of the Tolosa nucleus, supported by Jordi Solé—in terms of organization he had no qualms with advocating for them to openly structure themselves as a specific group:

> I understand armed agitation, insofar as it is constituted by a specialized group, as a dialectical relation between our own practice and the radical communist movements.[6]

Later, over the summer, he delivered more explicit proposals. In the moment, though, his undertakings did not bear fruit, and the majority of the group, including Puig Antich, decided to end their association with Ignasi Solé. The latter does not offer any more resistance, and, with a brief goodbye note, not without sarcasm, he leaves the group and soon after becomes closely involved with the OLLA.[7]

But much more important and crucial to the life of the MIL-GAC than Ignasi Solé's exit is the anarchist drift of the members of the armed sector who had left Barcelona and provisionally established themselves in Tolosa, where they edited the first issue of what they publicly presented as the magazine of the group, *CIA (Conspiración Internacional Anarquista)*. The title, the topic of the articles, the focus of some of them, the omnipresence of armed activity in the pages, and certain illustrations were such that the first impression one got from the magazine was that it was the official publication of an anarchist organization. It was not for nothing that Jordi Solé qualified it decades later as "the greatest theoretical error of the MIL."[8] *CIA* no.1 came out in

---

6. Ibid.

7. Later, after the arrests in September 1973, Ignasi Solé was one of the driving forces of the solidarity committees with the prisoners of the ex-MIL.

8. Interviews with Josep Lluís Pons and Jordi Solé, March 21, 2001 and

April, before the rest of the Barcelona members had relocated to Tolosa, and their impression when they saw it was negative. Santi Soler disliked how the first explicit publication of the MIL-GAC suddenly self-identified as anarchist. Pons criticized the inclusion of a chronology detailing the group's actions, including the names of Oriol Solé, Jean Claude Torres, Jean-Marc Rouillan, and Salvador Puig Antich.[9] Puig Antich, who labeled it a "joke," like Pons especially criticized the publication of the chronology and the names, as well as the acritical attitude of using the chronology as a letter of introduction to the world, rather than any clear political statement.

> And to cover up the "joke," a few publish some texts written by "others" without criticism or anything, and with the ever-present action list, which is to say offering us up (one cannot elude one's fate) as sacrificial victims for any reformists (referring to "Solidarity Committees" controlled by the Communist Party).[10]
> [...]
> With a relation based on actions we have wanted to open a rupture in the political world, and it is not enough. To think that we can resume actions without minimally elaborating our tactics is suicide.[11]

A debate was initiated then that surpassed the issue of the magazine and attempted to analyze the impasse in which the group found itself after the intense months of activity over the winter.[12] Within these discussions, three camps were identified:

April 25, 2001; and "Responses to the MIL Questionnaire," March 2001.

9.   Ibid.

10.   Trans: At that point, most of the solidarity committees were controlled by the Communists, who used the prisoners as martyrs to position themselves as spokespersons for the movement.

11.   Salvador Puig Antich, "From the brilliant idea to dismember the group..." (draft), spring 1973 (copy in CDHS-AEP). Salvador Puig Antich, "Who can revive a corpse?" (draft), spring 1973 (copy in CDHS-AEP).

12.   The first publicly distributed text (though it was still illegal) to point to this crisis was "Notes for a historical clarification of the autonomous workers'

the first was the "organizational-immediatists," the second was the "library-affinityists"—both of them terms used by the members of the MIL-GAC themselves—and the third tried to create a bridge between the first two.

The first camp, composed of Rouillan and the rest of the Tolosa members, identified with the practice begun the prior summer. They wanted to begin a new phase of armed actions, reinforcing their guerrilla structures and organizing themselves as an autonomous combat group, while advocating a closer relationship with anarchist sectors to be able to build other GACs. The third camp, for its part, accepted an intensification of the group's practice and the beginning of a new phase of struggle, as well as the consolidation of the politico-military organization, though they also criticized the behavior of the Tolosa sector, favored tightening the relationship with the sector in charge of the library, and advocated better political education for members of the group.

Santi Soler, who found himself practically alone as a representative of the library amongst the rest of the activists, represented the second camp, which criticized the groupuscular tendency of the armed sector. He defended the concept of an open group of individuals united by affinity, "without logos," against the institutionalization of a specific activist group that tended towards groupusculization with the creation of a magazine that served as the organizational mouthpiece and that, to top it off, publicly presented itself as anarchist. He also criticized the lack of political strategy behind the continual practice of robberies, and the

---

movement in Barcelona," included in the pamphlet "C.O.Ñ.O.!" (published in 1975 by members of the autonomous groups in Barcelona that had attempted actions to free Puig Antich), in which it was written that *CIA* no. 1 "was not accepted unanimously as 'legitimate,'" setting off a month-long debate in which those responsible for the publication finally won acceptance for its distribution as an "effective medium for propaganda" (p. 3). In this way, Rouillan recalls how Oriol Solé himself distributed it in a CNT event on July 19, 1973 in Tolosa de Llenguadoc (letter from Rouillan to the author, November 6, 2001), but the next month, its distribution "was suspended by the Congress of Summer '73 of the 1000," as written by Oriol Solé ("Study on Repression" [unfinished manuscript], December 1973 [copy in CDHS-AEP]).

excessive power of Rouillan, whom he thought was trying to become a leader and occupy Oriol Solé's place.[13]

Additionally, Santi Soler, as well as Núñez and López when they got copies of the magazine, were not happy about having to distribute it with flyers that were published by Ediciones Mayo del 37, since it constituted an extra risk for them, as the police could connect the two publications. In other words, the magazine adding the risk of association with a "terrorist organization" to the risk of distributing "clandestine literature." They tried to alleviate this concern as well as the anarchist façade of the magazine with the publication of a pamphlet that was distributed jointly, under the same publishing name, as an annex: *On Revolutionary Violence: The Baader Gang, From Prehistory to History*, a critical text by Jacques Baynac ("Émile Marenssin") about the RAF, which had just been dismantled by the German state (with a large number of the members subsequently assassinated). The pamphlet had been prepared by those who ran the library with the intention of it being published by Ediciones Mayo del 37, but it was released with the rather explicit stamp, "Published by the MIL."

The third position had common ground with the second regarding criticisms of the actions carried out up to that moment; nonetheless, they arrived at a strategic perspective different from that of Santi Soler in that they proposed to continue in the consolidation of the group, transforming it into a politico-military organization; what's more, they also proposed breaking through "the ceiling" of only robbing banks. The primary proponent of this position was Puig Antich. Several drafts written by Puig Antich in this period have been saved, as have two of his texts presented to the group ("The emancipation of the proletariat will be the work of the workers themselves, or it will not be" as well as another one, untitled but dated April 25, 1973, and signed with the seals of the MIL-GAC and the GAC-Insurrección Libertaria).[14] Taken

---

13. "Diagram of the history of the MIL" August/September 1973 (CDHS-AEP); letter from Santi Soler to Ignasi Solé, July 14 ,1975. (UB-Fons MIL).

14. The seven following drafts: "Abans de preguntar-se: què fem?, millor dir: què passa?"; "Agitación armada—movimiento real"; "Desde la genial idea

together, they are a valuable testimony of the crisis the MIL-GAC was going through in that moment, of the positions defended by Puig Antich, and of his personal reflections.

In contrast to the idea—unfortunately so widely held—that Puig Antich was an anti-Francoist champion of democracy, even a nationalist, these drafts present the truth of his views like a gust of fresh air:

> Why am I here? I believe in the validity of armed struggle as a medium for destroying the present society. As such, I search for or try to create an organization that agrees with my principles and I carry out a daily revolutionary practice. In my mind, what is the role of armed struggle and political organization for arriving at the ends previously mentioned?
>
> ...
>
> By armed practice, I mean the ensemble of political actions or expropriations that demonstrate the contradictions of a structure based on the exploitation of man by man, and that implicitly offer an alternative, which is to say an explanation of what we do and where we are going. I understand armed agitation, insofar as it is constituted by a specialized group, as a dialectical relation between our own practice and the radical communist movements.[15]

In general, these drafts demonstrate theoretical confusionism and a flagrant contradiction with the organizational principles of the MIL-GAC. But they also offer a clear political proposal for a new path after the anxiety of the previous months, with an analysis that does not skimp on adjectives in the course of its self-critique, as is seen, for example, in the following idea, repeated various times throughout these manuscripts:

> Before asking ourselves: what do we do? Better to ask:

---

de desmembrar al grup..."; "Encara no es veu l'horitzó"; "Historia 'terrible,' diciembre 72–julio 73"; "Organización pol.-mil"; and "¿Quién resucita un muerto?" (copies in the CDHS-AEP).

15.   Puig Antich, "We still can't see the horizon."

what's going on? The impasse is symptomatic at every level. Not even action serves to justify anything....

After attempting an evaluation, in which each member carried out their own functions, the measuring stick itself broke, a victim of its own inadequacies. We were and we are a gang of delinquents politicized at the individual level. Because of our lack of group consciousness and the consequent authoritarianisms, we do not move as a compact body, but rather follow the personal decisions of the most capable.[16]

The drafts allow us to discover that Puig Antich saw no problem with the organizational aspect, which is to say, in the consolidation as a "group," nor with the theoretical aspect, with the group openly declaring itself anarchist—though he recognized that it was for tactical reasons, deriving this anarchism from its practice, from the actions carried out—nor in the need to shift to another phase of armed practice.[17] What he did criticize was the most activist sector, especially the one in Tolosa, on a number of important points: their tendency to act separately (he believed that the move to Tolosa by part of the group after the bank robbery at Fabra i

---

16.   Salvador Puig Antich, "Before asking ourselves: What do we do? Better to ask: What's going on?," (draft), Spring 1973, (copy in the CDHS-AEP).

17.   It seems to be at this moment that Puig Antich adopted the anarchist slogan, "*Salut i anarquia!*," which he used in his final letters. However, this should not lead one to deduce that Puig Antich, or the MIL-GAC, were anarchist. Rouillan, the most anarchistic member of the group together with Torres, believes that Puig Antich was always a council communist, even if he also claimed anarchy (letter from Jean-Marc Rouillan to the author, January 21, 2002). [Trans: Here, Sergi Rosés is falling into an ideological dispute, what Salvador might describe as "fighting over the inheritance." In order to deny the clear anarchist heritage of the MIL, which, equally clearly, was mixed in with a dissident Marxist heritage, he ignores Salvador's explicit self-identification as an anarchist and contradicts the testimonies of other anarchist members of the group, also incorrectly identifying Rouillan as the most anarchist member to boost the credentials of his argument. This is another example in a long line of Marxists, from Pannekoek to Dauvé, who were forced by experience to move away from the authoritarian and reformist positions integral to Marx, and mischaracterized the anarchist positions they moved towards to satisfy their dogmatic qualms and insist that they weren't "becoming anarchists."]

Puig constituted a dismemberment of the group and a disconnection with those who remained in Barcelona); the way they flaunted group consensus to advance personal agendas and the concentration of power in certain individuals in the exterior; their consideration that the non-activist members did not actually belong to the MIL-GAC (the "pragmatism at any cost" that negated the validity of debating);[18] their attitude towards the people in the interior, seeing them as mere infrastructure; and their tendency towards carrying out actions without a well-defined, strategic plan.

Definitively, Puig Antich criticized the failure of the MIL-GAC to politically materialize their strategy.

> [Our] political positioning is surpassed by the radicalization of practice, as an armed agitation group without a capacity for political analysis.... And on the internal level, there was an immediatism ... and self-interested justifications that took precedence over an objective analysis of the situation of the proletarian movement. It should be underscored that starting once we disencumbered ourselves of a certain comrade, we were capable of expressing—at a very low level, of course—our political position or line....
>
> I think that the best critique of the prior period is as follows: An extremely tough practice that we developed to the utmost, alongside a practically non-existent political labor.[19]

And he admonished that the political organization had to prevail over the military one, proposing a clear planning of the political work and future actions in order to establish the connection between the armed actions and the workers' struggle, without having to "break this isolation handing out papers and

---

18.   In a draft he writes: "We henceforth deny the preeminent position of the military groups. All the comrades have their commitments with the revolution and each one labors from their own position. There is no difference between a political comrade, a military one, a worker, etc. These denominations only indicate the level each one works on, nothing more. We all form part of the proletariat in struggle for the emancipation of all the exploited." Salvador Puig Antich, "Armed Agitation—Real Movement" (draft), Spring 1973 (copy in the CDHS-AEP).

19.   Puig Antich, "Terrible' History, December '72–July '73."

ringing doorbells"; for Puig Antich, the quandary was clear: to continue with a sterile activist practice, or to consolidate the links with the revolutionary movement and elevate the politicization of the activist sector:

> The question has two possible solutions. 1) An acceleration of individual action (Sabaté, Bonnot, Ravachol); or 2) The creation of a political infrastructure with the aim of maintaining contacts in the revolutionary movement and politically consolidating a military group."[20]

According to Puig Antich, revolutionary violence (to which he applied the terms "armed struggle" and "guerrilla conflict") had to shift, without abandoning the bank expropriations, into another phase of actions that would be "selective, exemplary, and hard," like actions "with explosives" and attacks on police stations and armories, executions, etc., in which they should not reject occasional collaboration in specific actions with other revolutionary organizations that accepted the need for armed struggle.

In the document titled with Marx's phrase, "The emancipation of the workers must be the task of the working class itself, or it will not be," Puig Antich resumed the theoretical discourse of the group and recalled how the affirmation of class self-organization was born out of the struggle against the Leninist principle of organization, and from there he criticized all the vanguardist formations, including not only the Marxist ones but also "anarchism when elevated to an ideological category." The text followed through on the argumentation already expressed in the collective text, "Evaluation and perspectives of the workers' struggle," according to which the class struggle had been radicalizing in Spain and internationally, entering into an offensive phase in order to face the stronger reaction from the State-Capital. In this context, the most conscious militants had to take up arms to support and accelerate the revolutionary process, a moment in which Puig Antich takes the opportunity to affirm that armed agitation

---

20. Puig Antich, "Who Can Revive a Corpse?"

"must be understood on a political level, without falling into merely technical reductionism, as often happens." As such, the primordial task of armed agitation groups is to bind themselves to this offensive struggle of the working class through a "broad mass organization."

But it was probably the document he presented to the rest of the group at the end of April that best synthesized all the positions sketched out in the drafts and the prior text, maintaining a mix of self-critique and theoretical confusionism, with a clear line in favor of strengthening the MIL-GAC as a politico-military organization; as such, it is pertinent to quote it extensively:

> The present text attempts to present a prompt for a discussion in which we might all elaborate together a strategy as an autonomous combat group.
>
> 1) Bossism...
>
> If we go back in time, part of our history is conditioned by bossism, and it is no paradox that this coincides with the time when the fewest actions were carried out and the group was at its most disunited, consumed in internal disputes based on mistrust, differing tendencies, and supposed schisms.
>
> This reflection is a product of last week, when I saw the scourge that paralyzes so many groups be reborn among you. One could point to the disorganization of the group, how individuals do not present clear positions, etc., all of which are true, but none of these should impede the comrades in the exterior from having clear relations, nor make it seem—and I hope this isn't the case—that the only thing they want from comrades in the interior is the infrastructure they possess. The bureaucratic secret, sabotaging attempts at discussion, scorning those who do not adhere to the correct label, has re-emerged after the recent drama, with some leaving and others storming out. What is truly dramatic is that they gave the same reasons for leaving the group and the same mistakes are being committed.
>
> The fact that currently the group declares itself openly

anarchist is nothing special, or is it that the entirety of our practice up to this point, correct or not, hasn't been anarchist? Our positions have been conditioned by action and not by supposed ideological purism. I do not understand, therefore, the discomfort of some of the comrades. In any case, I think that adhering to a label brings serious problems. If, for tactical reasons, we have declared ourselves to be anarchists, this does not have to imply a disdain for other comrades who work with us, accepting the validity of armed struggle. We are going to work together and I demand total clarity and trust between comrades.

2) Called bluffs. We have spoken at great length about the isolation that tormented the group. I don't know to what extent it is correct to attempt to break this isolation handing out papers and ringing doorbells....

3) Past experience. We can ask ourselves the following question: Why has our practice not inserted itself into the class struggle? On the one hand, there have not been any clearly political actions and only these have the possibility of demonstrating the effectiveness of the practice.[21] The actions were all expropriations and they did not go beyond the framework of immediate necessities. Therefore, the actions did not go beyond themselves and did not have any subsequent effect.

There have been no new GAC or we do not know about them (Mallorca).[22] It is our practice itself that has isolated us.

4) Armed agitation. Any acceleration of actions, if they are not attached to clearly defined objectives and our own limitations, would be to "go up against the wall" ("*se faire*

---

21. Trans: An expropriation serves to finance other activities, and the relation between such actions and the activities is not visible. A clearly political action would be some kind of sabotage or attack that intervened in an ongoing workers' struggle, and though the MIL directly supported those struggles, they, unlike the OLLA, did not end up carrying out such actions.

22. Trans: Salvador's partner Margalida was from Mallorca, but the conditions on the island were hardly ripe for setting up an autonomous combat group. I consulted with a former member of the MIL, but he could not remember what this was in reference to.

casser la guele"). The results of subsequent stages will not improve just because we have separated from a comrade. It was necessary, but insufficient, and with a new dose of volunteerism, a consequence of the new situation....

The most important condition is the union (direct relation) between the guerrilla struggle and the economic and political struggles of the masses. The guerrilla conflict, as such, has no chance of developing if this relation does not become the essential nexus of the guerrilla practice.

To pose the question in terms of whether or not the armed struggle is necessary right now, is false. The armed struggle is a strategic objective of the class struggle...

The armed struggle is not exclusive, it must have a relation to the workers' sphere and the popular struggle.

Objectives:

1) Exhaust the forces of repression.

2) Support the radical struggles.

3) Support the creation of GAC in a way that tends towards their unification.

4) Create an information and propaganda apparatus.

Immediate objectives:

1) Complete infrastructure.

2) Expropriations.

3) Actions with explosives.

4) Release of books—library.

Without a political base capable of explaining the actions carried out within a historical perspective, we will repeat past errors.

The actions are conditioned by events and not by any visionary of the moment.

I repeat that the purpose of this text is to provoke discussion, clear and sincere, between comrades, however... The Movimiento (Ibérico de Liberación) demonstrates itself by the path it takes.

Anarchist greetings[23]

---

23.   Salvador Puig Antich, "Prompt for discussion." April 25, 1973 (copy

Puig Antich does not stop with the formulation of a general outline of the new path to follow; he also elaborates what design the new politico-military organization should have, structured on two levels: "intensive or military" and "extensive or the creation of a political infrastructure, 'Solidarity Committee.'" The first should have three sub-levels: "ultra-hard," "hard," and "paramilitary or semilegal," and the second should take charge of the library, the contacts, etc. These two political and military levels would unify in an executive committee, which would be the maximum organ overseeing the different cells of five or six individuals and that would place a special emphasis on the MIL's political practice, with the publication of a magazine ("above all theoretical"), the political training of militants, and propaganda.[24] These structures enjoyed the advantage of, if it were accepted by all, being able to impose political control on the armed actions and to favor the preeminence of the political organization over the military one; nonetheless, it was evident that beyond strengthening the MIL-GAC as a formal group, it reproduced the classical scheme of any party or groupuscule (cells, executive committees, specialization...) and went against one of the basic postulates of the MIL-GAC regarding organization.[25] The temporary acceptance of the proposal during the spring and summer of 1973 owes more to a desire to maintain the truce within the group until a definitive solution could be found, which it was believed would arrive with the intervention of Oriol Solé after he was released from prison.

Effectively, the debate in the spring did not solve the discrepancies, as was seen a few months later, in the summer, and the reason the group did not dissolve itself then and there is because of the impending release of Oriol Solé, an especially charismatic person who was respected by everyone in the organization.

---

in the CDHS-AEP).

24.   Salvador Puig Antich, "Politico-military organization." (draft), spring 1973 (copy in the CDHS, AEP).

25.   Puig Antich even proposed a name change, since the GAC already existed (the Grupos de Acción Carlista), though he does not suggest an alternative (Puig Antich, "Who can revive a corpse?"). Regarding this point, it is necessary to clarify that, contrary to what is affirmed in one Carlist book, there was no collaboration between the MIL-GAC and the Carlist GAC.

Faced with this situation, the sector charged with the publications, opposed to the ones who had adopted the dynamic of
armed struggle and opposed to the shift to a traditional armed
group, settled on a compromise and accepted Puig Antich's proposal, via the creation of a "politico-institutional arm," while they
awaited the arrival of Oriol Solé to try to reorient the trajectory of
the MIL-GAC.[26] The other sector also awaited his arrival, trusting
that he would reinforce their position.

One of the elements that should be underscored in this whole
episode is, obviously, the ascending role of Puig Antich within the
group, not only in light of his intervention in the internal arguments, but also his comrades' acceptance of his proposal for overcoming the crisis, and the responsibility subsequently placed on
his shoulders of acting as the contact person with other groups.
As such, Puig Antich was a far cry from the simple driver during
the bank robberies or, worse yet, the "poor boy" he is often portrayed as. These documents demonstrate his complete theoretical
and vital implication in the group, as a conscious revolutionary
trying to act consistently with his political beliefs and with a full
comprehension of the unity of revolutionary theory and practice.

---

26.   In a personal document, Santi Soler recognized the role played by Puig
Antich—without mentioning him, obviously—in achieving consensus, at the
same time as he recorded the fragility of the situation:

"In this moment, more or less correctly, more or less hurried, more or
less improvised, the strategy of combat groups is formulated, and of defining
ourselves openly anarchist, etc. The diverse tasks that were carried out in a
dispersed manner ... had a few points in common ... the assignment of new
people to positions of militant responsibility ... have demanded and given form
to this strategic formulation.... We have saved ourselves from a stumbling block
that seemed insurmountable thanks to the political perspicacity of certain
comrades and their ability to build consensus around a new alternative, and to
materialize it with precision in tactical criteria, concrete tasks, daily dedication,
sufficient means, etc.... Today as yesterday, a simple, everyday problem can
wreck any pretension the group has to a strategy: the political void and the
isolation were not, therefore, the fruit of an inability, in my mind, but of the
rhythm of permanent risk that was assumed." (Santi Soler Amigó, "Sobre la
práctica política," June 18, 1973 (CDHS-AEP).

Puig Antich, in another draft, affirmed that the preservation of the group—
which is revealed to only be temporary—was earned by everyone: "unity has
been maintained thanks to the absolute will of the group's members to carry out
our task" (Puig Antich, "'Terrible' History, December '72–July '73").

Shortly after they had arrived at the precarious compromise, Santi Soler set out to put Puig Antich's proposal for creating a politico-military organization in practice, taking charge, on June 8, of drafting a document to establish a "solidarity committee," which is to say, the political infrastructure proposed by Puig Antich. In this document, titled "On the constitution of the Committee X," he proposed the creation "of a politico-institutional arm of the MIL that would be formally independent" and would serve to solve the present dynamic by creating another independent entity that would be connected to the struggle of the working class. The solution, then, would consist of creating a committee formed by MIL members and people who did not belong to the group, and that would ensure that the movement would benefit from the political fruits of the armed actions and the distribution of texts.

Definitively, the purpose was to reinforce "the real movement" by creating a semi-legal organization that would broaden the base of the MIL-GAC and work for self-organization within the workers' movement, on the basis of a real intervention. However, this committee was never formed, though the proposal was brought up with the groups Topo Obrero, Estudiantes Libertarios (thanks to the contacts of Garriga's companion, Pilar García or "Eva"), and the OLLA, and new contacts were made.

Puig Antich was the main person responsible for keeping contact with the other groups, and in July he got a request from the Comissió Central de Solidaritat for a donation of fifty million pesetas to be distributed amongst the anti-Francoist movement, supposedly after a proposal that had originated with the MIL-GAC.[27] The figure of course was well beyond the group's means, but it squared with the "legend" built up around "the Sten gang," which was evidently well known to the entire opposition in Barcelona.

Obviously, the MIL-GAC never made such a proposal, and after informing his group, Puig Antich gave a response to the

---

27. This was probably the "Comissió de Solidaritat de Barcelona," an organization connected to the Assemblea de Catalunya.

request in which he denied they had ever made the offer—
which he attributed to police provocateurs—and after expressing his "unconditional support for the magnificent work that
the Commission was carrying out on behalf of victims of repression" and an offer of economic aid more in proportion to their
means, asked the organization to help clarify the facts of the
miscommunication.[28]

The MIL-GAC had bigger problems than the requests of the
Comissió Central de Solidaritat: with the release of Oriol Solé
at the end of June, they set a date in July for the next meeting
of all the members (the "congress") in Tolosa, though the gathering had to be postponed to August due to one of the periodic
health crises of Santi Soler. The debate quickly came to revolve
around the question of the dissolution of the MIL-GAC, and several group members—including Puig Antich—consulted with
"Jean Barrot" (Gilles Dauvé, one of the principal theorists and
supporters of the group, part of the milieu of the bookstore La
Vieille Taupe) in Paris on the need to separate the propaganda
project from the expropriations. At the end of the "congress," the
MIL-GAC dissolved itself, unable to find any other solution to
the crisis that had been dragging them down since the beginning of that year when they realized they were becoming just
another "groupuscule." The dissolution was more an organizational measure than a change in practice, as Dauvé pointed out
in his correct critique, but each sector—the one connected to the
actions and the other connected to the publications—decided
to continue with their prior practice, only separated from each
other.[29]

Santi Soler explains that the conflicting sectors were not
"activists" versus "theorists," but rather those who defended
the need, explicit or not, to strengthen themselves as a military
group and continue with an armed practice that grew beyond the
robberies to also embrace sabotage actions, against those who

---

28.   "To the Comisión Central de Solidaridad," Barcelona, July 1973 (copy
in the CDHS-AEP).

29.   Jean Barrot, *Violencia y solidaridad revolucionarias: el proceso de los
comunistas en Barcelona* (Ediciones Mayo del 37 [1974?]).

defended the traditional proposals of the group from its origins in 1970: self-organization and an opposition to groupusculiza-tion, which they understood as remaining an open group with a link to the real movement and an emphasis on the library. That is to say, it was basically a repetition of the arguments staked out during the crisis in April and May, revealing the latter not to have been resolved. Within each sector there were "activists" and "the-orists" with an important sector in between. According to Santi Soler, among the supporters of continuing the dynamic of the prior months were the theorist Garriga, the activists Rouillan and Torres, and the "logistician" Entremont. Among the supporters of turning more to the "actual movement" were Santi Soler, the activists Jordi Solé and Oriol Solé, and the "logistician" García, as well as the "distributors" Núñez and López. The sector in between, principally Pardiñas, Pons, and Puig Antich, would end up supporting the proposal for dissolution.

Rouillan gives a different explanation of the process and affirms that everyone, except for Oriol Solé in the beginning (given his disconnection from the history of the MIL-GAC due to his two successive prison terms) was in favor of dissolving, as this would permit the definitive separation of the two projects connected to the MIL-GAC and as such would allow them to intensify their practices: the realization of armed actions and the publication of revolutionary texts. Turning the page on the his-tory of the MIL-GAC, definitively eliminating the MIL acronym and only conserving the "GAC," they could materialize coordi-nation with other "autonomous combat groups," principally through Rouillan in Tolosa and Puig Antich in Barcelona. At the same time, the relation with the publications would no longer be based on a common connection and each project would achieve its autonomy.

Santi Soler and Garriga pursued the same objective of reducing the danger to the publishing project, such that in the end the decision was unanimous. Barrot was not present in the decision, as the visits to Paris by Rouillan, Entremont, and later, Puig Antich, occurred after the congress and the dissolu-tion; their purpose was to consult with "ultra-left" tendencies, the ORA, Spanish refugees (with Pierre Guillaume, not Barrot). Subsequently, Santi Soler and Garriga wrote the statement for the dissolution, to which they added a postscript with ideas expressed essentially by Rouillan and Puig Antich.[30]

In any case, whatever the exact progression of the "congress for the dissolution of the group," as far as Puig Antich is concerned, Rouillan's version once again demonstrates the importance of "the Doctor" both in the debate process and in the articulation of the postscript to the statement of dissolution, as does the role he was given to organize collaboration and coordination with other groups.

But there would not be time for him to fulfill that role or for the group to embark on its new course: just one month later, on September 25, Puig Antich was arrested together with Santi Soler and Garriga (as Oriol Solé and Pons Llobet had been ten days earlier, after a robbery in Bellver de Cerdanya), and a cop died during his arrest. He was judged by a war tribunal for that incident and the robberies, and condemned with two death sentences, one for the death of the cop and the other for a robbery, though the latter was commuted. Finally, as is well known, he became the last person legally killed by *garrot vil* in Spain, on March 2, 1974.

The killing of Puig Antich was a brutal shock that moved many people. But this shock remained at the incipient stage of a mere rejection of Francoism's brutality, without following Puig Antich's political orientation. Since a large part of the Catalan population, especially the youth, were "anti-Francoist" to a greater or lesser extent, many people could experience the human drama and take interest in everything related to the spectacle surrounding Puig Antich's killing: the weapons, the robberies, the fire fight, the arrest, the trial, and the execution. Quickly, "Puig Antich products" began to appear, from posters to books

---

30. Letters from Jean-Marc Rouillan to the author, November 6, 2001 and January 2, 2002; on the "postscript," there are different versions on where to attribute its authorship or inspiration (for example, the text "¡C.O.Ñ.O!" attributes it to "*affines*" (p. 4)); in any case, its authorship and its inclusion at the end of the "definitive conclusions of the congress" were unanimously approved.

and countless articles and stickers in between, creating a myth similar to "Che Guevara products." In the beginning, there were certainly "good intentions" behind these posters and articles, but these gave way to a morbid literature that culminated in the cinema, the modern spectacle *par excellence* (and years later there was an attempt to do the same with Oriol Solé). The description given by Santi Soler just one year after the murder of Puig Antich unfortunately remains completely current:

> After the complicit silence of the revolutionaries, the "1,000" has become a minor myth, a fashion, a spectacle, a festival of martyrology, merchandise, a gadget. Not long ago I read the Dossier from '73: it belongs to another era. Now, on March 2 they were selling a poster of the "martyr," like the Che Guevara fashion but more "made ours" (as they say), for ten bucks and with a text by Maragall on the back about the death of Ferrer i Guàrdia:[31] a doctor for ten bucks... What I mean is that capital recuperates everything, and even finds ways to silence its troubled conscience.[32]

In this entire process of appropriation (moreso than recuperation), there is another element besides making money, and it is about constructing a historical narrative that agrees with the era we live in: Puig Antich is repurposed into an anti-Francoist "good guy," a sort of Robin Hood who came to help the workers and was tragically finished off by the brutal dictatorship. The same way that Oriol Solé was subsequently presented as a hyperactivist motivated by his opposition to all dictatorships and his love of Catalunya and of freedom, and who met the same fate. In both cases, these are real falsifications of history, but they are

---

31.   Trans: Joan Maragall (1860–1911), modernist poet and Catalan author; and Francesc Ferrer i Guàrdia (1859–1909), anarchist educator and founder of the Modern School, executed as a scapegoat for the Glorious Week insurrection (recorded by mainstream historians as the Tragic Week due to all the churches that were set afire).

32.   Letter from Santi Soler to Ignasi Solé and Beth Calsapeu, March 21, 1975 (UB-Fons MIL).

not innocent: at their root, the negation of the deep revolutionary anticapitalism of Puig Antich and Oriol Solé serves to create
a historical narrative in which what happened (the Transition)
was what had to happen, with the bad guys—Franco and the
fascists—losing to the good guys, who included everyone who
opposed the bad guys and wanted "freedom," democracy, and
the nation. By eliding the struggle Puig Antich and Oriol Solé
dedicated themselves to, a struggle against capitalism and for
proletarian emancipation, they have tried to hide the fact that
there are revolutionary alternatives to the current socioeconomic
order.

The fact should give us pause that, while large mediatic
groups, political parties, and so on, continuously memorialize
over Puig Antich (and starting more recently also Oriol Solé),
Jean-Marc Rouillan did not receive practically any media cov-
erage during his campaign to be released from prison. How
was it possible to claim Puig Antich and Oriol Solé and ignore
Rouillan? The answer is obvious: by falsifying history. The lack
of interest in his case on the part of those who had no problem crying crocodile tears for Puig Antich and Oriol Solé reveals
their hypocrisy.

During the petition for reopening his case, it was stated
again and again that the process had been plagued by irregularities, that the body of the cop had bullets of different calibers,
etc. All of this is not only possible, but highly probable; however,
here we have two questions to consider. The first is that none
of it negates the evidence that Salvador Puig Antich consciously
carried out an action, which was to shoot a cop; trying to present
Puig Antich as a good boy who against his will found himself
in a bad situation is to falsify the facts. His commitment to the
politics of the MIL-GAC only increased qualitatively and quan-
titatively in the final year of the group, until he became one of
the key members of the organization in 1973. Puig Antich was
an anticapitalist fighter who understood that the struggle had
to make use of and increase revolutionary violence against the
agents of capital, and that is why he drew the second pistol he
had hidden on him (a pistol that had belonged to Oriol Solé and

that was given to him by Santi Soler; already, Txus Larrenea had showed him how to hide guns on his person).[33]

The second question to consider is precisely the never-ending petition to revise or annul the trial, a crusade for which several political professionals have appointed themselves the executors and guardians: if we analyze this from the political point of view the MIL-GAC adhered to, this revision/annulment makes no sense, as how can one ask the bourgeois State to determine if Puig Antich had been unjustly executed? Framing things in this way means remaining trapped in the pincers of antifascism, thinking in terms of the regime (Francoist *versus* bourgeois democracy), when the MIL-GAC framed things in terms of struggle against the bourgeois State, independently of its political regime. In other words: Salvador Puig Antich does not need to be rehabilitated by the bourgeois State. The anticapitalist revolutionary movement has always recognized him as one of their own.[34]

---

33.   Trans: Txus Larrena was a Basque comrade from one of the groups that split from ETA.

34.   Trans: Most of the documents the author of this article refers to are stored in the CDHS-AEP, that is, the *Centre de Documentació Històrica i Social* in the *Ateneu Enciclopèdic Popular*, an important "aetheneum" founded by the workers' movement in 1903, closed by the Franco regime, and reopened in 1978 by a group that included the anarchists Abel Paz and Cipriano Damiano. It is the second largest archive of the workers' movement in the world, after the IIHS in Amsterdam.

11.

Remembering Salvador Puig Antich Over the Years

Ricard de Vargas Golarons

"It's possible that we lose our next battle, that we lose it in the bourgeois sense of the word, but losing a battle in this way should never affect a revolutionary, because a revolutionary knows that their principal weapon is that of struggling for the cause they believe in: for a revolutionary, action is the progress of the social motor, and in this sense the simple act of initiating combat is a victory already..."

Buenaventura Durruti

Statement on the Eight Year Anniversary of his Execution

Eight years ago today, the 2nd of the March 1974, Salvador Puig Antich, member of the MIL-GAC (Movimiento Ibérico de Liberación—Grups Autònoms de Combat), known by his friends as "the Doctor," was executed by *garrot vil* in the Modelo prison in Barcelona. At that time, at the tail end of Francoism, Puig Antich's death was used in an opportunistic way by a large part of the anti-Francoist left, then in the opposition and now in parliament, in how they presented him as an antifascist, thus recuperating him for the anti-Francoist cause. Evidently, it did not interest them to reveal the true revolutionary, anticapitalist meaning of the actions of the MIL or the Grups Autònoms. And perhaps it is necessary to remember that the MIL, deeply connected to the workers' movement since before 1968, was one of the best things to come out of the revolutionary movement in the past years. Its contributions are still valid today, and corroborated by our recent experience of "democracy."

The MIL was an anticapitalist movement that fought against Capital in all its forms, that strengthened the practice of self-organization and workers' autonomy, that overcame the division between manual labor and intellectual labor and favored direct action and the autonomy of the social struggles, as well as spreading a relentless critique of Leninism, bureaucratic methods, professional militarism, and all the vanguardist tendencies, as reproducers of class domination within the current system of oppression.

It also criticized and overcame, in its own practice, the hierarchical conception of social life and the individual, and criticized syndicalism as a tool for integration and control over the working class within capitalist society, as we have seen over the last years. It criticized and combated the division between leaders and followers and threw itself into the transformation of daily life.

The years have passed when the Francoists gave us the current "democracy," which was then held up by the workers' parties, blocking the workers' struggles and defending Capital, leaving large sectors of the working class who struggled and expected a change in their situation defenseless, disarmed, and demoralized. The left-wing parties have propped up "democracy," that same democracy that is "incompatible with decision making in assemblies," as Felip Lorda, leading bureaucrat of the FETE-UGT, declared in an assembly of teachers who had voted to strike against the hierarchalization of the education sector, along with other labor-related demands. Evidently, their democracy is not that of the working class.

The years have passed, and under the neo-Francoist democracy, the murder of workers continues, as do torture and corruption at all levels. It is now fashionable to speak of disappointment. Could there be any other reality? Surely those who speak of disappointment or who are disappointed are those who had high hopes for this "democracy" that denies our national existence in the Catalan countries and generously condemns us to regionalization, to the role of marionettes or flunkies within the political and social life of the State. Many of these hopefuls must have been dazzled by the new "democratic" façade, they must have delegated their desire for freedom and their protagonism to the professional representatives of the hierarchical political bureaucracy, which does nothing but serve and strengthen the system of oppression and capitalist exploitation that all the pariahs and the disinherited of our country suffer.

Deals, pacts, consensus, sales, integration of the authoritarian and pro-capitalist left within neo-Francoism: they have all considerably weakened and demoralized the workers' movement, and the weaker it is, the more disorganized and impotent it becomes, and they grow fatter off us every day. Now more than ever they want us to integrate into the system, they deny us as a separate nation, and they refuse us the capacity and the possibility to be ourselves, the oppressed and the exploited, to be the only protagonists of our lives and our history.

Eight years after the execution of Puig Antich, his memory lives in all those who fight against the domination exercised by Capital in all its forms. His memory and his life cut short exalt and ennoble this struggle, which is unequal, but also inevitable and unbeatable, against all the forms, apparatuses, and servants of the domination of Capital, on the path to our individual and social liberation.

Diario de Barcelona, March 2, 1982.

Thirteen Years after the Execution of Puig Antich

Tomorrow marks thirteen years since Puig Antich was executed at Modelo prison in Barcelona and buried in the Montjuïc cemetery, in niche number 2,737. Revolutionary and unequivocally Catalan, his extreme generosity brought him—just like his comrade Oriol Solé Sugranyes, killed by the Guardia Civil in the Basque mountains—to a tragic end.

Today, with the historical perspective given to us by the time gone by, we can better comprehend the MIL, in which Puig Antich was active. Three books have been published on the topic. The first, in 1977, by Telesforo Tajuelo, *El MIL, Puig Antich y los GARI*, was published by El Ruedo Ibérico; though incomplete and with historical and interpretative errors, is the first work of reference. The second, published in Catalan by the collective Carlota Tolosa and with a prologue by Ramon Barnils, is *La torna de la torna, Salvador Puig Antich i el MIL*, published by Editorial Empúries in February of 1985 and with several editions already printed; it is an excellent journalistic-historical book that offers strong documentation and sheds light on what the MIL really was. And finally we have another book, this one in French, *1.000 histoire désordonné du MIL*, by the French historian André Cortade, published in December of 1985 by Dérive 17, a rigorous study as far as its historical and political analysis are concerned, offering some previously unpublished documentation and a good chronology of the MIL.

What was the MIL, to ask succinctly?

It must be said that the MIL was not an isolated group practicing armed struggle, rather it was connected and related with the most radical part of the workers' struggle in that era. The MIL was connected to the revolutionaries of 1937, presenting itself as the heir of the best libertarian traditions, the continuation of anarchist insurrectionalism and of the Catalan guerrillas of the post-war period, like Quico Sabaté; it was the promoter of newer subversive ideas as well, offering a new revolutionary focus in a different and changing reality.

We must remember that with the expropriated money, they financed strike funds and supported fired workers and clandestine activities. According to the French historian André Cortade: "it is often forgotten that the MIL represents the greatest experience of the revolutionary movement in the Spanish state in the last twenty-five years."

The best way, perhaps, to define the MIL would be to use their own text, published in August 1973, in their final congress, where they dissolve themselves as a politico-military organization:

The MIL is a product of the history of class struggle over these past years. Its appearance is united to the great proletarian struggles that have demystified the bureaucracies—reformist or groupuscular—that wanted to integrate this struggle in their party program. It is born as a specific group for the support of the most radical struggles and fractions of the workers' movement of Barcelona. It keeps in mind, at all times, the necessity to nourish the proletarian struggle, and the support it gives as a specific group is material and propagandistic, through agitation, through word and deed...

Currently, a film is being prepared about Puig Antich and the MIL, to be directed by Manuel Muntané, who for a while now has been searching for documentation, information, and testimonies regarding the MIL, with a true eagerness for historical reconstruction, which makes us think that the first film on Puig Antich and his movement will be trustworthy and authentic.[1] Likewise, the ARDHC (Asociació de Recerca i Documentació d'Història Contemporània) is beginning to set up a great exhibition on "The autonomous, radical workers' movement and the MIL, 1967–1974," which will present testimonies—with a large quantity of magazines, pamphlets, flyers, posters, manifestos, books, and all sorts of documents—and analyze the time period that was so important for the radical workers' movement that gave birth to the MIL.

This exhibition will be inaugurated this year and will be accompanied by the publication of a catalogue with an explanation of the history, a chronology, bibliography, and a large part of the most significant documentation. They will also release a cassette presenting the exhibition. We hope that the movie and exhibition introduce new generations to the revolutionary past, with details and full of the hope and strength of the working class in our country, such a contrast with our present.

---

1.   Trans: It seems this film was never released in the end, or at least not widely distributed, as I can find no trace of it.

Still today, on the thirteenth anniversary of his death, Puig Antich remains in the popular memory, close to all those who make Lluís Llach's song their own:

It is not this, companions, it is not this,
that so many flowers died for...[2]

Avui, Sunday, March 1, 1987

Thirty Years after the Execution of Salvador Puig Antich

On March 2, thirty years will have passed since the execution by *garrot vil* of Salvador, member of the MIL (Movimiento Ibérico de Liberación), in the Modelo prison of Barcelona. The PSUC, the hegemonic party within the Assemblea de Catalunya, which had a great capacity to mobilize people, did nothing, not even the final night when the Committee for Solidarity with the Prisoners of the MIL asked for help. We should not be surprised by the attitude of the "democrats," given that Salvador was not the anti-Francoist fighter they tried to convert him into after his death. Salvador was a revolutionary anticapitalist. And the Assemblea de Catalunya wanted to make a deal with the very fascists who murdered him, in order to get a larger slice of power. Before he was executed, the libertarian, autonomous, Trotskyist, Maoist, and independent communist groups took action; after he was executed, university students and workers inside and outside Catalunya led massive protests.

At the end of the 1960s and beginning of the '70s, many important workers' struggles arose that were autonomous and self-organized, like the strikes at AEG, Camy, Harry Walker, SEAT, the Besòs power plant... They created factory committees

---

2.   Trans: Lluís Llach (1948) is a Catalan musician, singer, and writer who was critical of the Francoist regime. He wrote a song in homage to Puig Antich in 1974.

and self-defense pickets that broke with the dirigist and reformist tendency of Comissions Obreres, represented by the PSUC and by the Trotskyists and Maoists. In this way, they developed a revolutionary consciousness that was reflected in how the distinction between leaders and the base disappeared, thus recovering the old phrase of the First International, that "the emancipation of the workers must be the task of the workers themselves." In December 1971, the Theoretical Team, the Workers' Team, and the Exterior Team founded the MIL-Grups Autònoms de Combat and radicalized the class struggle, participating in the great battles that demystified the reformist bureaucracy. The MIL was born as a specific group for the support of the most radical struggles and fractions of the workers' movement of Barcelona, under the influence of May '68, the autonomous workers' movement in Italy, and the wildcat strikes around Europe. Through Ediciones Mayo del 37 it distributed revolutionary texts that had been unknown in the Spanish state, like the works of Anton Pannekoek, Camillo Berneri, and the Situationists, as well as radical texts from the workers' movement in Catalunya. The various revolutionary bank expropriations during 1972 and 1973 had the objective of supporting workers' struggles, raising money for solidarity funds and for the publication of texts authored by workers in the movement. For the MIL, every new step of the workers' movement demanded another step forward in the theory, which was a product of the movement itself.

The MIL overcame militarism and dedicated itself to the transformation of daily life: "Everyday life must become an extraordinary affair so that the extraordinary becomes an everyday affair." Therefore it approached an anarchist framework through its anti-authoritarian, assembly-based, and self-organized practice. Salvador himself said that "the anarchists are the ones who have best known how to imagine a communist world." As such, there was no conflict between anarchism and communism. The politics of "the left" claimed that the MIL was utopian and unrealistic. They should be reminded of Bakunin's phrase, "By striving to do the impossible, man has always achieved what is possible. Those who have cautiously done no more than they believed possible have never taken a single step forward."

The MIL, however, was wrong to believe that, in that era, the working class in Catalunya had enough class consciousness and that, through the proliferation of armed autonomous groups within the proletariat, we might attain a revolutionary insurgency. This led to the dissolution of the MIL as a politico-military group in August 1973. The announcement of the group's disbandment is one of the strongest, most radical texts of the 1970s: it opines that part of the group had adopted a professional activism that had isolated them from the real movement of the working class. Practically all the journalists and historians who have studied the MIL agree. Telesforo Tajuelo affirms that "the MIL was the most radical group of the Spanish workers' movement since the Civil War." André Cortade says that "the MIL represents the greatest experience of the revolutionary movement in the Spanish state in the last twenty-five years." Sergi Rosés clinches it by saying "the MIL represents one of a limited number of authentically revolutionary formations within the political panorama of that time, because its objective was never to topple Francoism and achieve a democratic regime, but rather, completely connected to the revolutionary Marxist tradition, struggled directly against the bourgeois State, against Capital, for class motives that via self-organization should put an end to wage labor and the class division of society. Definitively: the emancipation of the proletariat."

Thirty years have already passed. As Fraga Iribarne said, adopting the phrase of Giuseppe Tomasi de Lampedusa, "something must change for everything to stay the same." And this is what has occurred. They have conceded us, with the inestimable aid of progressivism, a democracy made out of Francoist elements in which you can express yourself "freely" but you cannot change anything. This quarter century of parliamentary democracy without citizen participation has brought us to the point where the combative youth that is only familiar with this new reactionary framework—above all in the past few years, in which the most brutal and exploitative capitalism, baptized "globalization," reigns—begin to organize themselves in ways that strongly remind us of the MIL's theoretical contributions. They are the new movements of social transformation that have taken root in the Catalan countries, especially in the principality, and they create liberated spaces and a global network of alternative counterpower through anti-authoritarianism and direct action, since, to topple capitalism, action must be global.[3]

In conclusion, the dissolution of the Moviment de Resistència Global de Catalunya reminds one, despite some differences, of the dissolution of the MIL:

> It was born as a network and a space for communication between collectives and initiatives. Today, however, it becomes to turn into an identity, a static structure, and so we think it has become necessary to destroy it! We want to go well beyond resistance: we want to explore paths of rebellion.

El Punt, March 9, 2004.

Salvador Puig Antich, Thirty-Two Years Later

Thirty-two years have passed since Salvador's execution, and certainly many things have changed, have transformed, while many of the hopes from that time have been frustrated and betrayed. They can kill us as people, but they can never kill ideas. They are reborn as long as the constant exploitation and oppression persist. And the current reality is hardly flattering: the unleashing of the most brutal real estate speculation, the most savage capitalism, social and labor precarity as have never been seen, while layer after layer of the popular classes are shunted into poverty as a minority grows richer and richer. Our daily lives are more fully directed and controlled from above, as lies, manipulation,

---

3. Trans: The old designation for the part of the Catalan countries that today is identified as Catalunya. See the Glossary.

and corruption are not only tolerated, but incentivized. We also witness the accelerating destruction of the land, at the same time as our legitimate and democratic linguistic and national rights are denied.

Returning to Salvador, it is necessary to insist—beyond any "democratic" and party-oriented recuperation—that he, like thousands of young people from his time, were not and did not define themselves as anti-Francoist. A product of the most radical workers' struggles of the moment, Puig Antich was an anticapitalist revolutionary: on the path to radical social transformation following an autonomous practice, he confronted not only capitalist exploitation at every level, but also the reformist and vanguardist parties and groupuscules that wanted to direct and control the workers' movement and the struggle in the neighborhoods.

The most radical part of the working class and the MIL broke with the vanguardism that was dominant, they opened a path to the self-organization of the class and to decision making in assemblies, among other contributions. It should also be said that, at the beginning of the 1970s, there were many like Salvador Puig Antich willing even to give their own lives if necessary to achieve a truly free and liberated society. A large part of the MIL's contributions, its revolutionary project, are still valid today, despite the time that has passed. All those who currently struggle for a real liberation, who spontaneously and rebelliously stand up to the current system of capitalist domination—the social movements, squatters, the anarchist movement, neighborhood and village assemblies—work within a self-organized, autonomous, anti-hierarchical, assembly-based, and anticapitalist framework.

Today, after so many years of "democratic" silence imposed on our immediate past, it seems that the way is now clear for the recuperation of historical memory.

Those who are familiar with the content of the movie *Salvador*, soon to be released, and which is based on the manipulative, deceitful book *Compte enrere* (*Countdown*) by Escribano, which presents a falsified, manipulated, and mythical vision of Puig Antich's life, intentionally isolating him from the autonomous and anticapitalist workers' struggles of the early '70s, without which his life and his death make no sense. And as sick as we are of other ideological, party-aligned interests appropriating and recuperating the struggles of libertarian, anti-authoritarian movement, in the face of this new provocation, the release of this film, all those who are still alive—ex-MIL, ex-OLLA, former members of the autonomous groups, ex-GOA, ex-Platforms, and so many thousands of anonymous workers, the true protagonists of the history that has been hidden from us, all together and in a moment of our choosing, with firmness and historical objectivity, will respond in the way we see fit.

We will respond with a forceful denunciation of this flagrant historical falsification. We will neither tolerate the manipulation and deliberate confusion of the youth, who are unfamiliar with the history, nor the manipulation of the rest of the population. One need not agree with the methods of struggle or with the aims of the MIL and a large part of the Catalan workers' movement at the end of Francoism, but what must never be done is to cut out, hide, and erase a part of the history of our country. A people, a country, who are unfamiliar with their own history have no future and will not get anywhere.

El Punt, March 25, 2006.

12.

Letters

Salvador Puig Antich

Letter to Merçona

Barcelona, December 1973

Merçona:

To write... to write... Breathing comes with difficulty. My thoughts are such a jumble that relating details or ideas is a real battle.

I know that behind the clouds, out there, very far away, they are waiting for me. Who can walk on the sea or jump over a mountain? Why does fog obscure the landscape? And the sun, will it ever rise? Where have the fairies from the tales hidden? Have they lost their magic wands?

Questions, question marks, ellipses. Does imagination help or is the fog covering the landscape? So many things to tell you! But what to tell you?

We can say everything we need with just a glance!

One day I will tell you about myself, but wait. Wait until I explode, squeeze myself out, and leave the dregs to settle. The older the wine, the better the taste: more "bouquet."

Now the battle begins. "At war with my insides" (A. Machado).[1]

No. I don't want to put one word after another (too easy). I want to show my feelings. How can I thank you for so much?

---

1. Trans: Antonio Machado Ruiz (1875–1939). Modernist poet and writer from Andalucía, died in exile having fled the fascists.

Sometimes—curse my years!—I am tempted to give you advice. I? About what? Why? I know few things and can explain even fewer. You are you, and you alone... and "because we live at blows" we—each and every one of us alone—make ourselves. I remember your questions (so many questions!), your eagerness for learning. I know, even if you don't, how your answers impressed me.

And the dog (Xic), the parrot, the horse, there in the stable, and you. Studies, homework, friends, and you. The house, the family, the brother-in-law (if you'll pardon the expression), and you. You and I. Siblings. Goddaughter and godfather. Without irony, that's how we seem. That and more. And more. So much more...

Have you already finished reading it? Keep it, rip it up. But never stop looking, over there, far away (horizon, sea, mountain). It is projecting ourself into the future, feeling the weight of the present, that we find our reason for being.

"I feel this night/ the words/ mortally wounded."
(R. Alberti)[2]

I love you,
Salvador

Letter to Joaquim

"Je vais mettre en chanson la tristesse du vent." (Ferré)

Beloved Kim:

---

2.   Trans: Rafael Alberti Merello (1902–1999). Poet and Communist from Andalucía who fought in the Civil War.

The news is simple: sentenced to death. It would be very difficult to express my feelings in this moment. Perhaps, it is an affirmation of that for which I have fought and which now, when I am most put to the test, I believe only more firmly. They are carrying out an irrational vengeance. Disgust, disgust is what I feel.

For a long time now I have asked myself what I was doing in this world, where there is not yet a place for me. It will arrive, without a doubt, and don't think I am being dogmatic. Where the situation becomes too brutal is where it is forced on all the people I love. It is too hard a test for all of you.

So, to not digress into metaphysical ramblings about life, accept these lines as an affirmation of my feelings for you and yours (you, Lee, Michele). I have broken with everything and accept my responsibilities. Blood will be spilled, but not uselessly.

Well, boy, everything that I could possibly say to you is between these lines and in the sadness on the wind.

I love you,
Salvador
Salut i anarquia

Letter to the Antich-Segura Family

Antich-Segura Family:

As you can imagine, I wish I could explain everything to you directly.[3]

Accepting responsibility can sometimes be quite difficult, but in these moments it is you who have to bear a violent situation you have been placed into without seeking it out.

---

3. Trans: Salvador was viciously smeared in the media as a gangster, and with his correspondence censored, he could not explain his life decisions to family members who had no idea he was in an anticapitalist group.

It is difficult to speak now, I just wanted to tell you all that I love you and ask you not to lose heart.

> With love
> Salvador Puig
> *Salut i anarquia!*

Letter to Margalida Bover

Barcelona, November 1973

Hey girl![4]

How to begin? It is strange for me to write you, as I miss your mischievous eyes that watched and, without words, told me everything.

Don't be afraid to send me sad letters (as you called them). The situation is sad, so just keep in mind that getting word from you is a vital safeguard for my barely stable morale. Your letters in my hands acquire an extraordinary vivacity. Hearing from you, feeling you close, are injections of strength for me.

The day Oriol brought me news from you, I was struck dumb, excited and lyrical. It was like getting you back, feeling your gestures... In a word, having you here! Returning to my cell and there alone (lately, solitude is a good friend) I exploded. In a burst of joy, full of deep feelings, I wrote the following (I am copying exactly what I wrote in my diary):

> Everything began... (what a ridiculous beginning). Do you know what is "l'amour-éclair"? It is this: "Cupid's arrow, certain and precise."

---

4.   This and the following letter are from the archive of Xavier Cateura i Valls.

It is a woman (terrible, terrible, am I not capable of describing her?). I do not want to be rational with feelings. They arise spontaneously and that is what is valid. Affectionate, incredibly so. With an imagination that breaks all moulds. Sincere. Spontaneous. With a certain layer of toughness (which we all need to "keep moving forward"). Sweet. "Petite voleuse de magasins." (Life is rough!) Normal for a Spaniard, but short if we were to enter the Common Market.[5] Funny (you can't tell I'm in love, can you?). I like her. Mischievous, sweet eyes. I don't know what color, she always looked at mine. She does this little gesture with her nose that could bring the bravest to his knees (which is to say, me). She talks and talks and talks. She can't keep quiet. She is afraid of silence, being alone. She has an immense need for affection. She loves because she enjoys it, because it seems good to her, it's a pleasure. She knows how to make love, passionately and delicately (Salvador and you?). She doesn't know what to do. Working for a wage bothers her. And, a warning, she doesn't know how "TO REPRESS HERSELF." Isn't that true, Margalida? We haven't repressed ourselves!

After the second letter, I decide to reply. I am, I was, a little afraid to write to you. I feel the danger of crossing the line, of becoming ridiculously sentimental or falling into the role of the star or victim.

As much as I exert myself, it is impossible to overcome our gazes, our laughter, or even our silences. Talking about myself is so difficult! How to express thoughts, hatreds, feelings? I wanted to tell you without any pat phrases, any clichés.

Now, after the whole disaster with the fall, the hospital, the interrogations, and threats, I am in an apparent state of tranquility. I am not frightened of the future. Whatever may come, I have enough freedom of spirit and faith in myself to face it. I know

---

5. Trans: The European Common Market, the precursors to the European Union. Salvador is making a reference to how people in Europe tend to be taller than in Spain.

that one way or another they will try to destroy me little by little, but I am prepared to face all these trials. Why?

Because, though I have made many mistakes, I believe, I believed, in what I was doing. Because I know that, no matter how many painful occurrences we have to go through, I have you. Because my little sisters are taking it so well. Because Oriol is not only acting as a lawyer, we are slowly becoming friends. Because I take responsibility for everything they accuse me of, but I don't feel guilty of anything.

I regret not having confided in you what I was doing, and now you and my sisters have to suffer and bother yourselves over me.

Perhaps these murderers dressed in legality destroy the man but not Salvador. The struggle will be very difficult, dramatic at times, but I'll get through it... I have to get through it!

And now I have to tell you off a little. It is impossible to express in words what you mean to me. I have the sensation that they ripped me away from you right in the moment when we had found the support we needed to confront a multitude of situations. My diary again:

> I think our fortune was that we both had a great need for affection and sweetness without limits. We gave of ourselves completely, and we received to the utmost. What does it matter how we call it, what was said or done. It was there. We spoke more with our eyes than with our mouths. It is so difficult to express!

But I want to analyze your words in detail. Margalida, I don't know how to thank you for saying you wished you had gotten pregnant. It is no small thing that my breath caught in my throat, given the difficult situation I was going through... and I think: I love her so much!

I also want to see you, but for security reasons wait until they transfer me to a different prison, then I'll take the necessary steps so you can visit, but I don't want you to go beyond your means. Even if all goes as we hope, not even God could get me out of 10–20 years of prison. I'm not exaggerating. Marry you?

Good thing I don't have a weak heart, but, when I read that, I had to go back to it three times. I was somewhere between laughter and tears. Between reality and fantasy. I stretched out my arms to hug you... Where are you, Margalida? I asked myself. Despite it all I felt you so close by. Your sweet way of speaking, your capricious nose, your arms, your lips coming closer.

No, Margalida. The fact that I am screwed doesn't obligate you to make decisions like these. It can be fixed, I hope, in other ways. I know that signatures on a marriage certificate are just a formality, but I don't want you tied to an absurd situation. If you think about it carefully you'll see it's a completely unnecessary action.

I tell you this with a certain feeling of shame. As though I were telling you off when I should be thanking you. And if I have this feeling, it is because your spontaneity (well beyond what I could ever muster) borders on the heroic.

Girl, I place a great value on your proposal, even though I have to turn you down one more time. I know what it means to you and I accept this action as a lyrical expression of frustration and impotence as they steal from us what we most want: to live together. But the situation is too deplorable to be of any help. Girl, live and love hard, and I know that the fortitude of our feelings will persist in your freedom.

And don't let it get under your skin if a few idiots accuse you of "having a lover... freeloading" or similar rubbish. These "voices of good conscience" are focusing on the most superficial, a false image. And you know absolutely that behind that false image there is a true love story that's worth more if you hold onto it for yourself. Alright?

I wish you all the best with work as with your studies. Keep your head up, girl! Ah! And thanks, many thanks for the shirt. I feel like I have a little bit of Margalida right next to me.

Well, I'll bring this to a close. I'm the first one to be surprised at having filled up two pages without realizing it.

Kisses and greetings to Xavier, Marga, Felip. I hope that __ has found a job they like. I miss all of them, as it was at their house... and we hit it off so well.

You can decide for yourself who to give kisses to etc., to ___,
___, ___, and so forth.

> I love you.
> Salvador Puig
> P.S. As Miguel Hernández says: "Who
> could put bars on a smile?"
> *Salut*

Letter to Margalida Bover

Barna, New Year 1974[6]

I have here a long quote from Henry Miller's "Nexus"

> *If there is anything which deserves to be called miraculous, is it
> not love? What other power, what other mysterious force is there
> which can invest life with such undeniable splendor?*
>
> *The Bible is full of miracles, and they have been accepted
> by thinking and unthinking individuals alike. But the mira-
> cle which every one is permitted to experience some time in his
> life, the miracle which demands no intervention, no intercessor,
> no supreme exertion of will, the miracle which is open to the
> fool and the coward as well as the hero and the saint, is love.
> Born of an instant, it lives eternally. If energy is imperishable,
> how much more so is love! Like energy, which is still a complete
> enigma, love is always there, always on tap. Man has never cre-
> ated an ounce of energy, nor did he create love. Love and energy
> have always been, always will be. Perhaps in essence they are
> one and the same. Why not? Perhaps this mysterious energy
> which is identified with the life of the universe, which is God*

---

6.   Trans: "Barna" is slang for Barcelona.

in action, as some one has said, perhaps this secret, all-invasive force is but the manifestation of love. What is even more awesome to consider is that, if there be nothing in our universe which is not informed with this unseizable force, then what of love? What happens when love (seemingly) disappears? For the one is no more indestructible than the other. We know that even the deadest particle of matter is capable of yielding explosive energy. And if a corpse has life, as we know it does, so has the spirit which once made it animate. If Lazarus was raised from the dead, if Jesus rose from his tomb, then whole universes which now cease to exist may be revived, and doubtless will be revived, when the time is ripe. When love, in other words, conquers over wisdom.

How then, if such things be possible, are we to speak, or even to think, of losing love? Succeed though we may for a while in closing the door, love will find the way. Though we become as cold and hard as minerals, we cannot remain forever indifferent and inert. Nothing truly dies. Death is always feigned. Death is simply the closing of a door.

But the Universe has no doors. Certainly none which cannot be opened or penetrated by the power of love. This the fool at heart knows, expressing his wisdom quixotically. And what else can the Knight Errant be, who seeks assault in order to overcome, if not a herald of love? And he who is constantly exposing himself to insult and injury, what is he running away from if not the invasion of love?[7]

Beneath a clear blue sky, where a timid cloud, feeling alone, dissipates, the sun pumps through my veins. I feel strong, hot. Hungry lips caressing the sun, my love grows stronger. Whole love, infinite without barriers or morals. Love we're ashamed to confess and that, as the fool, the coward, the hero, and the saint, we intimately desire. Why do we not, for once, turn all our cards over?

---

7. Trans: Henry Miller, *The Rosy Crucifixion. Book III: Nexus* (Paris: The Odelick Press, 1960).

I am attaching a RETURN receipt.[8]

> Trust and courage. I love you...
> Salvador

Letter to Margalida Bover

Barna, 3 1974

Beloved Marga:

Once more we must separate, perhaps definitively. The word of some gentlemen who speak a language I do not understand has all the appearance of vengeance. The important thing is that no one can break these feelings.

You will understand that I find it so difficult to say everything I want to you. The words don't appear.

Take heart, girl, it will be a difficult blow for you, but I have no doubt that little by little you will grow and become strong.

> I love you
> Salvador Puig
> *Salut i anarquia*

Greetings and thanks to Francesc-Magda-Ricard

---

8.   Trans: Probably a reference to a book taken from the prison library.

13.

The Texts of Salvador Puig Antich

Before Asking Ourselves: What Do We Do?
Better to Ask: What's Going On?

Before asking ourselves: what do we do? Better to ask: what's going on?[1] The impasse is symptomatic at every level. Not even action serves to justify anything. Is the impasse political, then? Yes. But acknowledging this requires us to comprehend a situation that has gotten out of hand, and no putative practice will solve this imbalance.

After attempting an evaluation, in which each member stuck to their own functions, the measuring stick itself broke, a victim of its own inadequacies. We were and we are a gang of delinquents politicized at the individual level. Because of our lack of group consciousness and the consequent authoritarianisms, we do not move as a compact body, but rather follow the personal decisions of the most capable.

What is armed agitation? What is the difference between it and armed struggle? What is the MIL? What is singular function, specialization? I will attempt to answer these questions:

1) What is armed agitation? (every day it gets harder to express myself)

---

1. Trans: Most of these texts were written by Puig Antich for internal debate within the MIL. They were not intended for publication and propaganda, and though they provide a window both into his thinking and into the conflicts and dynamics of the group, they are not always polished, nor is every reference to specific group realities explained for a broader audience. Additionally, some of the texts are drafts or notes for debates, with phrases repeated and recycled, fragments and incomplete paragraphs, and outlines sketched out on the fly. They are offered here to provide a window into the internal debates of the MIL, and not an example of their theoretical production.

It is a military struggle not aimed towards creating an army or an extensive organization, but rather an intensive military practice carried out, or attempted, by few individuals with a high degree of preparation (specialization) without organizational connections with any other radical spheres, and who are committed to the struggle for a new, communist society.

What political characteristics give shape to their activity?

We can underscore:

— A direct relation, not a relation of dependency, with the most radical sectors of the proletariat.

— The multiplication of combat groups.

This direct relation means that the actions are carried out according to a tactic, or more precisely a strategy, in which attention is given not only to the needs of the group, but also to the general situation in a given moment. It does not imply that we await orders or suggestions from other radical spheres in order to engage in our practice.

2) What, then, is the MIL?

The *Moviment Ibèric d'Alliberació* is a combat and action group formed by capable individuals specialized in military struggle.[2]

Its propositions are:

— Exhaustion of the forces of repression.

— Multiplication of the combat groups.

—Support for different radical sectors engaged in the struggle.

— Self-financing.

— Connections with different radical sectors.

Current situation? Need for a strategic and tactical line that maps out our future labors. There exists, beyond doubt, a dangerous paralysis in the group, not provoked by individual positions but by the lack of a clear line, as well as the low level of political education of its members.

---

2.   Trans: MIL in Catalan. Though the MIL's published texts were usually in Spanish, a higher-status language and legible to a broader portion of the working class, Puig Antich generally wrote in Catalan.

These last months have been marked by immediatism, with all actions carried out on the fly, and thus, always being pulled along in the wake of events, a material and political inability to carry out clearly political actions, given the lack of strategy. Now is the time when, if the repression does not take us down first, we can answer these pending questions. We cannot take actions that are lucidly political without a political preparation that enables us to explain and disseminate our position.

What does it mean when one comrade "takes fright" and another poses a question? What it means is flight to France. The shit has hit the fan.

We Still Can't See the Horizon

We still can't see the horizon. The fog is thick as the purée we ate for lunch, but everyone has something to say, and wants to say it because there is no room for temporary solutions.

My position, halfway between two tendencies (or more precisely, individuals), puts me in a situation of contradictory aspects:

a) counterweight
b) intermediary
c) concretion

Neither counterweights nor intermediaries are valid. The latter is impossible among individuals who, for better or worse, are aiming for the politico-military organization of their practice. The posture isn't feasible because it impedes the formation of the group and, simultaneously, I would become the tool of one of the two tendencies. And to act as a counterweight is to walk a tightrope, considerably increasing opportunist positions by permitting an eclecticism to the death.[3] Neither of the two positions is valid, because even if we constituted ourselves as a

---

3.   Trans: Eclecticism in the sense of permitting contradictory postures in the same group.

group, I would end up on the outside in order to maintain these positions.

Concretion: there is such a pile of personal shit that any proposals, if there actually are any, can be boycotted by one side or the other. How can one or the other personal position become decisive, when only personal arguments are advanced in order not to accept, or at least to argue against, a particular proposal? We would have to go back in time to analyze all the actions and things that have happened in this group to try to justify the unjustifiable positions that exist at present.

This is not the right moment to do so. We will not find a solution (a super optimist word in this situation) in the past, but on the other side of the fog, because our labor will be effective and valid when we are conscious that we are working for the future, or more precisely, our work has a future. And this will not occur without a concretion of the present. We cannot forget all the personal problems we have had, but it is on a political level and only on a political level that our arguments will become useful means for continuing onward. This, therefore, is my task over the next few days.

The current state of the group is unsustainable. As such, we can be rid of all this burden and on the basis of individual decisions, form a new group on a new foundation, even if we are the same individuals. What is failing to function now are not the individuals but the principles, which should spell out clearly what we are doing and why (simple and dramatic question!). The important thing is to answer the why, which is nothing other than the exposition of our strategy. Tactics are a consequence of the latter, which must be coupled to the moment. In a quick reading this might seem very linear, but it is more an inadequacy in knowing how to express myself than an ingenuousness of thought.

It is immoral to remain so nonchalant as we hear affirmations, that I wish would be unwarranted, like:

"I don't give a damn about political problems, I am leaving because I don't want to work with a certain individual." Or, "I might understand better what you think, but I am leaving for personal shit." Are you crazy? Blind?

You are dirtying us by using up the greater part of your strength on internal conflicts, such that a comrade becomes more of an enemy than the true enemy. What romantics we are that with such a panorama, we still want to continue! What is it that we want? This is the only question that makes sense. And who can answer it? At the moment I cannot. (But keep your eyes open for the next chapter.)

I would like this chapter to be an exposition of my personal position regarding the present situation. I say I would like it to be, because I do not know if I will express myself clearly. At blows... we live at blows. These days, more than blows, it's lethal mishaps.

I have gotten the good news that one of the comrades is about to get out of prison, but it would be positive if there weren't other comrades willing to lean on this individual and what he represents, relying on him to provide a new direction. I hope the individual in question does not lend himself to play this role.[4]

The general exhaustion is accentuated when I can barely trust in my ability to offer an alternative. If the connection that theoretically united us has died and everyone is preparing to take away the biggest chunk of the inheritance, do we really need to pose the question of who won the match? If that seems to make sense then we really should just destroy it all.

Why am I here? I believe in the validity of armed struggle as a means for destroying the present society. As such, I search for or try to create an organization that agrees with my principles and to carry out a daily revolutionary practice. In my mind, what is the role of armed struggle and political organization for arriving at the ends previously mentioned?

I think that first it is necessary to explain my situation. As an individual not integrated at any level in a class organization or mass movement, I engaged with the proletarian movement from the outside. It was through my practice that I integrated into this non-exclusive movement of the working class.

For armed practice, I understand the ensemble of political actions or expropriations that demonstrate the contradictions of

---

4.   Trans: A reference to Oriol Solé Sugranyes.

a structure based on the exploitation of man by man, and that implicitly offer an alternative, which is to say an explanation of what we do and where we are going. I understand armed agitation, insofar as it is constituted by a specialized group, as a dialectical relation between our own practice and the radical communist movements.

We do not try to build a party or an army. Rather, the action serves to raise awareness, as they say nowadays, among those individuals who are committed to a revolutionary labor as well as those who are not. In this light, our action is quite exemplary. It would not rise above terrorism if not for the organization and the direct relations with the most advanced movements. The organization serves to explain and support our positions through publications, be they flyers, bulletins, or newspapers. And direct relations means our practice has an impact in the struggle.

What politico-organizational forms should these principles adopt? As a group we need to express and adopt political positions that materialize as a strategy in the long term and that seek to have an impact on the real and present movement in the most adequate way possible.

Armed Agitation—Real Movement

We have always posed the question, "What is armed agitation?"[5] Before responding to this question, I think some preliminaries are necessary.

Armed agitation supports and facilitates revolutionary movements without trying to dominate and appropriate them; rather from a place of military struggle it inserts itself into the development of the revolutionary process. Armed agitation is not about creating an army or an organization that would lead

---

5.   Trans: This text is a draft of the subsequent one, "The emancipation of the proletariat..." Readers interested in a more polished analysis might skip to that essay; those interesting in a sketch of the evolution of a political argument might read both.

the workers to their emancipation. On the contrary, the emancipation of the working class will be achieved by the workers
themselves: the essential question is how the groups of armed
agitation, operating at a military level, can and must support the
proletarian struggle. In this struggle for emancipation, various
spheres coincide, each with their own dynamic. The military
sphere, given its radical practice and stronger rhythm, can lose
itself in adventures at any moment, throwing itself towards false
objectives after being deluded by its apparent strength. Actions
are dictated by events.

***

Our prior practice has shown to us that a military group cannot be
viable without a political organization. And not an organization
in the sense of a party (whether a reformist one or a revolutionary groupuscule); rather, the military group needs a determined
political line and the channels for developing its practice. I think
the expression "military group" has been given too narrow and
instrumental a meaning. A military group is absolutely not the
armed wing of any organization that completes just a few concrete, practical functions. The military group departs from an
analysis of the situation, political theses, and defined tactics, and
on this basis takes up arms in order to pursue its political line.
Since the revolution will be violent, the armed groups adopt this
strategy as a practice to support and accelerate the revolutionary
process. Nonetheless, the armed struggle is not exclusive, it must
exist in relation to other fields of struggle both by workers and
by the popular classes as a whole. Only arising from an intimate
relationship (the politico-military practice) will the military struggle have an impact on the actual movement.

***

The current economic situation of fluctuations between inflation,
stabilization, and inflation (stagflation), permits the capitalist
State to control the class struggle through integration (collective

contracts, negotiations, CNS delegates, etc.) or through repression (Ferrol, Vigo, Granada, Barcelona, Sant Adrià, etc.).[6]

At the same time, the parties and reformist groupuscules (PC-PSUC, BR, PCI, etc.) attempt to channel workers' struggles into reformist demands (horizontally integrated labor unions), sucking up to the system and converting themselves into mechanisms of integration.[7]

Only when the workers' movement has learned how to impose syndicalist goals by taking over the streets have they eluded the mechanisms of control (integration/repression). Its answer has been given the ephemeral form of wildcat strikes that smash through the framework of reformist demands, or the creation of strike pickets that clash with the repressive forces.

Both the radicality of workers' struggles these last few years and the level of revolutionary violence have increased. And this is not an isolated fact, but the product of the whole preceding history. The workers' movement has seen how the organizations that declare themselves *vanguard*, parties that claim to be the genuine representative of the class consciousness, have betrayed them in order to conquer political power and suck up to the capitalist system.

The battle lines are well drawn. Arrayed against us, the system and all the reformist organizations backing it up, though they may use a pseudo-revolutionary language. Thus, it makes perfect sense to speak of a class strategy for the destruction of the capitalist productive system and the self-liberation of the exploited the world over.

This strategy has an anti-authoritarian character insofar as it rejects all lines that do not arise within the class itself. And the forms of self-organization the class adopts are nothing less than the logical consequence of this strategy.

All "revolutionary" experiences up until now have limited

---

6.   Trans: All the cities named are places where workers had recently been killed in the course of strike actions.

7.   Trans: The Brigadas Rojas or Red Brigades, a Maoist split from the PSUC, and the Partido Comunista Internacional, a Trotskyist group. On the PSUC, see the Glossary.

themselves to replacing the managers of Capital without destroying the system of capitalist production. In the so-called "socialist" countries, they continue to steal the surplus from the workers in the name of an abstract entity: The State.

Embattled on these two fronts, which in fact constitute a single enemy, are the organizations that advocate and practice armed agitation. This concept must be understood in a political sense without falling into merely technical reductionism, as often happens.

The task, therefore, of all revolutionaries today is to reject all forms that are alien to their class and to participate in the self-organization of the class with the aim of destroying capitalist production.

When the workers' cause has broken the reformist framework and spilled out into the street, the repressive forces have acted criminally, murdering comrades. Faced with this situation, the most conscious militants take up arms in order to support and accelerate the revolutionary process.

The movement of these groups is nothing more than the class's partial response to capitalist violence. The development of the latest struggles has created an objective necessity for the appearance of these direct action groups that respond to the provocations of repression.

The class strategy is a totality with various fields, and one of those is military. The groups today cannot map out a military strategy by themselves. Since the strategy is determined by historical circumstances, and the birth of the groups is indeed an expression of a historical necessity, we find ourselves situated within a historical contradiction. The groups of armed agitation today become groups of self-defense of the class with a capacity for immediate response. That is to say that today, in the development of the struggles, there is no clarity regarding the military strategy of the class, and the non-existence of a military strategy is conditioned by the insufficient framework within which radical struggles develop. The fact that the wildcat strikes that break out are usually destined to fail is due to the current impossibility of generalizing the struggle.

Faced with this situation, the armed agitation groups adopt as a tactic the military strategy of the class that was generalized during insurrectionary periods.[8]

Nonetheless, the action of the autonomous combat groups is not geared towards the creation of a party, army, etc. Rather, our commitment is with the daily combat of the proletariat in struggle. We therefore reject any proposal external to the class and that does not seek the destruction of the current society on every level.

As such, the functions of armed agitation are:

1) Harmonious development of a military and political practice.

2) Exhausting the forces of repression (military...)

3) Support for the nuclei of workers in struggle.

4) Strengthening and multiplication of the autonomous combat groups.

We believe, however, and our prior experience has demonstrated, that the groups up until now have been constructed without a broad mass organization, which so far has been impossible to develop practically and politically.

The character of this mass organization:

We henceforth deny the preeminent position of the military groups. All the comrades have their commitments with the revolution and each one labors from their own position. There is no difference between a political comrade, a military one, a worker, etc. These denominations only indicate the level each one works on, nothing more. We all form part of the proletariat in struggle for the emancipation of all the exploited.

---

8.   Trans: What Puig Antich is trying to express is that the armed groups, as he conceives them, are not carrying out a strategy based on small, specialized armed groups, which would be vanguardist and probably doomed to fail. Rather, the effective strategy would be for the entire working class to strike, to take the streets, and to arm itself in order to defeat the repression, as it had done in previous insurrectionary moments. The armed groups are carrying out actions—expropriations, armed self-defense, counterattacks against repression, support for wildcat strikes, the dissemination of illegal ideas—that the entire movement would need to adopt. In other words, with their tactics—the kind of actions they carry out—the MIL and similar groups are trying to *prefigure* a strategy that must be adopted by the entire class.

It is not a question of determining right now the concrete form that this mass organization will take—self-organization, unions, councils—but rather its functions.

On this point, the groups are trained by their political practice to act as organs of political interpretation. In other words, the direct contact between the struggles and the practice of armed agitation makes possible an analysis of the development of the struggles of the workers' movement, and with this movement and nothing else as their point of departure, the armed agitation groups can set themselves tactical objectives, identifying the needs of the revolutionary movement.

The Emancipation of the Workers Must Be the Task of the Working Class Itself, or It Will not Be (K. Marx)

Within the most radical struggles of these last few years, the workers' movement has begun to understand clearly that all vanguardist forms are nothing but means of integration and discipline within the capitalist system and our only interest, as the working class, is to reject them permanently.

From the anti-Leninist struggle—Leninism being the superior expression of the practice of disciplining and integrating the class and its struggle—to the affirmation of class self-organization and the identification of all other vanguardist forms (all the ideological formations that proclaim themselves to be any variant of Marxism, as well as anarchism when elevated to an ideological category) the class struggle has achieved lucidity within a most profound radicalization, here in Catalunya as in the rest of the Peninsula and across the industrialized countries of Europe.

While the struggle of the working class has radicalized insofar as it begins to abandon the reformist struggles, or more precisely, begins to lose faith in the necessity of a reformist struggle, its radicalization necessarily entails an astuteness with regards to the State and Capital, especially as to the danger of not correctly disciplining the class and its struggle. The bourgeoisie goes on the attack. Their flirtation with the traditional reformist organizations becomes more and more apparent, although, on the other hand, the bourgeoisie has no problem with disciplining the class struggle independently of those organizations. This offensive turn by the State and Capital translates simultaneously into a hardening of the fascist forms of power, which are selective forms only utilized against radical fractions of the class struggle (the vanguard of the movement for proletarian liberation are its most radical struggles).

It is not a gratuitous affirmation to say that today the class is entering into a very important radical moment, given that both classes are on the offensive, in a radical, lucid stage. The struggles of the working class at every level begin to dissociate themselves from those struggles that seek integration in the capitalist system, and the final objectives of the struggle (destruction of capitalism's productive process) are already present in concrete struggles. The general wildcat strike is a struggle with a pre-insurrectionary character. Unified class consciousness is a radical communist substance. The self-organization of the class is a form-substance of worker pre-power, of the destruction of the State.

Faced with the intensification of selective capitalist repression, the working class needs to organize its self-defense, the defense of its struggles, of its organizations, and of its interests as a class. The first organized offensive-defensive groups arise from the internal dynamic of the workers' movement, as products of history, the same way the first theoretical works appeared. And just as the elaboration of theory cannot be carried out externally to the actual struggle, the defensive struggle cannot be delegated to external groups and elements outside the class struggle. The self-organization of the class is a whole that must assume all the organizational tasks of the proletarian struggle.

The current economic situation of fluctuations between inflation, stabilization, and inflation (stagflation), permits the capitalist State to control the class struggle through integration (collective contracts, union representatives, etc.) or through repression (Ferrol, Vigo, Granada, Sant Adrià, etc.).

At the same time, the parties and reformist groupuscules

(PC-PSUC, BR, PCI, etc.) attempt to channel workers' struggles into demands that can be assimilated, sucking up to the system and converting themselves into mechanisms of integration.

Only when the workers' movement has learned how to impose radical goals by taking over the streets have they eluded the mechanisms of control (integration/repression). Its answer has been given the ephemeral form of wildcat strikes that smash through the framework of reformist demands, or the creation of strike pickets that clash with the repressive forces.

Both the radicality of workers' struggles these last few years and the level of revolutionary violence have increased. And this is not an isolated fact, but the product of the whole preceding history. The workers' movement has seen how the organizations that declare themselves "party" and "vanguard," betrayed them and continue to betray them in order to conquer political power and enlist in the capitalist system.

Thus, it makes perfect sense to speak of a class strategy for the destruction of the capitalist productive system and the self-liberation of the exploited the world over.

This strategy has an anti-authoritarian character insofar as it rejects all lines that do not arise within the class itself. And the forms of self-organization the class adopts are nothing less than the logical consequence of this strategy.

All "revolutionary" experiences up until now have limited themselves to replacing the managers of Capital without destroying the system of capitalist production. In the so-called "socialist" countries, they continue to steal the surplus from the workers in the name of an abstract entity: The State.

The task, therefore, of all revolutionaries today is to reject all forms that are alien to their class and to participate in the self-organization of the class with the aim of totally destroying the system.

When the workers' cause has broken the reformist framework and spilled out into the street, the repressive forces have acted criminally, murdering workers. Faced with this situation, the most conscious militants take up arms in order to support and accelerate the revolutionary process.

The birth of these groups is nothing more than the class's partial response to capitalist violence. The development of the latest struggles has created an objective necessity for the appearance of these direct action groups that respond to the provocations of repression.

Today the battle lines are well drawn. On the one side, the system and all the reformist organizations that back it up, though they may use a pseudo-revolutionary language. On the other side, facing these two fronts, which are in fact a single enemy, the organizations that advocate self-organization and practice armed agitation (this concept must be understood on a political level, without falling into merely technical reductionism, as often happens).

The class strategy is a totality with various fields, and one of those is military. The groups today cannot map out a military strategy by themselves, as strategy is determined by historical circumstances; yet if the birth of the groups is indeed an expression of a historical necessity, we find ourselves situated within an apparent contradiction. That is to say that today, in the development of the struggles, there is no clarity regarding the military strategy of the class, and the non-existence of a military strategy is conditioned by the insufficient framework within which radical struggles develop. The fact that the wildcat strikes that break out are usually destined to fail is due to the current impossibility of generalizing the struggle.

Faced with this situation, the armed agitation groups adopt as a tactic the military strategy of the class that will generalize during insurrectionary periods.

Armed agitation, arising as a necessity from the development of the recent struggles, becomes the self-defense of the class, granting the possibility of an immediate response to the provocations of repression. Faced with organized capitalist violence at every turn, the only response can be revolutionary violence. And the refusal of every kind of imposition is expressed in the daily practice of the groups that practice armed agitation.

As such, the characteristics of armed agitation are:

1) Anti-authoritarian.

2) Capacity for immediate response.

3) Proletarian violence. Intensive and selective.

4) The objectives of armed agitation are those of the class itself. The tactic for reaching those objectives is not a fully defined whole, but rather something in constant evolution, because "men make history, but in circumstances not of their choosing."

5) The actions are dictated by events.

6) Permanent contact with sectors in struggle.

7) Development of a harmonious military and political practice.

8) Radicalization of the workers' struggle.

In general, the functions of armed agitation are:

A) Exhaustion of the forces of repression (military or otherwise).

B) Support for the nuclei of workers in struggle.

C) Strengthening and multiplication of the GAC (Armed Combat Groups).

We believe, and our experiences have demonstrated, that the development of the GAC, practically and politically, is impossible without a broad mass organization. The question is not to determine, right now, whether the concrete form of this organism should be self-organization, a union, etc., but rather its functions.

On this point, the groups are trained by their political practice to act as organs of political interpretation. In other words, the direct contact between the struggles and the practice of armed agitation makes possible an analysis of the development of the struggles of the workers' movement and with this movement and nothing else as their point of departure, the armed agitation groups can set themselves tactical objectives, identifying the needs of the revolutionary movement.

Who Can Revive a Corpse?

[...] March '73, no news, contact with the group is lost. There has not been continuity, because we are not supermen. With a relation based on actions we have wanted to open a rupture in the political world, and it is not enough. To think that we can resume actions without minimally elaborating our tactics is suicide. There has been a complete disconnection between the interior and the exterior, placing the interior in a situation of dependency that has turned into desperation as they lack the possibility for action given the reduced number of militants. This limbo has been negative, as they have lost their few options for political work and the drive that gave us our practice. The values have inverted, which is to say, the motor of any group is its field of action (Barcelona, in this case), whereas the exterior only has a purpose while work is being carried out in the field of action. The exterior turned into the decision-making center, but it had nothing to decide about, given that it did not have sufficient force, including numerically.

The question has two possible solutions. 1) An acceleration of individual action (Sabaté, Bonnot, Ravachol); or 2) The creation of a political infrastructure with the aim of maintaining contacts in the revolutionary movement and the political consolidation of a military group.

1) I do not agree with the first solution, the practice all-consuming, as even the pointedly political actions do not have a capacity to politically explain themselves nor to socialize their results. I do not think this point requires further discussion. We have all read about and, I believe, assimilated the insufficiencies of this kind of practice, which is the purest and most romantic, but experience shows it self-destructs, being dismembered by repression. Two approaches have coexisted within this experience (July '72–March '73). One functions as a politico-military group, at least in appearance. The other functions as a gang of delinquents (though they may be politicized on a personal level, on the group level they act just as I have described): the lack of

responsibility of the members, the lack of control over money, justifying any behavior (the attitude: "we are all military and those who aren't, aren't part of the group"), etc.

Which is the "good side" that justifies the six million expropriated pesetas? The role of full-time military members was mystified in order to justify all their caprices.[9] The obstinacy of letting all their members live off the funds demonstrates a political inadequacy, as they failed to see how to make use of and support individuals who are or could be valid on other levels.

2) At this moment I think it is more important to consolidate a political infrastructure (the political base), rather than focusing on grand military actions that we won't be able to reap the consequences of nor socialize the benefits of, given our lack of such a base.

I will try, then, to express my ideas and expound a planning process for the immediate future.

Armed agitation arises as a historical necessity within the anti-authoritarian strategy of the workers' movement for the destruction of the capitalist system of production. The politico-military groups seize this historical necessity, in counterrevolutionary periods like the present one, as a tactic to support and accelerate the revolutionary process towards the armed insurrectionary strike.

Armed agitation is an anti-authoritarian struggle against all impositions of any strategy alien to the proletarian movement. As such, it is anti-Leninist, it denies the need for a party to serve as the consciousness of the working class. Such a party replaces reality with its own will.

Armed agitation does not aim for the creation of an army, but rather supports and maintains the development of autonomous defense groups. Armed agitation is, therefore, the tactic of

---

9. Trans: "Military" here and in the prior paragraph refers to group members specialized in armed actions; "full-time" to the practice of paying their living expenses with group funds so they can dedicate themselves to their actions; the "other levels" are group members focusing on other activities, like the library. Salvador is criticizing, among other things, placing these other group members on a lower level.

politico-military groups with a capacity for immediate response to the provocations of repression and the ability to support and maintain the partial victories of the workers' movement.

The current economic situation of fluctuations between inflation, stabilization, and inflation (stagflation), permits the capitalist State to control the class struggle through integration (collective contracts, union representatives, etc.) or through repression (Ferrol, Vigo, Barcelona, Granada, Sant Adrià, etc.). At the same time, the parties and reformist groupuscules (PC-PSUC, BR, etc.) attempt to channel workers' struggles into reformist demands (horizontally integrated labor unions), sucking up to the system and converting themselves into mechanisms of integration. Only when the workers' movement has learned how to impose radical demands by taking over the streets have they eluded the mechanisms of control (integration/repression).

Therefore, we pose the question of how to break this control that permits the exploitation of man by man. The answer has been given in ephemeral form with wildcat strikes that break the framework of reformist demands, or the creation of strike pickets that confront the repressive forces (police, Guardia Civil).

How do we assure the continuity of this struggle? Currently, the wildcat strikes have not been able to generalize their struggle (Ferrol, Vigo), being appropriated by the reformist parties and groupuscules that, casting themselves as the "vanguard," find themselves in complete dissonance with reality.

It is evident that in the face of organized military repression (the police, Guardia Civil, the army, etc.), only a military organization (groups of armed agitation for now, popular militias in revolutionary periods) can respond with sufficient force. It is necessary to respond to capitalist violence with organized proletarian violence.

Nonetheless, the experiences on the Peninsula show that military groups either depend on some party (ETA, PCI), or they carry out a terrorist practice isolated from the mass movements (ARUM, FAC, etc.). This dynamic of dependence or isolation has caused a mistrust of armed action even among the most radical sectors of the workers' movement.

Specifically, on the topic of armed responses to repression in counterrevolutionary periods, the question arises of how revolutionary minorities can intervene in the class struggle.

As such, the armed struggle is not exclusive and the development and consolidation of autonomous combat groups is intimately related to the development of the workers' movement. How can these different dynamics be synchronized?

As their tactics are more intensive, the dynamic of the revolutionary minorities should be based on an analysis of the situation, which is to say, they cannot force an advance beyond what the actual movement permits. Historical revolutionary possibilities are created by events and not by the visionaries of the moment or false vanguards. I believe this point to be fundamental. So, actions are conditioned by events and the tactics of the armed groups must always focus on the development of the class struggle, and must create and strengthen contacts with different radical sectors in the revolutionary movement. It is not a relationship of dependence, but rather a direct relationship with the workers' movement.

Without the broad understanding and support of the revolutionary movement, the actions will be isolated. As such, it is necessary for military practice and political practice to develop in harmony.

***

We have to change the name of the GAC as this acronym already exists. It belongs to Grupos de Acción Carlista, a paramilitary organization that is part of the Assemblea de Catalunya and the Taula.[10]

***

The politico-military groups do not adhere to any specific label, they are neither static nor definitive. Their process exists in a direct relationship with the development of the workers' movement. This is by no means an opportunist doctrine, but rather a

---

10. Trans: An initiative for coordinating dissidents to the Franco regime, pre-dating the *Assemblea*.

way of orienting a set of principles with the goal of organizing a given labor, which does not exclude collaboration with organizations of a distinct ideological tenor for specific actions (organizations that accept armed struggle). I do not think that ideological differences should at all impede such joint actions, as military groups are committed to the daily revolutionary struggle. After all, it is not the groups that impose the organization of the workers' movement, but this movement that creates its organization. In the most recent strikes (SEAT, Ferrol, Vigo), the demands surpassed the political organizations, and the workers' movement left them behind (CCOO), creating its own organizational forms that, when they failed to generalize the struggle, were recuperated by those organizations (once again!).

As such, the action of the armed combat groups occurs in three fields:

1) Political.
2) Military.
3) Organization—infrastructure.

1) Political

—The elaboration of a strategy to be followed, arising from the development of the class struggle.

—Contacts with the radical sectors of the workers' movement.

—Work towards the unification of tactics and strategy among the different autonomous combat groups.

—Creation of a propaganda apparatus. Any revolutionary must have access to it. There should not exist an ideological unity, but rather a daily commitment to the struggle.

2) Military

—Capacity to respond to any provocation by the repression (trials, the murder of workers or militants, etc.)

—Selective and exemplary actions (attacks on police stations, armories, executions, etc.)

—Guerrilla attacks, withdrawing from frontal engagements.

—Exact knowledge of the possibilities of each group, for the purpose of not carrying out actions beyond our means. Currently, we are more developed militarily than politically. Actions that exceed the means of any group are not only a partial defeat of the revolutionary movement, but also a step backwards, as they isolate us from the masses.

—This danger shows itself to be most pronounced in the kidnapping actions. The experiences in the Basque Country (ETA) show that, politically and despite their technical success, they have impeded the struggle as a political process.

3) The guerrilla practice emphasizes, above all: 1) A high capacity for mobilization. 2) Surprise. 3) Knowledge of the terrain.

Gathering and assimilating previous experiences (Tupamaros, Brazil, Baader, etc.), the autonomous combat groups organize in cells of three to four people, self-sufficient in every way to assure not only their own security but the security of all the groups.

—Apartments (good exits, adequate weapons for their defense, hunting rifles, etc.).

—Spaces (for meetings, printing presses, storage, etc.).

—Cars, etc.

Therefore, my proposal for the following months is as follows:

1) Few actions, but selective, exemplary, and hard.

2) Political offensive. Explanation of our strategy, texts.

3) Creation of infrastructure that meets our needs.

We will only move forward if our development is harmonious not only in these three fields but also with the development of the class struggle. In any case, I believe tactics are fundamental, given that the autonomous combat groups cannot draw up their own strategy to follow, given that their very development is a direct consequence of the radicalization of the workers' struggles in particular and of the revolutionary movement in general.

So, there should be no improvisational actions, and this summer, as the level of struggle diminishes (vacations, etc.), our principal objective is to prepare for the coming year.[11] And

---

11. Trans: The members of the MIL are not going on vacation, but amidst the extreme heat of August, many businesses close down, many workers get their vacations, and social struggles tend to subside.

I will repeat, that only with a political infrastructure can we face the new horizons that are on everyone's minds, but it is not a question of willing certain things to happen, but rather facing the present realities.

Greetings

Prompt for Discussion

"Without a clear understanding of objectives and of the forces (including ideological forces) impeding advance— in short without a sense of history—the revolutionary struggle tends to become 'all movement and no direction.' Without clear perspectives, revolutionaries tend to fall into traps—or be diverted into blind alleys—which,with a little knowledge of their own past, they could easily have avoided." (M. Brinton, *The Bolsheviks and Workers' Control*. Collection El Viejo Topo—ed. Ruedo Ibérico).

The present text attempts to present a prompt for a discussion in which we might all elaborate together a strategy as an autonomous combat group.

1) Bossism. For me, there is a fundamental difference between bossism and leaders.[12] A leader is an individual who in a given moment knows how to correctly weigh the situation and takes the initiative. A boss is an individual who manages to keep the

---

12.   Trans: Puig Antich makes use of that unfortunate rhetorical habit of the Left in the '60s and '70s, identifying erroneous practices by taking a commonplace noun and tacking "ism" on the end. It is interesting that in the original, he uses the Spanish word for leader or boss, *jefe*, but uses the English word for leader, with that exoticism trying to signify a concept or a distinction that is hidden in the discourse of the dominant society.

entire infrastructure and apparatus under his control, so that he becomes indispensable, to which end he uses that secret trick of bureaucrats, the personal relation, never confronting the group as a whole, but trying to dominate the parts that constitute it.

If we go back in time, part of our history is conditioned by bossism, and it is no paradox that this coincides with the time when the fewest actions were carried out and the group was at its most disunited, consumed in internal disputes based on mistrust, differing tendencies, and supposed schisms.

This reflection is a product of last week, when I saw the scourge that paralyzes so many groups be reborn among you. One could point to the disorganization of the group, how individuals do not present clear positions, etc., all of which is true, but none of this should impede the comrades in the exterior from having clear relations, nor make it seem—and I hope this isn't the case—that the only thing they want from comrades in the interior is the infrastructure they possess. The bureaucratic secret, sabotaging attempts at discussion, scorning those who do not adhere to the correct label, has re-emerged after the recent drama, with some leaving and others storming out. What is truly dramatic is that they gave the same reasons for leaving the group and the same mistakes are being committed.

The fact that currently the group declares itself openly anarchist is nothing special, or is it that the entirety of our practice up to this point, correct or not, hasn't been anarchist? Our positions have been conditioned by action and not by supposed ideological purism. I do not understand, therefore, the discomfort of some of the comrades. In any case, I think that adhering to a label brings serious problems. If, for tactical reasons, we have declared ourselves to be anarchists, this does not have to imply a disdain for other comrades who work with us, accepting the validity of armed struggle. We are going to work together and I demand total clarity and trust between comrades.

2) Called bluff. We have spoken at great length about the isolation that tormented the group. I don't know to what extent it is correct to attempt to break this isolation handing out papers and ringing

doorbells. I do not deny the necessity of having contact with any organization, with an eye towards continuity, but on what basis? The head (the decision-making center) is being strengthened, but there is an important vacuum: THE ABSOLUTE LACK OF A BASE IN THE INTERIOR. We have lived through the consequences of making a play without the hand to back it up, and the price is high. I am not against keeping the decision-making center in the exterior if the purpose is to assure the continuity of the group, I am against playing with a strong hand that we do not have.

3) Past experience. We can ask ourselves the following question: why has our practice not inserted itself into the class struggle? On the one hand, there have not been any clearly political actions and only these have the possibility of demonstrating the effectiveness of the practice.[13] The actions were all expropriations and they did not go beyond the framework of immediate necessities. Therefore, the actions did not go beyond themselves and did not have any subsequent effect.

There have been no new GAC or we do not know about them (Mallorca). It is our practice itself that has isolated us.

Why the inability to intervene in specific moments like, for example, the Zaragoza trials?[14]

This inability to go beyond the level of immediatist actions is based on:

1) Lack of familiarity with the real situation.

2) Incoherence between politics and practice when we cannot fulfill all the responsibilities assumed out of an excess of volunteerism or triumphalism.

3) Mistrust among members.

---

13.   Trans: An expropriation serves to finance other activities, and the relation between such actions and the activities is not visible. A clearly political action would be some kind of sabotage or attack that intervened in an ongoing workers' struggle, and though the MIL directly supported those struggles, they, unlike the OLLA, did not end up carrying out such actions.

14.   Trans: One of many cases of repression against the movement in those years, though this trial did not result in death penalties.

4) Lack of tactical objectives (at the group level).

5) Overestimation of our strength.

6) Concentration of power in two individuals and the inhibition of the others.

I am not trying to sing a "mea culpa" nor get lost in a labyrinth trying to find explanations for everything, simply trying to not commit the same mistakes.

4) Armed agitation. Any acceleration of actions, if they are not attached to clearly defined objectives and our own limitations, would be to "go up against the wall" ("se faire casser la guele"). The results of subsequent stages will not improve just because we have separated from a comrade. It was necessary, but insufficient, and with a new dose of volunteerism, a consequence of the new situation.

The indispensable bases of a GAC are:

1) Their own tactics and strategy.

2) A direct, not dependent, relation with the radical sectors of the workers' movement.

The facts have demonstrated the invalidity of reformism, which has become a mere manager of capital within the working class, never exceeding the framework imposed by capital itself. The latest struggles (wildcat strikes) demonstrate an anti-authoritarian tendency with a strong increase in revolutionary violence. But it manifested as a response to the demands of the moment without any continuity. This is the source of the historical need for armed agitation, in the formation of autonomous combat groups capable of confronting repression in all its forms with proletarian violence.

The most important condition is the union (direct relation) between the guerrilla struggle and the economic and political struggles of the masses. The guerrilla conflict, as such, has no chance of developing if this relation does not become the essential nexus of the guerrilla practice.

To pose the question in terms of whether or not the armed struggle is necessary right now, is false. The armed struggle is a strategic objective of the class struggle; however, the revolutionary minorities take this objective as a tactic, in order to accelerate the revolutionary process and maintain the partial victories of the workers' movement. In this way, armed agitation as a tactical demand of the workers' movement corresponding to the present situation must be prepared to respond to repression in its distinct forms, without exiting the framework of the class struggle, as to do so would send it tumbling headlong towards other, false objectives.

The armed struggle is not exclusive, it must have a relation to the workers' sphere and the popular struggle.

Objectives:
1) Exhaustion of the forces of repression.
2) Support the radical struggles.
3) Support the creation of GAC in a way that tends towards their unification.
4) Creation of an information and propaganda apparatus.

Immediate objectives:
1) Complete infrastructure.
2) Expropriations.
3) Actions with explosives
4) Release of books—library.

Without a political base capable of explaining the actions carried out within a historical perspective, we will repeat past errors.

The actions are conditioned by events and not by any visionary of the moment.

I repeat that the purpose of this text is to provoke discussion, clear and sincere, between comrades, however... The Movimiento (Ibérico de Liberación) demonstrates itself by the path it takes.

Anarchist greetings

"Terrible" History, December 1972–July 1973

End of December 1972

Political positioning is surpassed by the radicalization of practice, as an armed agitation group without a capacity for political analysis.

We won't get into criticisms of bossism, etc. right now, which is nothing more than political inability plus a strong dose of subjectivism. Why? My personal opinion is that all the contacts we had were to justify our practice and not to help and support the different radical sectors in struggle. And on the internal level, there was an immediatism, carrying out actions to get out of our predicament, but on the other hand the problem also existed on a political level, our positions, the self-interested justifications that took precedence over an objective analysis of the situation of the proletarian movement. It should be underscored that from once we disencumbered ourselves of a certain comrade, we were capable of expressing—at a very low level, of course—our political position or line (as far as a representative text of reference for the group, in this period there is only the text by M.[15] I suggest the critical analysis of this text, as a simple political explanation the concepts are much more clear).

January–March 1973

Rupture with one individual, which signifies the rupture with a certain political practice, or in this case non-practice.

A text is authored in which we define ourselves negatively. Speaking plainly: we knew what we did not want, but we did not know exactly what we did want, or at the least there was an inability, product of the prior encumbrance, to express ourselves positively.

---

15.   Trans: "Montes," or Ignasi Solé Sugranyes.

Armed agitation. Direct, non-dependent relation, anti-Leninism, anti-groupusculism, self-defense, insurrectional strike, proletarian-revolutionary violence, anti-totalitarianism, etc. These are the concepts that, though they are insufficiently explained, delineate our political practice. One notices a will to elaborate these concepts but it is excessively theoretical. This first text is lacking a historical reference to the practice of these concepts; thus we can see that on the practical military level we continue to focus on immediate necessities, not knowing how—or not being able—to move beyond this stage due to a lack of clear political objectives.

In March of 1973, the rupture with M. is complete as far as joint practice goes; nonetheless, one comrade maintains contact with him for two reasons. 1) At the time, it was thought that a dismemberment of the group would be a failure in the task we had set ourselves. 2) Breaking out of our isolation was considered to be vital, and he as an individual had a series of contacts (the Basque, the OLLA groupuscules, etc.) that could help us.

Nonetheless, our practice was more radical than our positions. The action at Fabra i Puig was simultaneously the burial of the previous stage and a confrontation with the actual political and military reality.

Two positions opposed each other, and on this basis came to a common agreement: it was necessary to celebrate a congress to clarify our practice. However, they differed on the proper place for the meeting. Now, with five months of hindsight, I think holding the congress in the exterior was the correct decision, but at its root what was really being proposed was a power play between the two tendencies. The boycott imposed by the exterior tendency, frankly, produced positive results as it destroyed any possibility for maneuvers.[16]

All the thinking inherent in this position (Sebas–Sancho) came to light in April and May. It should be established that during this time, all the interior-exterior contacts were cut.

16.   Trans: In other words, it was such a patent manipulation that it helped bring about the dissolution of the group rather than allowing the Tolosa sector to maintain their hegemony within a false consensus.

Perhaps due to different strategic framings of the struggle, or perhaps, by defect, due to the disdain the exterior exhibited to the comrades in the interior, a disdain which signified political mistrust.

As such, the exterior initiates a political adventure with three aspects.

—Propaganda: CIA no.1.

—Political contacts: the French ultra-left.

—Library (I think this point requires its own investigation, given its political importance and history).

Propaganda: two pamphlets are written, one of which asserts our practice and the other of which consists of slogans.

***

I will try to summarize:

1) Library.

2) Armed struggle. Political foundations. Current possibilities. Strategy and tactics.

Library. To make this task easier, I will divide this topic into its different components.

A) Workers.

B) Technical-military.

C) Intellectual.

1) What are its origins? It is the product of a group of individuals, going back three years, who carried out a fundamentally theoretical practice.

The objectives of the library are as follows:

1) Fill in the theoretical vacuum.

2) Create a free platform.

3) Unite forces.

4) A bridge between different levels of the current movement.

5) Independence of the different levels. What unites them is revolutionary practice and not an organization unification.

The objectives identified, for me, are strategic. It is easy to imagine the eminently political difficulty in achieving these objectives.

Are the motives for our inability exogenous? I don't think so, although certain vices, product of an entire history, slow us down in overcoming the inability. But the delay is not solely and exclusively due to this history, though it has certainly come to mandate said delay. As exogenous factors we can identify the following:

1) Conditions proposed by the workers' sphere threaten a rupture if certain individuals participate. The interests, or better yet the personal sympathies, are prioritized over the duty all of us have imposed on ourselves, not as educators of the people, which would be to fall in the errors of Leninism, but in the role already spelled out in other texts, sufficiently expressed and critiqued.

2) Difficulty with direct contact, strict security measures that are required by the ruling system and the demands of clandestine struggle. This does not impede the publishing of texts, but...

It is not an act of prophecy or the insight of a visionary to say that unity has been maintained thanks to the absolute will of the group's members to carry out our task (though distribution automatically became the library's territory). As a military member, can I finance a publication that betrays my principles to conquer positions of strength as well as prestige?[17]

We define as revolutionary or communist (not at all in the Western, orthodox sense of the word, but in its more pure essence) the entirety of the movement that cannot be integrated into the system. Every wildcat strike that breaks with the limitations of the union, every group that does not try to barter its actions for future positions of prestige or political power, every

---

17. Trans: The phrasing of the question is jumbled; what was at issue was military members who expropriated the finances imposing criteria on what should be published or distributed by the library, furthermore placing the interests of the military group ahead of the interests of the working class, which the library should be representing.

intellectual whose work is delineated by the real movement, the proletarian movement.

The incomplete, negative definition has too many limitations and is difficult to apply to a socio-historical context. Therefore, we define as communist or real that movement that after an analysis of the current situation acts out of historical necessity. The defining characteristic is to not alter the course according to individual or group needs. The movement is not created, the movement is and it cannot be stopped (to use a graphic example).

I believe it is the moment to analyze, to elucidate, what the three spheres consist of, as well as the strategic objectives that have been set and the current practice. I should begin by clarifying that classifying the library as its own sphere is arbitrary and serves only to facilitate understanding the different components.

The description of each sphere can already be found in its name, so the question is: how to give each sphere its political content and to create the forms of interrelation between each sphere?

There are three points everyone agrees on:

1) Only the most radical sectors have access to and participate in the library's decisions.

2) Precisely due to this radicality, we are against any reification, whether it be political, ideological, organizational, etc.

3) There is a theoretical vacuum in all the radical movements. This shortcoming will not be "solved" by the library. I think all of us agree that theory must be conceived as a movement (when it is reified it turns into ideology).

As far as I understand, those are the three points everyone agrees on, and that's what keeps us united to give birth to this work.

Rather than analyzing the near future from a situation of strength, I think it is more valid to do so on a basis of caution and taking into account the political content of the different spheres that participate.

Objectives.

1) Fill in the theoretical vacuum, the task of every revolutionary. The question becomes delicate when we ask how to fill this void. It is the task of every person and every collective to improve the way they overcome their problems and difficulties, which is to say, the library's objective is to present to the public a series of works that would otherwise never spread widely due to well known causes. These are published as a self-imposed duty by the revolutionaries themselves in order to make them better known. Every individual will make use of them according to their ability and situation.

Perhaps I frequently warn of the danger that the library comes to be dominated by a single way of thinking, which would result, without a doubt, in the reification of our theory. The danger is there and always will be.

In order to be able to express all revolutionary thought, the second objective is included:

2) Free platform. Free insofar as any revolutionary can express themselves without obstacles. What is important is not to be in agreement with everything that is published, but for there to be channels and a capacity for expressing revolutionary theory.

3) Unite forces. This becomes a tactic and a strategy at the same time. Generally, individuals define themselves negatively, which is to say they know what they do not want but not what they do want. The library serves the purpose, defining it positively, of accelerating the regrouping of the forces of the extreme left that today are isolated and fragmented, not offering them an organization in this case but the theoretical means, which does not exclude the material they might need to organize the dispersed forces.

4) For all these reasons, it can serve as a bridge for coordination among all the forces of the left.

The consequential question, then, is the following: does situating oneself, at least theoretically, above the groups and organizations have a real chance of achieving this objective or is it the "queen," untouchable, standing above the misery of daily life?

If what is important now is for the library to create situations of strength (via distribution), it will never achieve the selected objective, it will only do so as an open and evolutionary entity. That is the question.

5) Independence of spheres that constitute the library. It is overly idyllic to propose organizational questions when this has no chance of existing. Beyond being committed in this task, each sphere carries out a struggle that their own situation frames and materializes. This is the root of the specialization of the different functions and, simultaneously, means that each sphere is a collectivity that develops a practice in its own field. (I don't know how to explain it very clearly).

Currently, the library has been directed by the intellectuals and on their periphery, the workers' sphere participates "from a distance" with infrequent incursions to propose some title that might interest them. The "machine" will function fully when the first books become a reality.

The most confused role has been that played by the military-technical sphere. Not being defined as a politico-military group, it is completely impossible to have a clear position in relation to the library. Naturally, the problem is much bigger, but at a minimum, these past months have demonstrated the falsity of altruistic positions that, to top it off, were triumphalist.[18]

Is it prudent for a military group to present itself as the supporter of a library, even at the material level? No. Aside from giving the sensation that it exercises total control (which is simply not true), it would provoke... [fragment]

In this first issue, we present various texts on experiences of armed agitation, in order to extract the consequences and assimilate the teachings these experiences offer. There is a constant in

---

18. Trans: Here, Puig Antich means that the attitude of the group specializing in armed actions towards the group running the library was almost one of charity, generously providing the necessary financing, when in fact that was their duty and their function; and that even though this group was in a morass without a clear theory or practice, they acted as though their actions were the most heroic, the most important, and as though they had the right to dictate how the money should be spent.

all of them and it is the relation between a revolutionary minority and a revolutionary movement.

1) Revolutionary minorities—Revolutionary Movement.

2) Armed agitation—armed struggle.

***

Autonomous combat groups emerge as a historical necessity of the anti-authoritarian strategy in the proletarian movement. This anti-authoritarian strategy has arisen in workers' struggles (wild-cat strikes) in which workers' demands backed up by the struggle in the streets has surpassed all the proposals of political parties and groupuscules. The examples are innumerable (Ferrol, Vigo, Bandas de Echevarri, Harry Walker, May '68). It is the proletariat in struggle that proposes the organizational forms capable of striving for the proposed objectives (anti-authoritarian strategy) and not the political parties and groupuscules, trying to impose a kind of organization that is a product of their own ideological assumptions (authoritarian strategy).

***

We have left legality behind to carry out actions in the terrain of illegality, which is the only path to the revolution. It is necessary to "to utilize all the means that are in conformity with this objective" (IWPA 1881).[19]

The proletariat is illegal.

We are radicalized workers.

Develop tactics [as part of the working class], not as a specific group.

We must know how to use all the weapons possible.

***

19. Trans: The International Working People's Association, or "Black International," formed by anarchist delegates in 1881, four years after the dissolution of the St. Imier International.

Nonetheless, all the experiences up until the present moment have not been able to generalize the struggle, as they were all ephemeral responses and were not able to use all the means necessary to accomplish their objectives. As such, faced with the organized repression of Capital (police, *Guardia Civil*, army), it is only possible to respond through self-organization, which is to say confronting the violence of Capital with revolutionary violence.

***

Nonetheless, a series of vices acquired in past experiences must be eradicated.

The capacity to make an immediate response is the basis of armed agitation, given that in a period of counterrevolution, actions have to be responses to the provocations of repression, or provocation in particularly difficult moments.

This political task materializes when supporting and accelerating the radical and spontaneous movements that arise. Actions become the means for materialization of a defined tactic. The library must convert itself into a political weapon usable by and for the anti-authoritarian strategy. If our practice is radical, the library must be radical, too. We are not exhibiting some texts as though in a marketplace; we are only distributing texts that serve to generalize the struggle. A bulletin is also necessary, whether weekly or monthly, for information and constant debate. The tactic to follow is not to create a political position that represents a step backward in our labors, accepting the rules of a political game. On the contrary, our tactics must consist of being present in the streets and in the struggle.

14.

Glossary

In Catalan and Spanish, people receive two last names, both the paternal and the maternal. In the example of Salvador Puig Antich, "Puig" is not a middle name, but the first surname; alphabetically, Salvador Puig Antich would be located under "P."

Arnau, Oriol: a social movement lawyer who represented Salvador Puig Antich against the charges that resulted in his death penalty.

Assemblea de Catalunya: a unified platform of opposition to the Franco regime that existed from 1971 to 1977, the Assembly of Catalunya included parties, unions, and other organizations from the pro-democratic right-wing, center, and left. The most important sectors were Catalan nationalists like Jordi Pujol, progressive elements of the Church, and the Communist-controlled socialist party PSUC. It was this latter sector that was hegemonic within the Assembly. The three points of its program were liberty, meaning an end to the dictatorship; amnesty, meaning freedom for political prisoners but not for social prisoners or any resistance members who had carried out actions that would also be crimes under democracy; and a statute for Catalan autonomy under a new democratic government.

The Assembly played a key role in legitimizing the smooth transition from fascism to democracy, neutralizing the sectors that favored a complete rupture with the old regime, or even the dissolution of the Spanish state into its constituent national groups, in favor of the "Statute for Autonomy" for Catalunya within a renewed Spanish state. After achieving major electoral victories in 1977, the dominant sectors had the Assembly dissolved, against the wishes of those sectors who favored some kind of rupture with fascism.

autogestion: standard fare in Italian, French, Catalan, Spanish, and Portuguese, this concept is increasingly being used in

English to refer to a collective that meets its own functional needs rather than relying on government support or being dependent on other institutional resources over which it has no control. An autogestioned social center does not rely on government subsidies to stay open; an autogestioned factory horizontally organizes its own supply and distribution. There is both overlap, and a great difference in nuance, between autogestion, self-organization (a collective that structures itself, free of the dominance of any institution), and autonomy (a collective that sets its own laws or norms, from *avto* and *nomos*, "self" and "law").

Autonomia Operaia: "Workers' Autonomy" in Italian, a network of autonomous, extreme left and anti-authoritarian groups active in Italy in the 1970s that fought against the government, the capitalist class, and also the PCI, the Italian Communist Party, that sought to dominate and pacify the workers' movement. There were many connections between this and the Catalan autonomous movement.

avingunda: "avenue" in Catalan.

Baiona: known internationally as Bayonne, a coastal city in the French-occupied part of the Basque country.

Barcelona: the capital of Catalunya and one of the largest cities in the Spanish state, as well as its chief industrial city. Neighborhoods of Barcelona mentioned in the book, or towns absorbed into the metropolitan area, include Badalona, Clot, Cornellà, Eixample, Gràcia, Guinardó, Sant Adrià del Besòs, Sarrià, Vallcarca, and la Verneda. Tibidabo is a small mountain that overlooks the city, and also the name for the surrounding neighborhood and an amusement park located there.

Carlist: the *carlins* were supporters of an alternative branch of the Bourbon dynasty that has supplied the Spanish state with its monarchs for much of the nineteenth and twentieth centuries. Described as an ultra-conservative political current, one of the most interesting things about the Carlists is how their politics predate and confound the typical framework of left and right arising with the liberal French Revolution at the end of the eighteenth century. Their original leader, Carlos V, favored a less centralized Spanish state, and their motto was "God, Fatherland, *Furs*, and King." The third term, all but untranslatable in English, refers to the prior, far more complicated property regime and localized law code of feudalism, in which commodity property rights do not exist, but rather, every piece of land is tied into a complex web of inalienable use rights: the commons. As such, the main supporters of Carlism were not only the middle and lower levels of Church hierarchy or regional power holders, who all would be diminished by the concentration of power in a centralized Spanish state, but above all the peasants, for whom liberalism was a death sentence.[1] As such, Carlism was strongest in the parts of the Spanish state with an independent national reality, like Euskal Herria and the Catalan countries, particularly València, and areas where peasants had had some successes in defending the commons, like the Pyrenees.

In the nineteenth century, there were several Carlist insurrections against the dominant State. In 1936, Carlists supported Franco's coup against the Second Republic in the hopes of bringing back their preferred monarchy and putting an end to the hated liberal regime, but they were quickly sidelined. Towards the end of the Franco dictatorship, the Carlists joined the opposition, including the Assemblea de Catalunya, and a large part of the movement became federalist and autonomous socialist.

carrer: "street" in Catalan.

---

1   On how liberalism and its private property regime has led to the erasure of the very vocabulary used in describing and organizing the commons, see Peter Linebaugh, *The Magna Carta Manifesto*, 2008. For one example of how liberal revolutions engaged in genocidal warfare against the peasants, and how peasants opposed these revolutions not out of conservatism or "backwardness" but due to their own intelligent interests in defending the commons, see Peter Kropotkin, *The Great French Revolution*, 1909.

Carrero Blanco, Luis: (1904–1973) An ultra-conservative from a long line of military officers, Carrero Blanco climbed the ranks during the Civil War to lead the operations of Franco's navy. He eventually became Franco's righthand man and attained the rank of admiral. Franco groomed him to be his successor, and appointed him head of state in June 1973. The Basque independence group ETA, however, had other plans, and they dug a tunnel under the street that was on Carrero Blanco's weekly route to church, filled it with explosives, and assassinated him in December of that same year. The explosion was so powerful, Carrero Blanco's car flew more than a hundred feet high over the surrounding buildings, landing in the courtyard on the other side. This prompted jokes that the Admiral had really always wanted to be a pilot and finally saw his dream come true.

Carrillo, Santiago: (1915–2012) Member of the Communist Party, Councilor for Public Order in the Madrid government during the Civil War, and Secretary General of the Communist Party from 1956 to 1982, he was a major proponent and architect of the reconciliation with the fascists that led to the Transition. As such, he was a key figure in the Communist policy of pacifying and institutionalizing the strike movement, and tacitly supporting the repression of autonomous sectors and militants like Puig Antich. In 1976, he returned from exile and staged his own arrest in order to raise his profile as a political prisoner. The following year, negotiating with the head of the fascist government in transition, he achieved the legalization of the Communist Party, was elected to Congress, and took part in drafting the new Constitution.

Catalan countries, Catalunya: The *Països Catalans* or "Catalan countries" are the four countries where some version of the Catalan language is spoken: Catalunya Nord, now under French domination; the *Principat* or simply Catalunya, under Spanish domination but with a fair amount of autonomy; the Balearic Isles; and València. The Catalan countries were a distinct political entity in alliance with the Kingdom of Aragón through most of the Middle Ages, coming definitively under the domination of the centralizing French and Spanish states in the seventeenth and eighteenth centuries, respectively.

It can be helpful to problematize the liberal commonplace that "separatist" movements occur in the richest regions of a country, a view that naturalizes the myth-making of liberal nation-states. In fact, the richest region of the Spanish state is Madrid, and the countries with strong independence movements are not only Euskadi and Catalunya (wealthier than the average), but also València and Galicia (one of the poorest).

The Catalan bourgeoisie for most of the twentieth and twenty-first centuries has tended towards a consensus on favoring greater autonomy within the Spanish state rather than independence, though of course it has exerted a great deal of influence on the independence movement; a large part of that movement has been rural and working class. In València, in contrast, the political and economic elite is Spanish-speaking, whereas the independence movement tends to be rural and working class.

In the time period examined in this book, there were numerous armed groups that were both anticapitalist and in favor of Catalan independence, whereas the Catalan bourgeoisie was instrumental in legitimizing the Transition and sabotaging the independence movement in favor of a compromise with the fascist Spanish state.

CCOO: *Comissions Obreres* (Workers' Commissions), founded definitively in Madrid in 1964 on the basis of earlier experiences of workers' commissions, its first formations were in Madrid, Asturias, the Basque country, and Barcelona. The Comissions Obreres began as workplace assemblies—especially in factories as well as the mining and construction sectors—that federated through committees of elected delegates. In their beginnings, they approached the experience of workers' councils, and arose as a tool for the organization of wildcat strikes and solidarity among workers. Quickly, different political formations tried to control the Comissions, with the Communist Party achieving hegemony around 1968, though it was only between 1973 and the organization's legalization in 1977 that it was effectively transformed into just another bureaucratic union and a direct tool of the Communists.

It is currently the largest labor union in the Spanish state, and not considered by anticapitalists to be a part of the workers' movement. For example, in general strikes, the CCOO and UGT must hold separate events, as they are booed and kicked out of demos by the other strikers due to their systematic practice of approving austerity measures and other deals that hurt workers.

CGT: *Confédération Générale du Travail* (General Labor Confederation), a French labor union that was originally anarcho-syndicalist, though by the 1970s was only moderately on the left. After the events described in this book, an unrelated CGT was also created in the Spanish state, arising from a split in the anarcho-syndicalist CNT.

CNS: *Central Nacional Sindicalista* (National Labor Central), a "vertical labor union" and the only legal labor organization under the Franco regime from 1940–1976, the CNS was initially controlled by the Falange to discipline Spanish workers and stamp out any autonomous labor movement, which before the Civil War had been largely anarchist in character.

CNT: *Confederación Nacional del Trabajo* (National Labor Confederation), an anarcho-syndicalist confederation of labor unions founded in 1910 that was central to the revolutionary movements in the Spanish state through 1936, when it played a key role in defeating the fascist military coup. Subsequently, CNT leaders gave their support to the antifascist government, revealing a bureaucratization that had produced a disconnection between effectively permanent delegates and the organization's rank and file. From there, most of the organization became increasingly conservative and immobilist.

COPEL: *la Coordinadora de Presos en Lucha* (Coordinator of Prisoners in Struggle), a group of anticapitalist, largely anarchist prisoners who launched a powerful struggle in 1976, that continued into the '80s. They demanded a general amnesty for all prisoners and a drastic improvement of conditions in the prison system, also organizing several prison rebellions.

The democracy in transition responded by accepting a watered-down version of some of their reforms in 1979, while also developing the FIES, probably the most brutal regime of isolation and punishment in any European prison system. In parallel, the government passed its Amnesty Law in 1977, only granting amnesty to those defined as political prisoners, which meant that those who had engaged in expropriations or armed actions against the fascist regime, and those not connected to a major political party, were left in prison: these prisoners were disproportionately anarchists.

Several members of the COPEL were assassinated or tortured to death, while many others were killed more slowly, with bad conditions and indefinite prison terms that went beyond the legal limits. Over the last dozen years, the anarchist movement has won the release of several veterans of the COPEL through strong campaigns of pressure, legal motions, and sabotage.

dirigism: a vanguardist and statist tendency in which the government directs the economy and until such time as the Party takes over the government, it closely controls the movement and the workers' organizations.

Ediciones Mayo del 37: (May '37 Editions), a publishing project organized by the MIL. The name references the date in the Civil War when the antifascist parties—principally the Stalinist-controlled Socialist Party and the Catalan left-nationalist ERC—openly attacked the anarchists and the collectivized workplaces. This onslaught put an end to the revolutionary period of the Civil War, accelerated the suppression of collectives and communes, and opened the way for an unbridled repression of all active anarchists and dissident Marxists on the antifascist side.

entryism: the tactic, typically used by Trotskyists, of entering a larger organization in a coordinated way, without revealing one's political affiliations or affinities, to try to sway or take over the organization from within. In the late '60s and '70s in the Spanish state, this strategy referred primarily to activists entering the CNS, the legal vertical union of the Franco regime. This was the method advocated by the dominant Communist sector in Comissions Obreres.

ERC: *Esquerra Republicana de Catalunya* (Republican Left of Catalunya), a leftwing political party founded in 1931 that played a large role in the Civil War, was illegalized under the Franco regime, and was also active before and during the Transition. It has frequently led the semi-autonomous regional government of Catalunya.

Euskal Herria, Euskera: The Basque country and the Basque language, respectively. *Euskadi* is also used, typically to denote the "autonomous community" within the Spanish state, consisting of the provinces of Guipuzkoa, Bizkaia, and Araba. Historically and culturally, the Basque country, however, also includes Nafarroa (Navarra), split off by the Spanish state as a separate region, and Lapurdi (Labourd) and Xiberoa (Soule), ruled by France.

ETA: *Euskadi ta Askasatuna* (Basque Country and Freedom), an armed clandestine organization that fought from 1959 to 2011 for a socialist Basque State independent from Spain and France. It was an important part of the resistance against fascism, carrying out attacks against the police forces and economic elite, as well as assassinating Franco's second-in-command. It was one of the organizations that refused to negotiate with the fascist regime and rejected the new Spanish Constitution, designed to allow a smooth transition from fascism to democracy. It was subsequently declared a terrorist organization by most Western governments. In fact, democratic Spain was one of the principal countries to develop the repressive strategies adopted by the US much later as "the War on Terror," with anti-terrorism being a key mechanism by which democratic governments selectively bring to bear the "state of exception" doctrine fundamental to fascism.

There were several schisms in the organization's history. One of these was ETA-VI Assembly, named after the organization's 6th Assembly, held in 1970 in Baiona, at which the majority decided that the military wing should be subordinated to the anti-capitalist workers' struggle. The military wing refused to accept the decision and broke off, though the new faction eventually regained control of the whole organization, putting end to any possibility of a truly anticapitalist, internationalist practice and converting ETA into little more than an authoritarian military group. VI Assembly, on the other hand, was a mix of authoritarian and anti-authoritarian currents, though the former predominated. It was with ETA-VI that the MIL maintained a relation.

ETA had strong popular support not only in the Basque Country but also in Catalunya until it fell into a spiral of increasingly specialized and terroristic actions, most significantly the placing of an explosive at a supermarket in a working class Barcelona neighborhood in 1987, under the naïve belief the police would deactivate the bomb if alerted. Twenty-one people were killed.

Thousands of Basque people were arrested and tortured by the Spanish government, some of them killed, in its campaign of repression. Under the democracy, the judicial system declared that any person who favored Basque independence and committed an illegal act—like an unpermitted protest—could be prosecuted as a member of ETA, even if they had no relation with the group. In 1983, the Socialist government formed the GAL, a paramilitary group that carried out assassinations, torture, and acts of terrorism against supporters of Basque independence, killing at least 23 people.

Disarming in 2011, ETA dissolved definitively in 2018.

FAC: *Front d'Alliberament de Catalunya* (Liberation Front of Catalunya), a Marxist-Leninist armed group founded in 1969 to fight for an independent, socialist Catalan state. The FAC carried out over one hundred attacks, though in 1973 its politics and structure changed under Maoist and Trotskyist influences and its focus shifted away from armed actions. It disappeared in 1977.

FAI: *Federación Anarquista Ibérica* (Iberian Anarchist Federation), a federation of anarchist affinity groups founded in 1927 in València, to promote and coordinate anarchist actions and also to prevent reformist syndicalists from taking over the CNT, an objective they helped achieve in 1932. (It is noteworthy that the reformist syndicalists did not form a labor union of their own after leaving or being expelled from the CNT, and instead formed a political party, lending credence to the criticism that their leaders were professional bureaucrats more than labor organizers).

However, in 1936, the FAI merged with the CNT in a sort of pro-government bureaucracy, led by authoritarian intellectuals like Frederica Montseny and Diego Abad de Santillán, subsequently acting as a counterrevolutionary force.

Falange: Falange Española, a Spanish fascist political party founded in 1933 and existing in different forms until the present day, the Falange adopted the basic positions of Mussolini: a fierce animosity towards anarchist and Marxist movements, totalitarianism, a corporativist organization of the State, patriarchal social organization, and a revanchist imperialism: in their case adopting the Islamophobic "Reconquest" ideology. The Falange formed an important part of the movement that backed General Franco's coup attempt, serving as paramilitaries during the early days of the Civil War and quickly integrating into the government, with Franco assuming direct leadership of the organization in 1937.

After the war, it was instrumental in organizing support for the regime and organizing the "vertical unions" that would be used to control the workers and prevent the reemergence of any workers' movement.

FC Barcelona: Also known as "Barça," Barcelona's football club, it has historically had a working class and somewhat more rebellious fan base. During the Civil War, the fascists executed the club president and the players collectivized the club; most of them subsequently fled into exile. Symbolically, the Real Madrid club has always been the team of the regime, as well as FC Barcelona's longtime nemesis.

FIJL: *Federación Ibérica de Juventudes Libertarias* (Iberian Federation of Libertarian Youth), the federation of anarchist youth organizations throughout the Spanish state founded in 1932, during the Civil War they were consistently more radical than the CNT leadership, and organized the first waves of resistance to the Franco regime, even before the beginning of World War II. To name one example, due to the fierce resistance organized by the local anarchist youth, it was not until ten years after the fall of Barcelona that the fascist police dared enter the especially proletarian ghetto in the Clot neighborhood that Ricard de Vargas hails from.

In February 1937, the FIJL had 82,000 members.

Franco, General Francisco: (1892–1975) Career officer in the Spanish military, Franco was active in the wars against Spain's African colonies in the early-twentieth century, and assigned by the Republican government to repress the workers' insurrection in Asturias in October 1934. In July 1936, he was one of the principal instigators of the military coup, assuming supreme control over the Nationalist side in October of that year and subsequently converting himself into the dictator of Spain until his death.

Much to the shame of antifascists and revolutionaries the world over, he died peacefully in his bed in November 1975. No one in his regime was ever punished for organizing the murder of hundreds of thousands of political dissidents (except via illegal direct action), and his family members are still extremely wealthy. Until 2019, Franco was buried in the massive monumental complex, the Valley of the Fallen, erected under the dictatorship to honor the fascists who died in the war. In 2019, the Socialist government had his corpse moved out of the monumental site, transporting it and reburying it with full honors in the lavish family cemetery.

FRAP: *Frente Revolucionario Antifascista y Patriota* (Revolutionary Antifascist and Patriot Front), a clandestine armed struggle organization created by the Communist Party in 1973 and dissolved by the same in 1978, the group carried out attacks against the fascist repressive forces calculated to push the regime towards negotiating a transition to democracy.

FOC: *Front Obrer de Catalunya* (Workers' Front of Catalunya) was a socialist, anti-imperialist, anti-Stalinist founded in 1961 and dissolved in 1971.

GAC: *Grups Autònoms de Combat* (Autonomous Combat Groups) anti-authoritarian, anticapitalist armed groups, when capitalized, the acronym usually refers to the group created by the MIL, and in lower case can also refer to other autonomous combat groups, like those the Spanish police designated the OLLA. There were also the Grups Autònoms, the decentralized autonomous groups that arose a little later and continued to fight throughout the Transition.

GARI: *Grupos de Acción Revolucionaria Internacionalista* (Internationalist Revolutionary Action Groups), armed anticapitalist groups that took action primarily in France, founded in 1973 by ex-members of the MIL like Jean-Marc Rouillan, as well as other anticapitalist revolutionaries.

Garriga Paituví, Xavier: member of the Forces Socialistes Federals between 1966 and 1968, then active in Comissions Obreres, he was a member of the MIL, where he had the alias "Carlos" or "the Secretary." He was arrested in the same ambush as Salvador Puig Antich.

***garrot vil*:** a form of execution used widely in the Spanish state during and before the Franco dictatorship, by which the condemned is strapped to a chair with a metal hoop put around their throat, and the executioner tightens a wheel or lever at the back of the hoop, slowly driving a screw into the back of the condemned person's neck until their spine is broken.

Generalitat: the seat of the semi-autonomous Catalan government.

gitana/gitano: an ethnic group that has inhabited the Iberian Peninsula for centuries, subjected to much racism and economic marginalization, but also occasionally honored for their cultural attributes, for example the development of flamenco. English-speakers might tend to name them "Roma" or "Romani," but this label does not come from gitana communities themselves and is inaccurate, as there are important cultural and linguistic differences between gitanos and Roma peoples who have immigrated to Spain in recent decades.

GOA: *Grupos Obreros Autónomos* (Autonomous Workers' Groups), an anticapitalist formation in the autonomous movement that arose from the Circles for the Training of Cadres in March 1971 and was led by José Antonio Díaz and Manuel Murcia, the GOA had relatively close relations with the MIL.

grupuscle, grupusculització: part of the vocabulary of 1970s dissident Marxism in the Spanish state, the concept of a groupuscule is barely current in English, and I could not find its derivatives, groupusculism and groupusculization, in any dictionary. It refers to a small, factious, formal political group; not merely a project within a movement that might be able to work with other initiatives, but essentially a sect with its own separate identity and usually with vanguardist aspirations. The derivatives refer, respectively, to a practice or ideology that leads to the creation of such groupuscules, and to the fragmentation that occurs in a movement with the proliferation of such groupuscules. A key element of the internal debate in the MIL was that the organization rejected groupuscules but in a way had begun to turn into one.

grey: slang for cops during the Franco regime, referring to their grey uniforms.

Guardia Civil: (Civil Guard), a military police force particularly active in political repression and control of rural areas during the Franco era, the force still exists today.

libertarian: a synonym for "anarchist." The word has only taken on the meaning of "liberal capitalist" in a handful of countries where the distortion of political speech is particularly pronounced, like the US (a country where, incidentally, "liberal" has come to mean "progressive," when it actually refers to a position that favors individual liberties in the Enlightenment sense, private property, and free markets). The original usage of the word "libertarian" can be traced to France, where it was invented as a way to get around government censors when use of the word "anarchist" would ensure the prohibition of a newspaper or other publication. Nowadays, it can be seen as a slightly broader term, also including those who would eschew a specific ideological identity like "anarchist."

Incidentally, any language enthusiast knows that slippage and change are inherent to word definitions; nonetheless, in the English language in particular, this process has been hijacked by the media, especially reactionary segments thereof, to deliberately hide and distort meaning and make reasoned debate impossible. As such, conscientious people need to resist it and fight for a historically faithful or at least lucid usage of politically charged words.

Lotta Continua: (Continuous Struggle), a network of extreme left, autonomous, anticapitalist groups that formed in Torino, Italy, towards the end of 1969. Lotta Continua arose from the student movement and radical factory struggles, created social centers and a newspaper, and engaged in combative actions. They centralized between 1972 and 1974, and disbanded in 1976.

maquis: originally a French word referring to rural guerrilla bands in the anti-Nazi Resistance, many of them were Spanish, Basque, and Catalan exiles who brought the term back with them in 1945 when launching a new wave of resistance against the Franco regime. While in many parts of the Spanish state, *maquis* came from a wide variety of political currents, in Catalunya the only *maquis* to take action were anarchists. The Catalan *maquis* consisted of thousands of combatants and supporters who carried out actions of propaganda, sabotage, assassinations, and support for the anticapitalist movement. They were especially active between 1945 and 1949, though the last Catalan *maqui*, Ramon Vila Capdevila, remained active until he was shot down in 1963.

MIL: *Movimiento Ibérico de Liberación* (Iberian Liberation Movement), the armed anticapitalist group active from 1971 to 1973, its original name was "Mil," which simply means one thousand in Spanish and Catalan and refers to the group's anonymous, diffuse nature as part of the autonomous workers' movement.

militant: in most Romance languages, variations of this word refer not to the use of violence, but to membership in a union, political party, or other formal organization. I have generally opted for "party member" or "union organizer" as the context allowed, but have used the original term when it was necessary to refer to those formally active in any type of organization. Members of the MIL often referred to themselves as "activists" to break with the connotations of "militant."

MSC: Moviment Socialista de Catalunya (Socialist Movement of Catalunya), a Catalan socialist political party founded in 1945 by old members of the POUM, discontents of the Socialist Party's Stalinist tendencies, and also some members of ERC and the CNT. It lasted until 1974.

OLLA: *Organització de Lluita Armada* (Armed Struggle Organization), a name made up by the Spanish police on the basis of a phrase that appears in seized propaganda, OLLA refers to a network of autonomous and anticapitalist armed groups.

passeig: a broad, straight avenue in Catalan.

PCE: *Partido Comunista de España* (Communist Party of Spain), the Stalinist political party that was the dominant force of the anti-Franco opposition until the Socialist Party surged ahead at the very end of the Transition.

Perpinyà: the Catalan name for the city rendered in French as Perpignan. The principal city of Rosselló, North Catalunya, the city changed hands multiple times throughout the Late Middle Ages and early Modern period between ruling dynasties based in Aragón, Barcelona, Paris, and Madrid. It was finally and definitively ceded by the Castillian crown to the French crown, together with the rest of North Catalunya, after the Reapers' War in 1659. Its self-government was suppressed by the French the next year.

plaça: "plaza" or "square" in Catalan.

Platforms: Plataformes de Comissions Obreres, an anticapitalist formation created in 1969 as an attempt to stymie Communist control of CCOO and push the workers' movement in an autonomous, anticapitalist direction. The Platforms were connected to the Circles for the Training of Cadres and the magazines *¿Qué Hacer?* and *Nuestra Clase.* The Platforms achieved a majority in some factories and were strong in several regions of Catalunya, as well as València, Zaragoza, and elsewhere, but in the end the Communists predominated, and the Platforms fell apart around 1978.

Pons Llobet, Josep Lluís: (1955) One of the younger members of the MIL, arrested with Oriol Solé on September 15 1974, escaped from Segovia prison in 1976 but recaptured shortly thereafter, and released in 1977 as part of a widespread amnesty.

popular classes, popular neighborhoods: the phrases *classes populars* and *barris populars* refer to the etymological root of the word "popular," meaning: "of the people." The term includes all who are not a part of the dominant classes, and as such are potential allies in revolutionary struggle. Aside from being slightly broader than the term "working class," there is also the specific denotation of *obrer,* usually rendered in English as the catch-all "worker," that actually signifies "manual worker" and is thus ill-suited to represent the entirety of the proletariat.

POUM: *Partido Obrero de Unificación Marxista* (POUM), a "revolutionary Marxist" party close to Trotskyism, but not part of Trotsky's International Communist League, founded in 1935, most active in Catalunya and València. The POUM joined the Central Committee of Antifascist Militias in 1936, sent militias to the front to fight the fascists, and fought alongside the anarchists during the May Days of 1937, opposing the authoritarian bourgeois government of the ERC and the Communists and advocating revolution. The party was mostly liquidated by the Stalinists in 1937.

PSOE: *Partido Socialista Obrero Español* (Socialist Workers' Party of Spain), founded in 1879 but effectively dismantled by the Franco regime, the PSOE scarcely had a presence in the anti-Francoist opposition. Nonetheless, it received a huge amount of financing from German social democrats and, it has been alleged, covert aid from the United States. In 1974, the party abandoned any symbolic commitment to Marxism and declared itself to be social democrat. In 1982, the party swept the elections and its leader, Felipe Gonzalez, ruled as president until 1996.

PSUC: *Partit Socialist Unificat de Catalunya* (Unified Socialist Party of Catalunya), a Stalinist party effectively controlled by the PCE, founded in 1936, the PSUC played an important role in the Catalan government during the Civil War and towards the end of the Franco dictatorship, achieved hegemony in Comissions Obreres in Catalunya by creating a higher level of bureaucratic "coordination" under their control, the same tactic used by Leninists to neutralize the workers' movement in Russia in October 1917, and, curiously, also a tactic that was used unsuccessfully to try and control the 15M movement in Barcelona. They managed to bureaucratize CCOO, discouraging wildcat strikes, combative actions, and revolutionary ideas. Amidst factionalism and the shift in power from the PCE to the PSOE, the PSUC largely fell apart after 1982.

Sabaté, Quico: (1915–1960) Francesc Sabaté i Llopart, "Quico," was the most famous of the anarchist *maquis* active in Catalunya.

During the Civil War he fought in an anarchist militia, killed a Communist commissar who prevented the anarchists from getting weapons, was arrested, escaped, joined another anarchist column, and fled to France at the end of the war. Already in 1944, he began establishing infrastructure for a guerrilla campaign around Tolosa and on the Spanish side of the border. His brothers were also active *maquis*, though they died in 1949. Sabaté was the most influential and famous *maquis* in the 1950s, carrying out bold actions in support of anticapitalist struggles, attacking regime targets, and helping set up resistance groups throughout Catalunya. He was declared the regime's "public enemy number one." With the aid of the French secret services, the *Guardia Civil* finally managed to ambush him in January 1960 and he and his group crossed over the Pyrenees. The other four members of his group were killed, but despite being surrounded by hundreds of soldiers, Quico escaped and made it clear to the other side of Catalunya, where, with a wound that had become badly infected, he was caught and killed.

Salut i anarquia: "Health and anarchy" in Catalan; in Spanish: "*salud y anarquía*." (Though "salute" in English now has military denotations, its origins are the same). A common anarchist substitute for "goodbye."

"Goodbye" in Catalan and Spanish, as well as in English, is a Christian phrase, though the semantic commendation of an interlocutor to God—*adeu, adios, God be with ye*—is far less obvious in English, given the latter's greater linguistic drift. To replace this religious leave-taking, workers' movements in Catalunya and throughout the Spanish state adopted *salut* or *salud*, which is broadly similar to the toast, "To your health," offered in English, though of course in a different context. I have left this phrase in the original throughout the book, as there is no substitute in English with a similar history.

Solé Sabaté, Felip: a member of the OLLA who also participated in actions with the MIL, Solé Sabaté was also a cousin of the Solé Sugranyes brothers. His nickname was *the Basque*.

Solé Sugranyes brothers: Oriol, Ignasi, Raimon, Jordi. Four of the brothers of this numerous family participated in the MIL and the OLLA. Oriol, the oldest, was known as the most charismatic and influential. He was arrested after an expropriation at Bellver de Cerdanya in 1973, escaped with a large group of prisoners from Segovia in 1976, and was shot down by the Guardia Civil just meters from the French border. Ignasi was an effective networker, but also a controversial figure, and was expelled from the MIL in 1973. Jordi, the youngest, was the only one to escape arrest after the expropriation at Bellver de Cerdanya in September 1973. Ignasi and Raimon joined the OLLA in the fall of '73.

Soler Amigó, Santi: (1943–1999) Alias "Little Guy" or "Fede," one of the members of the MIL, principally connected with the library, arrested shortly before Puig Antich in September 1973. He remained active in the anarchist movement after being released from prison at the end of the dictatorship.

SDEUB: Sindicat Democràtic d'Estudiants de la Universitat de Barcelona (Democratic Student Union of the University of Barcelona), part of the opposition to the Franco regime towards the end of the dictatorship.

Transition: (1975–1978/79) the transition from dictatorship to democracy in the Spanish state, also referred to by critics as the Transaction. Though the fascist regime had long been preparing for some kind of liberalization and integration into Western political and economic structures, the official dates go from the death of Franco on November 20 1975 to either the approval of the new Constitution in 1978 or the adoption of the Statutes granting partial autonomy to Catalunya, Euskadi, and Galicia in 1979. Others consider the Transition not to be complete until the recently ex-fascists running the government were replaced by the Socialists in the 1982 elections.

   The compromises that made up the Transition ensured that none of the mass murder, torture, and political repression of the Franco regime would be punished, nor would there be any redistribution of wealth affecting those who had profited immensely under the fascist government, though some properties seized by the fascists during the Civil War were returned. The police forces and judicial apparatus was left intact and turned against all the resistance groups that had refused to negotiate with the fascists.

On the left, the political forces that made the Transition possible were the socialists, the Communist Party, progressive Catholics, and nationalists like the ERC.

Tolosa de Llenguadoc: the Catalan and Occitan name for the city rendered in French as "Toulouse." Tolosa is the principal city of Occitània, a country on the northern side of the Pyrenees, controlled mostly by France. Occitan is a language closely related to Catalan, though few people still speak it, as France has been historically effective at nation-building, resulting in the near or total extinction of the languages of the many countries now within its borders. Tolosa was an extremely important city for the Spanish and Catalan exiles, and a hub of anarchist activity against the Franco dictatorship.

There is also a small town in the Basque country by the name of Tolosa, but all the references in the book are to Tolosa de Lenguadoc, except for one that clearly situates the Basque locale.

UGT: *Unión General de Trabajadores* (General Union of Workers), the second largest trade union in the Spanish state, founded in 1888. It has historically been controlled by the PSOE. Before the Civil War, it tended to largely represent white collar workers whereas industrial and construction workers largely affiliated with the CNT; however in some regions it was massively represented amongst miners and agricultural workers. This latter part of the rank-and-file sometimes acted in insurrectionary and revolutionary ways between 1932 and 1936, though the leadership generally played a stabilizing role in favor of a liberal democratic regime. After the first few years of the dictatorship, the UGT did not play a major role in the resistance or in the Transition.

Welzel, Georg Michael : Alias Heinz Ches, a dissident from East Germany who fled to the West and carried out a string of individual anticapitalist actions. He was arrested in the Spanish state after killing a Guardia Civil, and executed the same day as Salvador Puig Antich. Because he had no connections to local movements and no one knew who he was or even his real name, there was no support movement on his behalf, and the Francoist state succeeded in portraying him as a sort of psychopath. It is assumed he was executed the same day as Puig Antich in order to carry out the same smear against the latter.

15.

Photos and Documents

Salvador, Imma, and Quim

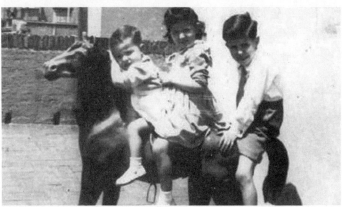

Salvador, Imma, and Quim on the terrace of their parents' house

Imma, Salvador, Montse, and Quim in the garden of their grand-parents' house in Vilafranca

At nursery school

Imma, Salvador, Montse, and Quim

Christmas at La Salle Bonanova

Singing with his mother on the piano

Acting as Merçona's godfather (1960)

With Merçona (1962)

On the football team (bottom row, first on the right)

Vaulting at the Salesians school in Mataró

With the family at Montserrat (1963)

At Montserrat (1963)

In the garden at Palautordera (1966)

Menorca (1968)

Menorca (1968)

Imma's wedding (1969)

Imma's wedding (farthest right)

Induction into the military (1970)

Completing his compulsory military
service (1970)

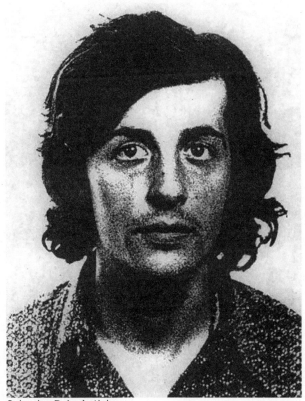

Salvador Puig Antich

DOCUMENT SOURCES FOR REMAINING IMAGES:

CS: Archive of Carlos Sanz
RVG: Archive of Ricard de Vargas Golarons
CDHS-AEP: Center for Historical Social
   Documentation- Ateneu Enciclopèdic Popular
FELLA: Fundació d'Estudis Llibertaris i
   Anarcosindicalistes

"Save three Spanish revolutionaries from the garrote!" French poster protesting his death sentence

FELLA

"Salvador Puig Antich, anarchist, revolutionary militant, has been condemned to death by the Spanish fascists! Unity, autonomy, and internationalist solidarity must snatch him from the hands of the fascist executioners!" Italian poster protesting his death sentence
FELLA

Salvador Puig i Antich condemnat a mort
i assassinat a Barcelona
el dia 2 de març de 1974

No gosaré parlar
en l'alta matinada
i odiaré els vostres
ulls
fins el darrer moment,
i en la mort.
El company que em recordi
sabrà del dolor sinistre
de les presons feixistes
i sabrà de les vostres
paraules
opressores i cruels.

M'assassinareu al matí...
d'amagat però,
i temerosos,
perquè sabeu què el meu nom
no l'embolcallarà el silenci,
perquè sabeu que el meu somni
no l'ofeguereu!
—Aquesta llibertat
que llavi a llavi,
passa a passa,
de mica en mica
us escapça el pas.

Poster illegally plastered throughout the streets of Catalunya
shortly after his execution
RVG

To make the revolution, you need money. How to get it?

You can beg. "This is going anywhere."

Or rob banks. "This gets a lot more!"

When we rob banks to meet revolutionary needs and we get arrested like Salvador Puig Antich, Oriol Sole Sugrañes, and Jose Luis Pons Llobet, we run the risk of being judged and executed amidst a general silence.

When we beg, we risk very little, and we reach the end of our days as dignified, respected revolutionaries. "For the revolution!"

To help those who chose the second solution, everyone to the streets!

Committee for Solidarity with the Prisoners of the MIL

CDHS-AEP

SALVADOR PUIG SERA CONDEMNAT A MORT A BARCELONA DINS DE POCS DIES

Salvador Puig, Oriol Soler, J.L.Pons Llobet Angustias Fernandez, militants del M.I.L., organització revolucionària que practica l'agitació armada (expropiació de bancs, col·laboració en accions dels sectors més combatius del moviment obrer, enfrontament davant la repressió, etc.) van ser detinguts el mes de setembre d'aquest any. El dia 16 la Guardia Civil va detenir Soler i Pons. Quan dies després la policia va sorprendre Puig en una cita a Barcelona, es va produir un tiroteig en el que Puig fou ferit de bala al cap i un dels policies resultà mort.

Una vegada més la premsa local, radio, televisió i altres mitjans de comunicació han facilitat una informació falsejada i han presentat els fets com un enfrontament entre la policia i una banda d'atracadors, quan en realitat les expropiacions no eren per robar diners en profit propi, sinó per treure'l dels llocs on els capitalistes el tenen acumulat, i utilitzar-lo en la lluita del moviment obrer.

Com en tants altres casos, també els militants del N.I.L., ja a la presó, han estat barbarament torturats, portant la policia en aquest cas la repressió al màxim; prova d'aixó és la reacció immediata d'un grup de policies que intentà linxar en Puig en el llit de l'Hospital Clínic on es recuperava de la ferida (aquest cas fou impedit per alguns dels metges i informeres que el cuidaven). Culminació d'aquest procés repressiu és el Consell de Guerra que es celebrarà dins de pocs dies (primera de gener). Es demanaran 2 penes de mort per S. Puig, 30 anys de presó per Pons Llobet, 2 penes de 30 anys per O. Soler i 6 anys per Angustias Fernandes.

La decisió del govern, davant la situació agreujada pels ultims esdeveniments,amb la petició de repressió per part dels feixistes i aprofitant les festes d'aquests dies, és la de matar S. Puig i fer complir les altres condemnes.

Només una reacció popular immediata pot salvar S. Puig i els seus companys.

DIVULGUEM AQUESTES INFORMACIONS ! DIVULGUEM AQUEST FULL ! EVITEM AQUESTS CRIMS ! SALVEM SALVADOR PUIG!!

P.S.A.N.

"Salvador Puig will be condemned to death in Barcelona within a few days." PSAN

RVG

ABAJO LA PENA DE MUERTE DE PUIG

Salvador Puig Antich, luchador antifranquista, militante del Movimiento Ibérico de Liberación, ha sido condenado a muerte por los "jueces" militares. A sus dos compañeros, José Luis Pons y Mª Angustias Mateos, les han impuesto penas de 30 y 5 años de prisión.

La Dictadura quiere así consumar el brutal asesinato proyectado al realizar los Consejos de Guerra. La historia de la Dictadura en los últimos años es una serie continua de derrotas, desde que en Burgos la clase obrera, a la cabeza de todos los oprimidos, salvó la vida de Izco y sus camaradas. La ejecución de Carrero es el más reciente golpe recibido por la Dictadura. Lejos de atemorizar y frenar las luchas populares, no puede más que estimularlas, mostrando la debilidad del franquismo.

El endurecimiento de la represión, con las más duras penas en el proceso 1001, con la condena a muerte en los Consejos de Guerra del M.I.L., es la última salida de la Dictadura, herida de muerte. El pretexto la ejecución de un esbirro de la brigada político-social. La campaña de prensa, intentando presentar a Puig y sus compañeros como vulgares atracadores o terroristas, olvida señalar quién es el auténtico terrorista: la Dictadura sangrienta que durante 37 años ha encarcelado, torturado y asesinado a los que luchan por sus necesidades y derechos.

Porque Puig se enfrentó a esta represión con sus armas, en una emboscada que le tendió la policía, la Dictadura lo condena a muerte. Porque hay que salvarle la vida, porque hay que impedir la maniobra de la Dictadura, la más potente movilización de masas debe ser puesta en pie.

La lucha ha comenzado ya. Los actos de propaganda y explicación en los barrios, las asambleas en la universidad, Institutos y E.F.P., las manifestaciones de cientos de luchado-

"Down with Puig's death sentence." Provincial Committee of the Revolutionary Communist League/ETA VI

RVG

res en la calle, marcan el camino a seguir. ¡Hoy es el momento de movilizar todas las energias. Ningún rincón donde resuene la lucha obrera y popular debe escapar al combate generaliza do: TODOS EN LUCHA POR LA LIBERTAD DE PUIG, PONS Y MATEOS.

Las Comisiones Obreras, los partidos y organizaciones obreras tienen la responsabilidad, con su unidad en la acción de masas, de la puesta en pie de una respuesta masiva y unitaria, para arrancar a los tres luchadores de las garras de los Verdugos franquistas.

ABAJO LOS CONSEJOS DE GUERRA !!
NO A LA PENA DE MUERTE DE PUIG !!
LIBERTAD PARA TODOS LOS PRESOS POLITICOS !!
DISOLUCION DEL T.O.P. Y LOS TRIBUNALES MILITARES !!
DISOLUCION DE LOS CUERPOS ESPECIALES DE REPRESION (Policía
Armada, B.P.S. y Guardia Civil) !!

LIBERTAD PARA PUIG PONS Y
MATEOS! ABAJO LA DICTADURA!

Barcelona, 10 de enero 1974
Comité Provincial de la
LIGA COMUNISTA REVOLUCIONARIA/ETA VIª
(organización simpatizante de la IVª Internacional)

Illegal leaflets distributed by revolutionary leftist organizations
shortly before the execution, trying to save Puig Antich's life
RVG

Puig Antich ASESINADO!

UNICA SOLUCION: L A   L I B E R T A D ! !

Franco, de nuevo, se ha manchado las manos de sangre. Arias y su go- bierno "aperturista" han ejecutado a garrote vil al joven catalán de 26 años Salvador Puig Antich. El mismo gobierno que ha subido los precios de la electricidad, gasolina, leche,...que pretende congelar los salarios!

El crimen ha sido premeditado, desoyendo el clamor nacional e inter- nacional que se ha producido entre los más amplios sectores populares, Iglesia, personalidades, colegios profesionales, entidades, etc. etc.

Desafiando el sentir de los pueblos de España, a la opinión interna- cional, Franco ha matado otra vez...¿Cuántas veces ya?

Acosado, aislado, enfrentado incluso con la Iglesia y su jerarquía y llegando al arresto del obispo Añoveros, impotente para cambiar el rumbo de España hacia la libertad, el caduco dictador pretende continuar hacien do del terror su arma de gobierno, prolongando mediante la violencia su agonía.

Por eso, las promesas aperturistas que Arias se ha visto obligado a reconocer como necesidad de los tiempos entran en abierta contradicción con las concesiones a las fuerzas represivas como única posibilidad de frenar la caída del régimen dictatorial.

Por eso, frente al camino de la violencia, de guerra civil que sigue constantemente la dictadura, urge poner en pie un amplio diálogo, una convergencia de cuantos estamos decididos desde unas u otras posiciones políticas y desde distintos intereses sociales a restablecer las liberta- des democráticas en nuestro país. Y PARA ELLO HAY QUE ACABAR CON LA DIC-

"Puig Antich Murdered! The only solution, freedom!"
RVG

TADURA! Esta no puede "evolucionar"

La respuesta a la violencia dictatorial comenczó ya el mismo sábado:
PAROS en el INP, sentadas en San Pablo y la Residencia, acciones en otras
empresas, Huelga en la Universidad, numerosas manifestaciones, asambleas..

Urge que la protesta de todo el pueblo de Barcelona cierre el paso
a este camino de guerra civil.

Urge transformar la indignación ciudadana en una amplia movilización
de masas: Idas al cementerio de Montjuic donde se encuentra enterrado,
asambleas y funerales en todos los barrios, en todas las iglesias; escri
tos delegaciones, exigiendo la supresión de la pena de muerte (HAY 4 PE-
NAS DE MUERTE PEDIDAS PARA 4 JOVENES DEL FRAP EN MADRID), delegaciones
a los militares, manifestaciones por toda la ciudad,...

Llamamos en primer lugar a la clase obrera, a las grandes empresas
(SEAT, PEGASO, OLIVETTI, FABRA Y COATS...) a responder con acciones de masas al asesinato, a la provocación que suponen los nuevos aumentos de
precios. El PARO GENERAL de 3 horas que este lunes martes y miércoles de-
cidieron los trabajadores del textil en asamblea debe ser una señal de
combate para toda la clase obrera de Barcelona.

Llamamos a los estudiantes, profesionales, a la Iglesia, a todo el pue
blo de Barcelona a ponerse en pie:

- por todas las reivindicaciones obreras y populares

- por la supresión inmediata de la pena de muerte

FUERA EL GOBIERNO ASESINO!   LIBERTAD!

3 de Febrero 1974   El Comité de Barcelona del
                                     PARTIT SOCIALISTA UNIFICAT DE CATALUNYA

PSUC, calling for protests after Puig Antich has been executed
RVG

CNT-AIT: "Let us avenge Puig Antich" 1974

CNT-AIT: "Let us avenge Puig Antich" 1974
CS

OFENSIVA PROLETARIA

N°6 MARZO 74

- **SALVADOR PUIG ANTICH ASESINADO POR EL CAPITALISMO.**

- salvador, camarada y hermano, tu sangre es parte de nuestra sangre, caiste por nosotros y con nosotros, tu has regado el camino y perteneces a esa legión de mártires de la causa proletaria, te vengaremos, porque vengarte es acabar con este sistema que te ha asesinado.

- **LUCHEMOS CONTRA LOS ASESINATOS** DE LOS COMPAÑEROS DEL FRA

- **LA LUCHA ANTICAPITALISTA HOY.**

PLATAFORMAS DE TRABAJADORES ANTICAPITALISTAS DE BARCELONA

Proletarian Offensive: "Salvador Puig Antich, killed by capitalism. Your blood is our blood. You fell for us and with us. You have prepared the way and joined the legion of martyrs of the proletarian cause. We will avenge you, because avenging you means ending this system that murdered you." March 1974. The Platforms of Anticapitalist Workers of Barcelona

RVG

"Salvador Puig Antich murdered. Save the comrades of the MIL"
CS

LA VÉRITÉ
EST RÉVOLUTIONNAIRE

"Libération" du 4 mars fait la constatation critique et autocritique suivante:
«...il faut avouer notre culpabilité...il faut dire que nous sommes tous coupables.
Qu'avons nous fait pour PUIG? Que chacun s'interroge et se souvienne du procès de Burgos... pour PUIG la rue est restée déserte de nos colères.... A gauche et à l'extrême gauche, les vieilles habitudes sont restées tenaces et le sectarisme est resté une manie quotidienne. Personne ne s'est demandé ce qu'était le MIL »...et en premier lieu "Libération"!

Si ce journal a toujours publié de petits comptes-rendus d'actions, il n'y a eu que 3 articles dignes de ce nom sur le MIL depuis septembre 73... et avant l'exécution bien sûr!

Le 3 décembre le comité de soutien invite à une conférence de presse: seul "Combat" est présent.

Le 25 janvier nouvelle conférence de presse: seule "Tribune socialiste" se déplace.

"Politique Hebdo" nous demande un article que nous envoyons le 22 janvier: cet article ne passera jamais.

Réunion à "Libération" le 13 janvier: promesse de publier un article juridique ainsi que 3 textes politiques du MIL. Seul l'article juridique paraîtra. Négligence ou censure politique?

Quant aux groupuscules et aux organisations ouvrières et démocratiques, la lettre ci-après leur a été envoyée... début décembre.
Inutile de s'étendre davantage.
Chacun peut constater par lui-même, à condition de ne pas regarder la réalité avec les lunettes idéologiques.

L'EXTRÊME GAUCHE FRANÇAISE FACE AU RÈGNE DE LA BARBARIE

Ainsi ils ont osé!
Ces criminels, ces assassins, ces fascistes, ces barbares.

Puig Antich, cet anarchiste espagnol, vient d'être garrotté, supplice médiéval qui consiste à broyer les vertèbres cervicales à l'aide d'un collier de fer.

Mais qui donc doutait de cette exécution? L'extrême-gauche française? Parlons-en! Après avoir gardé un silence criminel sur l'arrestation et la détention de Puig Antich, l'ensemble des organisations d'extrême gauche, se réveillent pendant le procès. Réveil plutôt dur: au cours de deux manifestations sans convictions tout le monde se jettera sur «le cadavre» encore vivant, «au cas où ça marcherait» (chacun pour sa boutique évidemment).

Salauds de «gôchistes». Je vous hais, toi de Rouge, toi de L.O. toi du FRAP, toi de Révolution, toi de l'ORA, et autres, révolutionnaires en peau de boudin, manipulateurs. En ce moment je vous hais peut-être aussi fort que je peux haïr Franco, «ce prolongateur de Hitler en 1974».

Il est probable que vous tous, réunis dans une harmonie de Prisunic allez appelé à descendre dans la rue.

Osez-le vous, pour une fois, d'avouer que c'est vous-mêmes...misérables.

...idéologues, que vous défendez, votre lâcheté que vous camouflez?

- Je vous conseillerais plutôt un peu de pudeur. Laissez pisser, contentez-vous, comme les partis du programme commun, d'envoyer un télégramme d'indignation. Cela aura au moins l'avantage pour vous d'être conforme avec votre idéologie religieuse. Vous ne serez pas obligés de vous forcer. De faire semblant d'être à l'aise alors que vous ne l'êtes pas: « Qu'est-ce qu'il ne faut pas faire tout de même pour la cause, on en vient à être obligé de défendre des attaqueurs de banques!»

Moralistes de «soriste» léniniste, vous ne pourrez vous en sortir (dans ce cas particulier comme pour le global), qu'en tablant, comme les oppresseurs de toutes sortes, sur l'ignorance des gens, et même de votre propre clientèle actuelle.

Je vous le hurle de fait: ceux qui descendront dans la rue, à votre invitation ou non, pour condamner ce nouveau crime de «Candillo», condamneront par la même occasion ce même complicité, qu'ils en soient conscients ou non, à moins qu'une fois de plus ils ne crient leur impuissance.

Ce matin, Puig Antich, 20 ans, mon âge, un ami, mon frère, est mort garrotté, étranglé.
Et j'ai pleuré.

Mehdi
Samedi midi

Call for a demonstration, in French and in Spanish, in defense of Puig Antich. Paris, January 18, 1974

CDHS-AEP

Index

Page numbers in italics represent illustrations.
Page numbers with *f* represent figures.

Alberola, Octavio, 9
Anguas Barragán, Francisco Jesús,
  82
Angustias Mateos, María, 139
Antich, Immaculada (mother), 79,
  80, *274*, *276*
Antich-Segura Family, 205–6
Arau, Oriol (lawyer): about, 249;
  fight for clemency, 43–4,
  58–60, 83; visiting Salvador in
  jail, 65, 66, 208
ARDHC (Asociació de Recerca
  i Documentació d'Història
  Contemporània), 195
Armed Struggle Organization. *See*
  OLLA
Assemblea de Catalunya, 89–90,
  195, 249–50
Autonomia Operaia, 98, 250
Autonomous Combat Groups. *See*
  GAC
Autonomous Workers' Groups.
  See GOA

Bakunin, Michael, 197–8
Bañeres, Jordi ("Parides"), 147
Barça (FC Barcelona), 258
Barjau (doctor), 55, 65, 68–9, 70, 82
Barnils, Ramon, 194
Barnuruntz group (The Block),
  91, 130

Barragán, Anguas, 65, 69, 70
Barrot, Jean, 88, 107, 131, 184
Baynac, Jacques, 173
Berneri, Camillo, 24, 91, 91n9,
  125, 135
Bocigas, Santiago, 132
Bover, Margalida (partner),
  179n22, 206–12
Brinton, Maurice, 234

Calderón, Ángel, 69, 70
CAM (Comité de Acción
  Marroquí), 13
Caminal, Francesc (lawyer), 69, 70
Cañestro, Manuel Antonio, 139
Cardan, Paul, 89
Cardona Curco, Irene, 28
carlins, about, 250–1
Carlos de Borbón, Juan, 95
Carlos V, 251
Carlota Tolosa, 194
Carrero Blanco, Luis, 29, 92, 93,
  252
Carrillo, Santiago, 153, 252
Castoriadis, Cornelius, 89, 89n
CCOO (Comissions Obreres):
  about, 253–4; and entryism,
  23, 255–6; forming, 85–6;
  history of, 21–3, 30; and new
  radical tendency, 88; 1966
  protest, 87; and Platforms,

264; *Proceso 1001* trial, 93; and PSUC, 265; structure of, 102, 102n. *See also* Platforms

CDC, 156n65

CGT (Confédération Générale du Travail), 254

cheka, 9, 13

Ches, Heinz, 94, 94n, 269

Christie, Stuart, 12–13

Circles for the Training of Cadres, 88–9, 103, 115n, 264

Civil Guard. *See* Guardia Civil

CNS (Central Nacional Sindicalista), 23, 99, 254

CNT (Confederación Nacional del Trabajo): about, 254; and adaptation, 137, 158; and Barcelona workers, 137; and bureaucratization, 12–3, 19, 144n; and Catalunya working class, 100–1; and conservatism, 19; counterfeiting, 18; and Defensa Interior, 20; disowning MIL, 131; in exile, 16; and FAI, 258; and FIJL, 259; forming joint antifascist committee, 10, 12n; history of, 8–9, 100n1, 136–7; and interior/exterior viewpoint, 19, 31; leaflets, 289; and Mujeres Libres, 28; 1965 protest, 86; and power, 11–2; reconstruction of, 158; reestablishing in Spain, 21, 23, 30–1; *Between the Revolution and the Trenches*, 126

Comissió Obrera Central of Barcelona, 85–6

Committee for Solidarity with the Prisoners of the MIL, 54, 56–7, 93, 152, *285*

Communist Party of Spain. *See* PCE

Communist Party of Spain International (PCE(i)), 87

Companys, Lluís, 148, 148n56

Congress of the Autonomous Groups, 149–50

Continuous Struggle. *See* Lotta Continua

Coordinator of Prisoners in Struggle, 254–5

COPEL (Coordinadora de Presos en Lucha), 151, 254–5

Cortade, André, 194, 198

Cortès, Jordi, 77, *279*

CRAS (Comunas Revolucionarias de Acción Socialista), 130–1

Creix, Antonio Juan, 120, 135

Cruyff, Johan, 121, 121n18

Cruz, Olga de la, 69

Dalmau, Father, 56

Dauvé, Gilles (aka Jean Barrot), 88, 107, 131, 184

Defensa Interior, 20, 85

Delgado Martínez, Joaquín, 85

Democratic Students' Union of the University, 86, 87, 257

Díaz, José Antonio, 115, 130, 261

"the Doctor." *See* Puig Antich, Salvador

doctors of Salvador. *See* Barjau (doctor); Latorre (doctor)

Durruti, Buenaventura, 191

Ediciones Mayo del 37: about, 4, 112, 123, 255; congress of 1973, 92; continuing to publish, 156; creation of, 121–2; and OLLA, 143; as provocation, 122, 123–4; various publications of, 123–8

Einstein, Carl, 140
ERAT (Ejército Revolucionario de Ayuda a los Trabajadores), 110
ERC (Esquerra Republicana de Catalunya), 148n56, 255, 256, 265
Escribano, Francesc, 67, 200–1
Escudé, Damià, 56
ETA (Euskadi ta Askasatuna): about, 256–7; and Carrero Blanco, 93, 252; commutation of death sentences, 59; execution of Manzanas, 87; execution of members, 96; Felip as messenger, 51; and first weapons, 18; and MIL, 117, 130, 143; prison escapes, 155; Trial of Burgos, 89
ETA-VI Assembly, 257, 286
Exterior Team (ET), 88–9, 90, 91, 111–2, 117, 132, 197

FAC (Front d'Alliberament de Catalunya), 155, 257
Facerias, Josep, 18
FAI (Federación Anarquista Ibérica), 9–10, 12–3, 20, 126, 258
Falange, 14, 254, 258
Farell, Duran, 121
FC Barcelona (Barça), 258
Fernández Grandizo, Manuel, 129
Fernández Márquez, Manuel, 146
Ferrer i Guàrdia, Francesc, 187, 187n31
FIES, 255
FIJL (Federación Ibérica de Juventudes Libertarias), 9, 15, 20, 259
1st of May Group, 20
FNC (Front Nacional de Catalunya), 90, 140

FOC (Front Obrer de Catalunya), 86, 88, 102, 260
Franco, Francisco: about, 259; assassination attempts, 16, 20; and capitalism, 28–9; and Carrero Blanco, 252; and democracy, 29–30; and Falange, 258; and guerrillas, 16; influence of, 5; murdering anarchist sympathizers, 18; and number of people killed, 14–5; and patriarchy, 28; punishing strikers, 22–3; reparations for victims of, 71
FRAP (Frente Revolucionario Antifascista y Patriota), 96, 259–60
French Communist Party, 150
FSF, 86

GAC/gac (Grups Autònoms de Combat): about, 260; bases of, 237–8; Black September-Red October, 134–5; creation of, 57, 79, 90, 117; and MIL conflicts, 184–5; 1972-3, 91–3; purpose of, 134
GAL, 257
Garcia Oliver, Joan, 20
GARI (Grupos de Acción Revolucionaria Internacionalista), 95, 154–5, 260
Garriga, Francesc Xavier, 139
Garriga i Paituví, Xavier ("Carlos") ("the Secretary"): about, 260; at Imma's wedding, 77, 279; "justice in the street," 167; meeting Salvador, 76, 163–4; and MIL dissolution, 185–6; political meetings, 78; as witness, 70

Gelderloos, Peter, 7–32
General Labor Confederation. *See* CGT
General Union of Workers. *See* UGT
Generalitat, 260
German Communist Party, 12
GOA (Grupos Obreros Autónomos): about, 261; created, 89; *Dictionary of the Militant Worker*, 106; end of, 157–8; and MIL, 115; number of members, 138; and texts, 115n
Gómez Bravo, Gutmaro, 71
González, Felipe, 161, 265
Granados, Enric, 68
Granados Gata, Francisco, 85
Grimau, Julián, 85
grups autònoms de combat, 57, 260. *See also* GAC/gac
Guardia Civil (Civil Guard), 35, 49, 146, 146n, 261
Guillamón, Agustín, 12n
Guillaume, Pierre, 131
Guillén, Abraham, 18

Iberian Anarchist Federation. *See* FAI
Iberian Federation of Libertarian Youth. *See* FIJL
Iberian Liberation Movement. *See* MIL
Internationalist Revolutionary Action Groups, 95, 154–5, 260
Iribarne, Fraga, 198
Italian Communist Party, 250

Juventud Comunista Revolucionaria, 87, 104

Lafargue, Paul, 125

Latorre (doctor), 55, 65, 68–9, 70, 82
Lefeuvre, René, 131
Liberation Front of Catalunya. *See* FAC
Llach, Lluís, 196, 196n
Lluïsa Piguillén, Maria, 139
Loher Rodríguez, Martina, 156
López, Marcelo, 4, 115, 167, 173
Lorda, Felip, 192
Lotta Continua, 88, 98, 106, 130, 262
Luigi, Bruno, 88

Machado, Antonio, 160
maquis: inspiring MIL, 114; at L'Entrecôte, 37, 37n10; overview, 16–21, 18n; and Sabaté's paths, 91n8; Salvador as, 53–4
Macri, Mauricio, 73
Manero (chaplain), 46
Manzanas, Melitón, 87
Márquez, Fernández, 110
Martín Escudero, Antonio, 57n
Martínez Ramos, Sebastià, 69
Martos, Cipriano, 110
Massana, Marcel·lí, 18
May '37 Editions. *See* Ediciones Mayo del 37
Mendieta, Timoteo, 73, 73n
Mera, Cipriano, 20
MIL (Movimiento Ibérico de Liberación): about, 4, 191–2, 194–5, 197–8, 263; and anarchism, 24, 175n17; as anticapitalist, 191–2; and CCOO, 22n; chronology of, 87–95; *CIA (Conspiración Internacional Anarquista)*, 170–3; and CNS, 23; CNT disowning, 131; as cut short,

158; direct actions, 114, 115–21, 145–6, 165–6; dissolution of, 27, 81, 132–5, 184, 198, 199; and ETA, 117, 130, 143; and ETA-VI Assembly, 257; exhibition on, 195; and GAC, 260; and GOA, 115, 261; and grupuscle, 261; history of, 23–4, 25, 25n (*see also* chronology of); ideological foundation of, 103–4; ideology of, 113–4, 116, 122, 124, 135, 165–6; and interior/exterior viewpoint, 19, 228; legacy of, 161–2; and Marxism, 163n; *MIL: The History of a Family with History*, 156; name of, 98–9; and OLLA, 79, 81–2, 81n, 90, 119, 139–40, 142–5, 147–50; origins of, 111–2; and patriarchy, 28; and PCE, 136; and Platforms, 115; and revolutionary texts, 97–8; and Sabaté's paths, 91n8; and sabotage, 236n13; and Salvador (*see* Puig Antich, Salvador: political biography); Salvador ideas for, 181–4, 182n; self-criticism, 135–9; tactics of, 129–30; Vargas Golarons memories, 97–101, 103–7, 111–36; and women's equality, 28, 141. *See also* Ediciones Mayo del 37; GAC

MIL-GAC. *See* GAC; MIL

Miller, Henry, 210–1

Miquel (comrade), 57–8

Mitterand, François, 150

Montseny, Frederica, 13, 19, 28

MSC (Moviment Socialista de Catalunya), 86, 90, 263

Mujeres Libres, 28

Munis, Grandizo, 129

Muñiz, Mati, 77

Muntané, Manuel, 195

Murcia i Ros, Manuel, 115, 130, 261

Mussolini, Benito, 258

National Labor Central, 23, 99, 254

National Labor Confederation. *See* CNT

No Alineats, 56

Núñez, Ernesto ("el Chato"), 115, 127, 167, 173

OLLA (Organització de Lluita Armada): about, 263; actions, 145–8, 149, 151–4, 157; and CCOO, 22n; chronology of, 90–4; and CNS, 23; collapse, 148–56; as cut short, 158; history of, 25, 140–1 (*see also* chronology of); legacy of, 161–2; and MIL, 79, 81–2, 81n, 90, 119, 139–40, 142–5, 147–50; name of, 99; number of members, 147; and patriarchy, 28; and sabotage, 236n13; and Salvador, 82, 83, 143, 149–51; 2nd Congress of the Grups Autònoms, 156–7; and specialization, 134n; Vargas Golarons memories, 119, 139–57; and women's equality, 28, 141–2

1,000. *See* MIL

ORA (Organisation Révolutionnaire Anarchiste), 131

ORT (Organización Revolucionaria de Trabajadores), 131

Pablo (chaplain), 46

Panyella, Jordi, 71

Pardiñas, Emili ("Pedrals"), 106, 139

PCE (Partido Comunista de España): about, 263; and Carrillo, 252; and combativity, 138; and Committee for Solidarity with the Prisoners of the MIL, 56; communism in Spain, 29–30; and FRAP, 259–60; Junta Democrática de España, 95; and MIL, 136; and monarchy, 161; as threat, 157

PCE(i) (Partido Comunista de España Internacional), 87

PCF (French Communist Party), 150

PCI (Italian Communist Party), 250

Peiró, Joan, 148, 148n56

Platforms (Plataformes de Comissions Obreres): about, 264; creation of, 88, 103; leaflets, 290; and MIL, 115; and propaganda, 106; workers pushing for, 23. See also CCOO

Plaza, Montse (partner), 76, 81

Pons Llobet, Josep Lluís: about, 264; arrest of, 48, 48n, 82, 92–3, 139; bank robbery, 82; and CIA, 171; and death penalty, 56; joining MIL, 167; objectives, 117; Salvador moving in with, 81

POUM (Partido Obrero de Unificación Marxista), 9–10, 265

prisoners in Copel, 151, 254–5

PSAN (Socialist Party for National Liberation), 90, 140–1, 286

PSOE (Partido Socialista Obrero Español), 13; about, 9, 265; and CAM/CNT joint struggle, 13; Catalan publishing houses, 155n64; and CCOO, 23; formation of, 102; legalized, 29–30; and money, 161; and Platforms, 88; and Stalinists, 12; and UGT, 268

PSU (Parti Socialiste Unifé), 150

PSUC (Partit Socialist Unificat de Catalunya): about, 265; and Assemblea de Catalunya, 89–90, 249; and Committee for Solidarity with the Prisoners of the MIL, 56; leaflets, 288; 1965 protest, 86; and Salvador, 153

Puig, Joaquim (father), 15, 78, 276

Puig Antich, Immaculada (Imma): pictures of, 271–3, 276; Salvador moving in with, 78; and Salvador's memory preserved, 63–74; saying goodbye to Salvador, 43–8, 83; wedding, 77, 279

Puig Antich, Joaquim (Quim) (brother): letter from Salvador, 204–5; pictures of, 271–3, 276; Salvador as driver, 77; and Salvador's memory preserved, 63–74; saying goodbye to Salvador, 43, 66; visiting mother, 80; visiting Salvador in jail, 83

Puig Antich, Maria Carme (Carme) (sister), 43–8, 63–74, 83, 276

Puig Antich, Merçona (sister): letter from Salvador, 203–4; pictures of, 275, 276; and Salvador's memory preserved, 63–74; saying goodbye to Salvador, 43–4, 83

Puig Antich, Montserrat (Montse) (sister), 43–8, 63–74, *272–3, 276*

Puig Antich, Salvador: 45th anniversary of death, 7, 26–7; as anarchist, 175n17, 178–9, 197; as anticapitalist, 31–2, 188, 191–2, 200; appeals, 66, 67–70; on armed agitation, 213–4, 217–9, 221–3, 222n, 226–7, 229–34, 237–8, 246–7; and Barcelona factory strike, 27; books on, 194, 200–1; on capitalism, 220–1; as Catalanist, 155; Che Guevara record, 166; chronology of life, 75–83; on *CIA*, 171; on class defence, 223–7; and commitment, 37, 164; and Committee for Solidarity with the Prisoners of the MIL, 56–7; as cook, 36; as council communist, 175n17; critiquing movement, 175–80; date of birth, 75; day of arrest/ Girona shootout, 64–5, 69; and death sentence, 83; as deliberate, 188–9; distancing from MIL, 166; as driver, 77, 167; eating out, 37; education, 75–7, 77n, 78; execution of, 43n2, 59, 73, 83, 152, 186; and expulsion of Ignasi, 168–9; and father, 15, 44, 78; Felip memories of, 52–60; and feminism, 3; films about, 195, 200–1; 43–8, 66; formation of new path, 180–4, 182n; Franco and death sentence, 59; friendships, 40–1; funeral, 48, 67, 83, 152; Guardia Civil dangers, 35; an hope, 59–60;

in hospital, 65; on interior/ exterior, 228, 236; Jean-Marc memories of, 33–42; joining CCOO, 76; language of writing, 215n; leaflets on, *286–92*; letters from, 203–12; on the library, 241–6, 245n; as maquis, 53–4; and marriage, 208–9; as martyr, 31–2, 67, 148–9, 186–8; and Marxism, 163–4; memories, 41; memory preserved by siblings, 63–74; and MIL, 78–9, 186, 214–5; military service, 77–8; and mother, 35–6, 79, 80; as nationalist, 174; and nickname, 34, 77; as nurse, 34; objectives, 117; and official history, 31; and OLLA, 143, 149–50, 151; overturning conviction, 67–73, 148, 188; overview, 3; partners, 38, 76, 81, 179n22, 206–12; personality of, 64, 68; pictures of, *271–81, 289–90*; plaza dedicated to, 71; political biography, 163–89; political ideals, 52–4; posters on, *282–5*; printing propaganda, 78; reflection on movement 1972-3, 237–8; sent to prison, 82; sentence of, 186; solidarity for, 59–61, 149–53; song about, 196, 196n; on strategy, 234–7; texts written, 80, 81, 163, 168–70, 171, 173–7, 212–48, 213n (*see also* Puig Antich, Salvador, texts of); Tibidabo school impression, 39; trial of, 65–6; Vargas Golarons statement of execution anniversaries, 191–201; waiting for commutation, 59–61

Puig Antich, Salvador, guerrilla
    actions: bank robbery, 54–5;
    day of arrest/Girona shootout,
    55, 64–5, 69, 82; Fabri i Puig,
    33–4, 167–8; losing vital
    documents, 138–9; robberies
    in 1972, 79–80; stolen cars,
    38–40; telegraph and postal
    office, 81
Puig Antich, Salvador, texts
    of: *Armed Agitation—Real
    Movement*, 218–23; *Before
    Asking Ourselves: What Do
    We Do? Better to Ask: What's
    Going On?* 213–5; *The
    Emancipation of the Workers
    Must Be the Task.*, 223–7;
    Prompt for Discussion, 234–9;
    *"Terrible" History, December
    1972–July 1973*, 239–47; *We
    Still Can't See the Horizon*,
    213–8; *Who Can Revive a
    Corpse?* 228–34
Pujol, Jordi, 155n64, 156n65

RAF, 173
Real Madrid club, 258
Republican Left of Catalunya. *See*
    ERC
Revolutionary Antifascist and
    Patriot Front. *See* FRAP
Revolutionary Army of Workers'
    Aid, 110
Revolutionary Communes of
    Socialist Action, 130–1
Revolutionary Communist League,
    286
Revolutionary Communist Youth,
    87, 104
Revolutionary Organization of
    Workers, 131
Rey, Carlos, 71

Rosés, Sergi, 28, 139, 142–3, 163n,
    175n17, 198
Rosés Cordovilla, Sergi, 163–89
Rouillan, Jean-Marc: *De Memoria
    I*, 140; memories of Salvador,
    33–42; on MIL dissolution,
    185–6; and Oriol, 172–3,
    172n; and Salvador, 78,
    175n17; support for, 188
Rovira, Bru, 43–8
Ruiz Villalba, Antonio, 89

Sabaté, Quico: about, 91n, 265–6;
    communiqué of memory, 91;
    homage to, 144; and media,
    155; resistance group, 18–9;
    *Sabaté: Quinze anys de guerrilla
    urbana antifranquista*, 155n64
Santillán, Diego Abad de, 13
Sardà, Joan (lawyer), 58–9, 60
SDEUB (Sindicat Democràtic
    d'Estudiants de la Universitat
    de Barcelona), 86, 87, 267
Self-Defense Group Ruiz Villalba,
    110
Servini, Maria, 72
Sindicat Democràtic d'Estudiants
    de la Universitat de Barcelona,
    86, 87, 257
Situationist International, 87, 107
Socialist Movement of Catalunya,
    86, 90, 263
Socialist Party for National
    Liberation (PSAN), 90, 140–1,
    286
Socialist Workers' Party of Spain.
    See PSOE
Solé Sabarís, Felip (uncle), 56, 60
Solé Sabaté, Felip ("the Basque"),
    49–62, 266
Solé Sugranyes, Ignasi: about, 267;
    expulsion of, 168, 170; leaflets,

55; meeting Salvador, 76; and
nationalism, 143; objectives,
117; organizing infrastructure,
167; Oriol border pick ups,
50; political meetings, 78;
recruiting, 164; 2nd Congress
of the Grups Autònoms,
156–7; *The Worker's Movement
in Barcelona*, 105
Solé Sugranyes, Jordi ("Sancho"):
about, 267; bank robbery,
82; escaping, 93; objectives,
117; political meetings, 78;
recruited, 164; and Tolosa
nucleus, 170
Solé Sugranyes, Oriol: about,
104–5, 267; arrest of, 82, 92–3,
139, 167; bank robbery, 82;
Camy ice cream direct action,
104–5; *The Catalan Che*, 155;
changing MIL, 164–5; and
CIA, 172n; and Creix, 120;
death of, 96, 155; and death
penalty, 56; and Felip, 49–50,
51; as martyr, 187–8; and MIL
teams, 111; and nationalism,
143; objectives, 117; political
strategy, 172–3; and prison, 78,
151, 164; and Rouillan, 172–3;
on Salvador and hope, 158–9
Solé Sugranyes, Raimon, 143, 167
Soler Amigó, Santi ("Little
Guy"): about, 105n, 267; anti-
authoritarianism sketch, 128;
arrest of, 139, 139n; as author,
105–6, 105n; and CAC, 117;
and *CIA*, 171; and Felip, 50;
and library, 167; and MIL,
182n, 184–5, 185–6; political
meetings, 78; on Salvador as
martyr, 187; support for, 95

Tajuelo, Telesforo, 198
Tamames, Ramón, 127
Téllez Solà, Antoni, 155n64
Theoretical Team (TT), 88–9, 90,
91, 112, 197
Torres, Jean Claude, 78, 117, 167

UDC, 90
UGT (Unión General de
Trabajadores), 9–10, 23, 30,
192, 254, 268
Unified Socialist Party of
Catalunya. *See* PSUC
Utrera Molina, José, 73

Vaneigem, Raoul, 87, 107
Vargas Golarons, Ricard de: as
anticapitalist, 31; father in
French camp, 15; as FIJL, 259;
on MIL and OLLA, 97–162;
Salvador execution anniversary
statements, 191–201; Salvador
overview, 1–5
Vila Capdevila, Ramon, 18–9, 85
Villalba, Ruiz, 110
Viola, Joaquim, 153

Welzel, Georg Michael (aka Heinz
Ches), 94, 94n, 269
Workers' Commissions. *See* CCOO
Workers' Front of Catalunya, 260
Workers' Team (WT), 88–9, 90,
112, 197

Xirinacs, Lluís Maria, 56, 118,
118n17

AK PRESS is small, in terms of staff and resources, but we also manage to be one of the world's most productive anarchist publishing houses. We publish close to twenty books every year, and distribute thousands of other titles published by like-minded independent presses and projects from around the globe. We're entirely worker-run and democratically managed. We operate without a corporate structure—no boss, no managers, no bullshit.

The **FRIENDS OF AK PRESS** program is a way you can directly contribute to the continued existence of AK Press, and ensure that we're able to keep publishing books like this one! Friends pay $25 a month directly into our publishing account ($30 for Canada, $35 for international), and receive a copy of every book AK PRESS publishes for the duration of their membership! Friends also receive a discount on anything they order from our website or buy at a table: 50% on AK titles, and 30% on everything else. We have a Friends of AK ebook program as well: $15 a month gets you an electronic copy of every book we publish for the duration of your membership. *You can even sponsor a very discounted membership for someone in prison.*

Email **friendsofak@akpress.org** for more info, or visit the website: **https://www.akpress.org/friends.html**.

There are always great book projects in the works—so sign up now to become a Friend of AK Press, and let the presses roll!